Theory and Practice in Vocabulary Research in Digital Environments

This collection is a comprehensive resource on the state of second language vocabulary learning today, building on earlier studies to spotlight the diversity of issues and foci in the field toward encouraging further advancements in both research and practice.

The volume foregrounds the importance of vocabulary learning in language teaching and learning and in effective written and verbal communication, charting the range of approaches and theories used to address the unique challenges of vocabulary instruction. While there exists a well-established body of vocabulary research, this book takes those lines of inquiry in new directions by exploring how technology has shifted the focus from teacher-led delivery to more activity-driven experiences. Chapters from prominent researchers and rising scholars feature studies on emergent approaches in virtual environments such as interactive whiteboards, CMC, virtual world learning, and mobile-assisted language learning. In offering a holistic portrait of technology-enhanced vocabulary learning, the volume makes the case for the power of technological tools in fostering optimal environments for encouraging vocabulary acquisition and in turn, the potential opportunities for future research and pedagogical applications.

This book will be of interest to students and scholars in second language acquisition, language education, TESOL, and applied linguistics.

Mark Feng Teng is an Associate Professor in Applied Linguistics at Macao Polytechnic University, China.

Agnes Kukulska-Hulme is a Professor of Learning Technology and Communication in the Institute of Educational Technology at the Open University, UK.

Junjie Gavin Wu is a Lecturer and Ph.D. Supervisor at Macao Polytechnic University, China.

Routledge Studies in Applied Linguistics

ELF and Applied Linguistics
Reconsidering Applied Linguistics Research from ELF Perspectives
Edited by Kumiko Murata

The Structure of Philosophical Discourse
A Genre and Move Analysis
Kyle Lucas and Sarah Lucas

Multimodality across Epistemologies in Second Language Research
Edited by Amanda Brown and Søren W. Eskildsen

Transnational Approaches to Bilingual and Second Language Teacher Education
Edited by M. Dolores Ramírez-Verdugo

Interdisciplinary Research and Innovation in Bilingual and Second Language Teacher Education
Edited by M. Dolores Ramírez-Verdugo

Self-Concept in Foreign Language Learning
A Longitudinal Study of Japanese Language Learners
Reiko Yoshida

Theory and Practice in Vocabulary Research in Digital Environments
Edited by Mark Feng Teng, Agnes Kukulska-Hulme, and Junjie Gavin Wu

For more information about this series, please visit: www.routledge.com/Routledge-Studies-in-Applied-Linguistics/book-series/RSAL

Theory and Practice in Vocabulary Research in Digital Environments

Edited by Mark Feng Teng,
Agnes Kukulska-Hulme, and
Junjie Gavin Wu

NEW YORK AND LONDON

First published 2025
by Routledge
605 Third Avenue, New York, NY 10158

and by Routledge
4 Park Square, Milton Park, Abingdon, Oxon, OX14 4RN

Routledge is an imprint of the Taylor & Francis Group, an informa business

© 2025 selection and editorial matter, Mark Feng Teng, Agnes Kukulska-Hulme, and Junjie Gavin Wu; individual chapters, the contributors

The right of Mark Feng Teng, Agnes Kukulska-Hulme, and Junjie Gavin Wu to be identified as the authors of the editorial material, and of the authors for their individual chapters, has been asserted in accordance with sections 77 and 78 of the Copyright, Designs and Patents Act 1988.

All rights reserved. No part of this book may be reprinted or reproduced or utilised in any form or by any electronic, mechanical, or other means, now known or hereafter invented, including photocopying and recording, or in any information storage or retrieval system, without permission in writing from the publishers.

Trademark notice: Product or corporate names may be trademarks or registered trademarks, and are used only for identification and explanation without intent to infringe.

Library of Congress Cataloging-in-Publication Data
Names: Teng, Mark Feng, editor. |
Kukulska-Hulme, Agnes, 1959– editor. | Wu, Junjie Gavin, editor.
Title: Theory and practice in vocabulary research in digital environments / edited by Mark Feng Teng, Agnes Kukulska-Hulme and Junjie Gavin Wu.
Description: New York, NY : Routledge, 2025. |
Series: Routledge studies in applied linguistics |
Includes bibliographical references and index. |
Identifiers: LCCN 2024026158 | ISBN 9781032434858 (hardback) |
ISBN 9781032434865 (paperback) | ISBN 9781003367543 (ebook)
Subjects: LCSH: Second language acquisition. | Vocabulary–Study and teaching. |
Web-based instruction. | Applied linguistics.
Classification: LCC P118.2 .T463 2025 | DDC 418.0071–dc23/eng/20240708
LC record available at https://lccn.loc.gov/2024026158

ISBN: 9781032434858 (hbk)
ISBN: 9781032434865 (pbk)
ISBN: 9781003367543 (ebk)

DOI: 10.4324/9781003367543

Typeset in Sabon
by Newgen Publishing UK

Contents

List of figures	vii
List of tables	ix
List of contributors	xi
Acknowledgements	xvi
Preface	xvii

1 Introduction to *Theory and Practice in Vocabulary Research in Digital Environments*   1
MARK FENG TENG AND JUNJIE GAVIN WU

PART I
Theories and synthesis   13

2 Intentional vocabulary learning through captioned viewing: Comparing Vanderplank's 'cognitive-affective model' with Gesa and Miralpeix   15
ROBERT VANDERPLANK AND MARK FENG TENG

3 Mapping the digital game-based vocabulary learning landscape: A comprehensive bibliometric exploration   39
ZHAOYANG XIONG, JUNJIE GAVIN WU, AND DI ZOU

4 Development of gloss studies in vocabulary learning research   60
MAKOTO YOSHII

PART II
Pedagogical practices 91

5 A corpus-based study of learners' language learning trajectories with captioned viewing: Implications for vocabulary learning practices 93
MARK FENG TENG AND JESSE W. C. YIP

6 L2 vocabulary learning with an AI chatbot: From linguistic, affective, and cognitive perspectives 115
SANGMIN-MICHELLE LEE

7 Training to use machine translation for vocabulary learning 132
YIJEN WANG AND GLENN STOCKWELL

8 Korean EFL learners' vocabulary development through asynchronous CMC and synchronous CMC in content courses 154
SUNG-YEON KIM

9 The anatomy of word lists in New Word Level Checker: Description and comparison 174
ATSUSHI MIZUMOTO

10 Mobile-assisted vocabulary learning in an EAP context 194
JEONG-BAE SON AND SANG-SOON PARK

11 Vocabulary learning with Netflix: Exploring intraformal learning practices through the lens of Complex Dynamic Systems Theory 211
ANTONIE ALM AND YUKI WATANABE

12 Using TikTok for vocabulary learning: Multimodal implications 230
YEONG-JU LEE

13 Conclusion: The next generation of studies in multimodal, multilingual, and multi-agent vocabulary learning 249
AGNES KUKULSKA-HULME

Index 257

Figures

1.1	Three emerging areas for TEVL	7
2.1	The model of attention with selection and grading factors	22
2.2	The model of 'Paying attention to the words'	23
2.3	A cognitive-affective model of language learning through captioned viewing	24
2.4	'Paying attention to the words' model	31
2.5	A cognitive-affective model of learning with media	34
3.1	The annual scholarly output in DGBVL	43
3.2	Top ten most prolific countries/regions in the field of DGBVL	44
3.3	Top ten most prolific institutions in the field of DGBVL	45
3.4	Visual mapping of keyword co-occurrence analysis	46
3.5	Visual mapping of keyword clustering in DGBVL research	47
3.6	Top 20 keywords with the strongest citation bursts	52
4.1	Changes in the numbers of SMG, MMG, and total gloss papers from the 1990s to the 2010s	75
4.2	Changes of results favoring L1, L2, and showing no differences	77
4.3	Changes of results favoring MMGs, SMGs, and showing no differences	78
4.4	Three conditions for L1 vs. L2	80
4.5	Three conditions for text and picture	81
5.1	Proposed model of the trajectory of language learning with captioned viewing	111
7.1	Students' awareness of vocabulary aspects for writing (N = 85)	139
7.2	Perceptions of the ethicality of using AI tools for English writing	142
7.3	Desire to learn appropriate usage of AI tools for English writing	143
7.4	Perception of ethical usage of AI tools for English writing	144

7.5	Perceived helpfulness of the training sessions	144
7.6	Perceived most helpful features of AI tools for English writing	146
9.1	Initial user interface of NWLC with text area and word list dropdown menu	175
9.2	Graphical representation of word level coverage rates in NWLC	176
9.3	Interface for user-created word lists with search and sort functionalities	177
9.4	Flowchart representing the algorithm of lemmatization in NWLC	181
9.5	Coverage rates of five word lists in NWLC	186
9.6	Demonstration of contextual word analysis using NWLC's KWIC feature	189
12.1	a Multimodal content on pronouncing contractions (left) b Multimodal content explaining confusing sounds (right)	237
12.2	a Short-form video content mainly edited with text (left) b Multimodal content mainly edited with text and emojis (right)	240
12.3	Screenshots of Jieun's short-form multimodal content	241
12.4	Shasha's user profile within which all the selected content is saved	243

Tables

3.1	Top ten keywords in terms of frequency and centrality	46
4.1	List of review / meta-analysis papers on gloss research	62
4.2	List of gloss studies in the 1990s	66
4.3	List of gloss studies in the 2000s	67
4.4	List of gloss studies in the 2010s	72
5.1	Frequency and dispersion of top 20 lexical words at Initial Stage	101
5.2	Frequency and dispersion of top 20 lexical words at Middle Stage	104
5.3	Frequency and dispersion of top 20 lexical words at Final Stage	107
6.1	Descriptive statistics of students' and chatbot's outputs	121
6.2	Paired t-test results of students' outputs in H-H and H-C interactions	121
6.3	Independent t-test results of outputs of the students and the chatbot	122
6.4	Survey results	123
6.5	Results of the reflection paper analysis	124
7.1	Training process	137
7.2	Usage of AI tools for writing before training	140
7.3	Frequency of students' MT tool usage	140
7.4	Student perceptions of teachers' attitudes toward AI tools. Item 17. Did your teachers recommend or discourage AI tools for learning English?	141
7.5	The affordances of the AI and MT tools	147
7.6	The limitations of the AI and MT tools (all responses are included as is)	149
8.1	Paired t-test of the lexical density measure between SCMC and ACMC	160
8.2	Examples of student postings across the two modes of communication	161

x *List of tables*

8.3	Paired *t*-test of lexical sophistication measures between SCMC and ACMC	161
8.4	Paired *t*-test of lexical variation measures between SCMC and ACMC	162
9.1	CEFR-J level, number of headwords and school levels in Japan	179
9.2	List of words with capitalized letters	182
9.3	List of words with apostrophes	183
9.4	List of words with periods	183
9.5	List of hyphenated words	184
9.6	List of compounds	184
9.7	Summary of word counting units and rules	185
10.1	Participant profiles	198
10.2	Average ratings of attitudes toward digital technologies and tools	201
10.3	Average ratings of mobile-assisted vocabulary learning experiences	202
10.4	Results of the pre-test and the post-test	204
11.1	Timeline of activities	215
11.2	Texting shortcuts recorded in Mario's blog	220
12.1	Participants' background information	234

Contributors

Editors

Mark Feng Teng is an Associate Professor in Applied Linguistics at Macao Polytechnic University. His research area mainly focuses on second language vocabulary acquisition, particularly in captioned viewing for vocabulary learning. He has published extensively in the topic area, including international journal articles, books, and chapters. His recent research has explored the cognitive processes/working memory involved in vocabulary learning in various input conditions. He is the author of *Language Learning through Captioned Videos: Incidental Vocabulary Acquisition* (2021, Routledge) and co-editor of *Researching Incidental Vocabulary Learning in a Second Language* (2024, Routledge).

Agnes Kukulska-Hulme is a Professor in the Open University's Institute of Educational Technology where she leads on research and innovation, with a focus on pedagogical transformations and future learning scenarios across informal and formal settings. She is Past-President of the International Association for Mobile Learning, and serves on several journals' editorial boards including *ReCALL*, *RPTEL*, and the *International Journal of Mobile and Blended Learning*. She has published numerous articles and books on the topics at hand.

Junjie Gavin Wu is a Lecturer (equivalent to Assistant Professor) and a Ph.D. Supervisor at Macao Polytechnic University. He is a Shenzhen High-Caliber Talent and a Vice President of PacCALL. Gavin sits on the organising committee of various associations such as iLRN, GLoCALL, and ChinaCALL. He is an Associate Editor of *IEEE Transactions on Learning Technologies* and *Computers & Education: X Reality*. Gavin has authored around 40 English publications, with over 20 papers appearing in SSCI journals. He has edited books with Routledge and

Springer and spearheaded eight special issues such as *Educational Technology & Society*.

Contributors

Antonie Alm (Ph.D., UCLA) is an Associate Professor at the University of Otago, New Zealand. Her research interests lie in L2 motivation, learner autonomy, and informal language learning. Antonie is on several editorial review committees and works as an Associate Editor for the *CALL Journal* and the *JALTCALL Journal*.

Sung-Yeon Kim (Ph.D., UT-Austin) is a Professor in the Department of English Education at Hanyang University, Seoul, Korea. Her research interests include technology-enhanced language teaching and learning, writing instruction, language policy, and teacher education. She has published her work in international journals, such as the *Asia-Pacific Journal of Teacher Education*, *Asia TEFL*, *British Journal of Educational Technology*, *Foreign Language Annals*, *Language Teaching Research*, *System*, *TESL-EJ*, and *Vigo International Journal of Applied Linguistics*.

Sangmin-Michelle Lee is a Professor of Global Communication and Graduate School of Metaverse at Kyung Hee University, Korea. Her research interests include a technology-enhanced learning environment, machine translation, L2 writing, game-based learning, and digital creativity. She is an associate editor of *JALT-CALL*. Her articles have appeared in *Computer Assisted Language Learning*, *ReCALL*, *Language Learning & Technology*, and *British Journal of Educational Technology*, among others.

Yeong-Ju Lee (Ph.D., Department of Linguistics, Macquarie University) is a teaching and research academic specialising in Linguistics and Language Education. She currently teaches in the Master of Applied Linguistics program at Macquarie University, the Master of TESOL program at the University of Wollongong, and the Bachelor of Education program at Australian Catholic University. Her research interests include informal digital language learning, technology use in language education including TESOL, digital literacy, multimodality, digital space, social media, and generative AI.

Atsushi Mizumoto (Ph.D. in Foreign Language Education) is a Professor at the Faculty of Foreign Language Studies and the Graduate School of

Foreign Language Education and Research, Kansai University, Japan. His current research interests include learning strategies, language testing, corpus use for pedagogical purposes, and research methodology. He has published articles in journals such as *Applied Linguistics*, *Language Learning*, *Language Teaching Research*, *Language Testing*, and *System*. He won the Award for Outstanding Academic Achievement from Language Education and Technology in 2017.

Sang-Soon Park (Ed.D.) is a Senior Lecturer in Pathways at the University of Southern Queensland, Australia. He teaches a range of courses related to academic preparation, study management skills, and research skills. His research interests include English for academic purposes, intercultural communication, international education, international students' language development, and widening participation.

Jeong-Bae Son (Ph.D.) is a Professor of Applied Linguistics and TESOL in the School of Education at the University of Southern Queensland, Australia. His areas of specialisation are computer-assisted language learning and language teacher education. His research interests include technology-enhanced language teaching, computer-mediated communication, mobile-assisted language learning, AI-powered language teaching, digital literacy, academic English writing, and language teacher development.

Glenn Stockwell (Ph.D. University of Queensland) is a Professor of Applied Linguistics at the Graduate School of International Culture and Communication Studies, Waseda University. He is author of *Mobile Assisted Language Learning: Concepts, Contexts and Challenges* (Cambridge University Press, 2022) and editor of *Smart CALL: Personalization, Contextualization, & Socialization* (Castledown Publishers) and *Computer Assisted Language Learning: Diversity in Research and Practice* (Cambridge University Press, 2012). He is Editor-in-Chief of *Computer Assisted Language Learning* and the *Australian Journal of Applied Linguistics*.

Robert Vanderplank is an Emeritus Fellow and Director of the Centre for the Study of Lifelong Language Learning at Kellogg College, Oxford University. Until his recent retirement, he taught courses and supervised research in applied linguistics and second language acquisition at Oxford, where he was also Director of the University Language Centre. He has been researching the value of captioned viewing for language learning since the 1980s and has published on this topic widely in books and journals. He has also published research on educational technology, adult language learning, listening comprehension, learner strategies, supra-segmental phonology, and first language development in children.

Yijen Wang is an Assistant Professor at the School of International Liberal Studies at Waseda University. Her main research was on the factors affecting technology adoption by teachers and students in language teaching and learning. She has published a number of research articles and book chapters in the field of technology and language education, specifically looking at learner and teacher motivation and the development of autonomy. She is currently the Editor-in-Chief of *Technology in Language Teaching & Learning*.

Yuki Watanabe is a Lecturer in Media, Film, and Communication at the University of Otago in New Zealand. Her research interests include intercultural communication, global media, the use of communication technology in education, and the construction/performance of gender in Asian popular culture.

Zhaoyang Xiong is a Ph.D. student at Macao Polytechnic University. Her research interests include technology-enhanced learning, game-based learning, and language learning.

Jesse W. C. Yip is a Research Assistant Professor in the Department of Linguistics and Modern Language Studies, the Education University of Hong Kong. His research interests include healthcare discourse studies, identity theory in professional contexts, corpus-assisted discourse analysis, and computer-mediated communication. He has published articles in peer-reviewed journals, such as *Journal of Pragmatics*, *Applied Linguistics Review*, and *Health Communication*.

Makoto Yoshii is a Professor at the Prefectural University of Kumamoto. He teaches English and Second Language Acquisition classes for the Department of English Language and Literature, Faculty of Letters. His research interests include SLA and second language vocabulary acquisition in particular. He has done studies on glossing and examined how it affects vocabulary learning through reading. His work can be found in *CALICO Journal, Language Learning & Technology*, among others.

Di Zou is an Associate Professor and Head of Centre for English and Additional Languages, Lingnan University. Her research interests include technology-enhanced learning, AR/VR-enhanced learning, game-based language learning, vocabulary learning, flipped classroom, computer assisted language learning, and learning analytics. She has over 150 publications in journals and books with international impact. She has been listed as one of the World's Top 2% Scientists by Stanford University in 2021 and 2022.

Acknowledgements

We would like to extend our gratitude to the following reviewers for their suggestions and comments to improve the chapters in this volume. Reviewers include:

Antonie Alm, University of Otago, New Zealand
Arif Altun, Hacettepe University, Turkey
Sung-Yeon Kim, Hanyang University, Korea
Alice S. Lee, University of Macau, Macau SAR
Sangmin-Michelle Lee, Kyung Hee University, Korea
Seongyong Lee, University of Nottingham Ningbo, China
Yeong-Ju Lee, Macquarie University, Australia
Warid Mihat, Universiti Teknologi MARA Cawangan Kelantan, Malaysia
Atsushi Mizumoto, Kansai University, Japan
Jeong-Bae Son, University of Southern Queensland, Australia
Morgana Valentina, Università Cattolica del Sacro Cuore, Italy
Kevin Wong, Pepperdine University, USA
Yijen Wang, Waseda University, Japan
Mokoto Yoshii, Prefectural University of Kumamoto, Japan
Gavin Bui Hiu-Yuet, the Hang Seng University of Hong Kong, Hong Kong SAR

Preface

Two years ago, while I was on the bus heading to a tourist attraction, Gavin, a fellow researcher whom I had met at a previous academic event and other informal occasions, approached me. He sent me a message, "Hi Mark, shall we collaborate on editing a book together? You have a knack for vocabulary, and my expertise lies in computer research". Intrigued by the proposal, I responded enthusiastically, "Sure, why not". As we delved deeper into our discussion, Gavin shared his vision of enhancing market awareness in Europe through inviting another editor. He then proposed bringing Agnes on board, a renowned CALL expert, to join our editorial team. Excited by the prospect of working as part of such a knowledgeable team, we collectively brainstormed and conceptualised the innovative idea of exploring digital environments as a focal point of our project.

The idea of digital environments comes from the integration of technology and digital devices that plays a transformative role in expanding our awareness, sparking new ideas, and nurturing our imagination. This digital revolution has revolutionised the way we perceive and engage with language learning, offering a rich and interactive learning environment that enhances the overall learning experience. Digital environments thus encompass integrated communication environments where a myriad of digital devices seamlessly communicate and manage content and activities. These environments can be accessed or generated using a variety of digital tools such as computers, tablets, or smartphones, reflecting the pervasive nature of technology in our daily lives. Of course, in this contemporary digital landscape, vocabulary learning has transcended the confines of conventional print-and-practice exercises. It has evolved into a dynamic and engaging experience that incorporates audiovisual elements, multimodal resources, entertainment, and creativity.

The process of working on this project with Agnes and Gavin was not only rewarding and fulfilling but also a testament to the dedication and passion we shared for our collaborative endeavour. We proactively reached out to potential contributors who were not only willing but eager to lend their expertise and insights to the project. Collaborating with Gavin, Agnes, and all the contributors proved to be a positive and enriching experience, as their profound knowledge, cooperative spirit, and diligent work ethic greatly contributed to the project's success. The synergy among our team members ensured that the collaboration proceeded seamlessly, fostering a harmonious and productive working environment. Without the invaluable contributions of Agnes and Gavin, as well as all the contributors, this book would have never reached its full potential. Their unique perspectives, expertise, and unwavering commitment were instrumental in shaping the content and direction of the project, making it a comprehensive and impactful resource for language learners and educators alike. In the realm of academia, where the pursuit of knowledge knows no bounds and the quest for excellence is ceaseless, it is essential to find joy, fulfilment, and respect in the scholarly journey. Academic work is too demanding and rigorous, but my wish is for academics to not only excel in their work but also to savour, cherish, and honour the academic pursuits that contribute to the greater scholarly community.

Returning to the essence of this book, it is evident that the digital environment holds a pivotal position in the lives of language learners, presenting a myriad of advantages including fresh educational avenues, avenues for creativity, and enhanced social interaction. As the world continues its rapid digitisation, educators may encounter difficulties in harnessing the full potential of both existing and emerging digital resources. Recognising the significance of embracing the marvels of our ever-evolving world, we have meticulously curated a comprehensive book aimed at supporting teachers and researchers on their quest for knowledge and innovation. Within the pages of this book, teachers will find a wealth of theories and practices designed to engage language learners in diverse exercises that not only broaden their understanding of the physical realm but also bolster their lexical proficiency through the utilisation of digital tools. By bridging the gap between traditional pedagogy and cutting-edge digital advancements, this book serves as a valuable resource for educators seeking to adapt to the changing educational landscape and empower their students with the skills and knowledge needed to thrive in a digitally driven environment for language learning.

Mark Teng
Macao Polytechnic University, Macau SAR, China

1 Introduction to *Theory and Practice in Vocabulary Research in Digital Environments*

Mark Feng Teng[1] and Junjie Gavin Wu[2]
[1]*Faculty of Languages and Translation, Macao Polytechnic University*
[2]*Faculty of Applied Sciences, Macao Polytechnic University*

Background

Vocabulary learning is often regarded as a crucial research area in applied linguistics. Vocabulary is the body of words that make up a language, and the importance of vocabulary in language teaching and learning cannot be overstated. Without a good working knowledge of words and their meanings, neither written nor verbal communication will be effective. A robust vocabulary improves all areas of communication, including listening (Stæhr, 2009), speaking (Uchihara & Clenton, 2020), reading (Qian, 2002), and writing (Olinghouse & Wilson, 2013). Successful vocabulary acquisition involves expanding both the breadth and depth of word knowledge (Schmitt, 2010). While vocabulary learning often occurs in a language classroom under the guidance of language teachers, it is now further developed through language input outside the classroom (Richards, 2015). Researchers generally concur that vocabulary growth is possible only after being exposed to meaning-focused input, meaning-focused output, context-aware learning, and fluency development (Nation, 2007). However, the effectiveness of meaning-focused input and output is dependent on the way that the language input is presented to the learners. Exploring technological tools in digital environments may offer a promising avenue for enhancing vocabulary acquisition, underscoring the necessity for innovative technological strategies and pedagogy in vocabulary learning (Miller & Wu, 2021; Morgana & Kukulska-Hulme, 2021; Teng, 2021).

Despite the effectiveness of vocabulary learning activities that are specifically designed to encourage students to focus on developing lexical knowledge, vocabulary instruction remains a challenging dimension of second language acquisition (Nation, 2022). Building up a second language (L2) vocabulary is more complex than mere memorisation of word meanings.

DOI: 10.4324/9781003367543-1

Although researchers have been exploring the potential of technology applications for vocabulary learning, the optimal tools and methods for technology-enhanced vocabulary learning (TEVL) remain ambiguous.

Vocabulary learning in the digital era refers to the adoption of a wide range of information and communications technology applications and approaches to vocabulary teaching and learning, from the "traditional" drill-and-practice programs to more recent manifestations in virtual exchange (Wu & Miller, 2021) and chatbot-empowered interactions (Lee & Jeon, 2022). It also extends to the use of interactive whiteboards, computer-mediated communication (CMC), language learning in digital gaming worlds, and mobile-assisted language learning (MALL). Along with the availability of new technologies such as artificial intelligence (AI) and extended reality (XR), opportunities for vocabulary learning have multiplied and far exceed what can be done in more formal learning environments (Kohnke et al., 2023; Wu et al., 2024a). TEVL beyond the classroom has emerged as an area whose development has been influenced not only by rapidly changing technology but also by a growing awareness of digital learning.

One important gap in the vocabulary research literature is the lack of diverse perspectives discussing the potential of vocabulary acquisition in digital environments. While vocabulary researchers agree on a great many aspects, each researcher brings a different perspective to the discussion. With so many studies on vocabulary learning being conducted, it is perhaps beneficial to classify research into distinct categories to reveal potential gaps in the literature, as well as to highlight areas that have garnered varying levels of attention in TEVL. One of the great benefits of technology in digital environments is the ability to expose learners to "real" or authentic language as it is used. The term "input" refers to all exposure to the target foreign language. While English is the most widely used language in the academic world, students in non-English-speaking contexts encounter challenges that negatively impact their vocabulary development, such as the lack of exposure to authentic English input and lack of opportunity to apply their vocabulary knowledge in an authentic fashion (Webb, 2019). Input appears to be not enough. If learners fail to notice or concentrate on the incoming flow of language, their comprehension would be limited.

Researchers in second language acquisition commonly make a distinction between input and intake. Despite the exposure to the language input, intake is limited to the comprehended input that impacts the learner's developing linguistic system. In this context, technology tools are crucial in exposing L2 learners to intensive form-focused activities that intrinsically induce a state of vocabulary acquisition. To enhance informal yet effective learning, a number of studies have appeared lending support to claims for captions (Teng, 2022a, 2022b, 2023a, 2023b, 2024), digital gaming (Zou et al., 2021), mobile concept mapping (Liu, 2016), multimedia annotations (Zou & Teng, 2023), and online reading (Korat, 2010; Teng, 2018) as robust techniques to enhance vocabulary learning. At the same time, educators have begun to explore the use of advanced technologies in augmenting the process of vocabulary learning, including the use of augmented reality (AR, e.g., Zhang et al., 2020), virtual reality (VR, e.g., Wu et al., 2021) and AI (Kukulska-Hulme & Lee, 2020). The potential for TEVL has begun to be unearthed, lending credibility to its potential for enhancing the acquisition and retention of various dimensions of vocabulary knowledge. Hence, technology provides avenues to increase the foreign language input that learners are exposed to and enhances the process of how input is converted into intake.

Goals of this edited volume

Our volume sets out to achieve the following research goals. First, we aim to explore innovative digital approaches for enhancing vocabulary acquisition. For example, this volume aims to help classroom practitioners apply the available technology resources to enhance English learners' vocabulary acquisition inside and outside the classroom. While much has been done about vocabulary instruction, the published literature has not sufficiently addressed the challenging issues related to vocabulary acquisition outside classroom contexts, particularly in digital environments. Given this oversight, it is time to discuss ways to support researchers in seeking a better understanding of vocabulary research. It is essential to find ways to disseminate good practice and, perhaps most importantly, to integrate innovative approaches across curricula, institutions, and contexts to broadly influence vocabulary learning to address the need for digital learning.

Second, we aim to understand learners' cognitive ability in speculating, predicting, and comprehending input when being immersed in a flow of foreign utterances in the "digital wild" in relation to the constraints of human cognitive processing ability. The vast amount of information available in digital environments presents both opportunities and challenges for vocabulary learning. Learners are often exposed to a wide array of linguistic and contextual cues that require them to make inferences, anticipate meaning, and decipher unfamiliar vocabulary in real time. This immersion in the "digital wild" can be particularly demanding due to the inherent constraints of human cognitive processing ability. Understanding the learners' cognitive processes and capabilities within this digital context is vital for designing effective vocabulary instruction.

Finally, this volume aims to showcase practices in conducting vocabulary research and suggest future directions or agendas for the field of vocabulary research. This purpose is meaningful, as vocabulary learning is a gradual and cumulative process (Nation & Webb, 2011; Nation, 2022). This project thus contributes to addressing the need for applied linguistics researchers to expand their methodological toolkit to study the complexities involved in vocabulary research and to respond to the needs of digital learning.

There are some core features of this volume. First, our edited volume represents a pioneering effort in the field of vocabulary learning in digital environments, making it a unique and valuable contribution to the existing body of knowledge. Unlike previous projects, which have primarily focused on broader aspects of language learning or technology integration, our project specifically targets vocabulary learning, addressing the micro-level and practical intricacies of this process. Second, drawing insights from investigations in digital learning, our project will provide empirical and theoretical foundations to inform the design and implementation of effective vocabulary learning interventions in digital environments. By leveraging the advancements in technology and pedagogical approaches, we aim to bridge the gap between traditional classroom-based vocabulary instruction and the emerging practices enabled by technological tools. Third, while some projects have touched upon the use of technology in language learning, vocabulary research in digital environments remains relatively underexplored. Our volume fills this gap by placing a strong emphasis on investigating vocabulary acquisition within the context of digital platforms and tools. We aim to generate up-to-date information on the adaptation of traditional vocabulary instruction methods to new teaching environments facilitated by technology. Finally, our volume adopts a comprehensive approach by incorporating both empirical and conceptual studies. This approach allows for a deeper understanding of the key issues surrounding vocabulary learning in digital environments. Through our investigations, we aim to uncover insights into the effective use of technological techniques, such as e-learning and m-learning platforms, to enhance vocabulary teaching and learning experiences.

In terms of practical values, one of the strengths of our volume lies in its integration of praxis-based, student-focused pedagogy into empirical research. By aligning our investigations with practical teaching practices and digital learning contexts, we aim to provide meaningful and applicable findings that can be directly implemented by educators and practitioners. This approach is particularly relevant in the current era of digital learning, where the need for effective vocabulary instruction in digital environments has become increasingly important. In terms of relevance to teaching, our volume seeks to establish a blueprint for enhancing vocabulary learning in the digital age. Through in-depth pedagogical research studies supported by a strong empirical foundation, we aim to uncover strategies and techniques that harness the full potential of technology for vocabulary instruction. By doing so, we hope to contribute to the advancement of vocabulary research and provide valuable insights for educators and researchers seeking to optimise vocabulary learning experiences in digital environments.

This volume mobilises an internationally stellar lineup of both seasoned and up-and-coming researchers and practitioners to make a concerted effort to push for vocabulary research in digital environments. Our initial approaches to some potential collaborators met with great enthusiasm and immediate agreement to contribute to our project. These researchers contributed their expertise and insights to moving the field forward. Their contributions have greatly enriched the volume, ensuring a diverse range of perspectives and expertise. Furthermore, their involvement enhances the volume's credibility as their expertise aligns with the interdisciplinary nature of researching vocabulary learning in digital environments. Their experience in conducting research, collaborating with international teams, and publishing in reputable academic journals further strengthens the volume's credibility and potential impact.

Outline of chapters in the volume

In the first part of this collection, we present the reader with three review studies, each addressing distinct research topics in vocabulary learning. In Chapter 2, Vanderplank and Teng compare Vanderplank's "cognitive-affective model" with the findings of Gesa and Miralpeix, shedding light on intentional vocabulary learning through captioned viewing, advocating for the use of captioned viewing in language learning, and opening up new avenues for inquiry suited to the evolving landscape of language learning. Digital game-based vocabulary learning has been a popular research domain. Chapter 3 by Xiong, Wu, and Zou thus provides a holistic overview of digital game-based vocabulary learning by reviewing 1,173 academic publications between 2008 and 2023, shedding light on potential research directions to explore. Chapter 4 by Yoshii examines gloss studies over the past three decades, tracing their evolution through the foundation, flourishing, and further exploration phases.

Transitioning to pedagogical implementation, in Chapter 5, Teng and Yip investigate 20 English learners' language learning trajectories through an approach of corpus linguistics, systematically analysing the advantages and drawbacks associated with language learning through captioned viewing. One key feature is a corpus-based model of language learning trajectories that outlines a phased progression consisting of three distinct stages, each elucidating the nuanced dynamics inherent in the integration of captioned viewing for language learning. Lee in Chapter 6 reports on 36 Korean university learners' use of an AI chatbot for vocabulary learning from linguistic, affective, and cognitive aspects. By employing a mixed-methods approach, the chapter discovers that chatbot-enabled vocabulary learning can be as effective as human-based learning. Also focusing on AI technology, Chapter 7 by Wang and Stockwell attempts to understand the role of machine translation with Japanese learners by examining the use of Google Translate, DeepL, and ChatGPT. One key takeaway from this chapter is that the alliance of attitudes between teachers and students should be treated carefully, and open communication between them should be encouraged to co-develop strategies and awareness of such tools for vocabulary learning. Kim in Chapter 8 investigates lexical development via asynchronous and synchronous CMC. It reports no significant differences in student use of advanced vocabulary but highlights greater lexical diversity observed in synchronous modes. Chapter 9 by Mizumoto introduces the New Word Level Checker (NWLC), highlighting the gap between vocabulary lists developed for researchers and material developers and the practical needs of learners and teachers, emphasising the role of tools like NWLC in bridging theory and practice. Through teaching English for Academic Purposes, Chapter 10 by Son and Park involved learners from an Australian university in mobile learning activities. The chapter provides readers with qualitative insights into MALL. Focusing on language learning in the wild, Chapter 11 by Alm and Watanabe explores the use of Netflix with Spanish learners in New Zealand. Informed by Complex Dynamic Systems Theory, this chapter uncovers the heterogeneous, context-dependent nature of developing vocabulary learning practices for three learners. Similarly, Chapter 12 by Lee delves into how international students in Australia improve their vocabulary learning via TikTok. It highlights the key role of multimodality in digital learning. This edited volume ends with a concluding Chapter 13 by Kukulska-Hulme that reviews this collection and proposes future uses for digital technology in vocabulary learning.

Future directions and implications

To end this introductory chapter, we would like to propose three research themes for future teaching and research (Figure 1.1).

Theme 1: The Metaverse and TEVL

a) Technological development
   While Apple Vision Pro has been introduced to the market, the Metaverse remains in its developmental stage within the technology

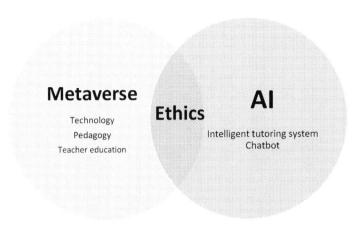

Figure 1.1 Three emerging areas for TEVL

industry. Envisioning a future of a shared Metaverse (Hwang & Chien, 2022), wherein individuals can create sub-Metaverses to suit their specific needs, the incorporation of various enabling technologies like XR and AI is essential. Despite this, we are yet to see Metaverse platforms available for vocabulary or language learning. Although it could be argued that the accessibility of new technologies is exacerbating the digital divide (or Metaverse divide, Wang et al., 2022) among learners in different disciplines, an alternative perspective suggests opportunities for collaboration and co-leadership in technological development. For example, the immaturity of Metaverse platforms targeted at teaching vocabulary presents a chance to involve students, teachers, educators, and researchers in co-constructing and shaping technological progression based on their feedback and suggestions (Wu et al., 2024b). This inclusion of educational stakeholders in technological development can contribute to a learner-friendly, pedagogy-driven Metaverse for vocabulary learning.

b) Pedagogy development

The majority of current language teaching approaches and methods are rooted in traditional classroom settings. Now, the revolutionised Metaverse calls for a re-evaluation of the effectiveness of these approaches and methods, ranging from the roles of teacher and learner, interactions between learners, avatars, and the Metaverse environment, and provision of feedback (Wu et al., 2024a). Developing a comprehensive knowledge of the features, affordances, and constraints of the Metaverse plays a pivotal part in shaping language pedagogy. In recent years, game-based learning and immersive learning have emerged as robust pedagogical methods across various disciplines. TEVL studies can also capitalise on these new methods so as to modernise current pedagogical practices. Yet one pressing issue in learning in the Metaverse is the cultivation of immersive literacies for learners (Pegrum et al., 2022), which warrants deeper exploration in TEVL studies.

c) Teacher education

Training both pre-service and in-service language teachers to use the Metaverse has yet to receive serious attention from teacher educators. Despite limited coverage in previous years, a recent report from South Korea provides insight into potential future research. Lee and Wu (2023, 2024) made use of one commercial Metaverse platform to train Korean pre-service and in-service language teachers. Guided by the TPACK (Mishra & Koehler, 2006) and SAMR (Puentedura, 2006) models, their studies emphasise the importance of updated teacher training programmes, even for technology-savvy language teachers born into the digital age. A forthcoming special issue, "Virtual Reality in Teacher Education: Innovations, Opportunities, and Challenges", of *Educational Technology & Society* promises additional insights into the needs of teachers when utilising the Metaverse in TEVL. However, further scholarly exploration is necessary to refine tailored training for teachers before it can be fully realised.

Theme 2: AI and TEVL

a) Intelligent tutoring systems

Intelligent tutoring systems (ITSs) have been popular among language educators and learners. There are two mainstream categories of ITSs on the market: automated essay scoring (AES) systems like Grammarly and educational applications such as Duolingo and Busuu. They are typically argued to simulate tutors and provide linguistic feedback to learners; however, one major criticism of ITSs is their heavy emphasis on automatic scoring at the expense of constructive human-machine interactions. In a certain sense, these ITSs reflect the concept of behaviourism, promoting excessive mechanical repetitive imitation. This approach may hinder the development of learners' autonomy and other humanistic learning objectives such as critical thinking and empathy. With the rise of ChatGPT, ITSs can anticipate technological improvements by leveraging new AI technology to facilitate interactive conversations and provide meaningful feedback to learners. This could potentially address the limitations associated with the current ITS models.

b) Chatbot

As an advanced AI, generative AI such as ChatGPT relies on GPT 4.0 or higher to empower chatbots to remember, create, engage, and grow with the user through natural language processing and deep learning algorithms (Yang et al., 2024). Differing from ITSs, chatbots powered by GPT have the capability to "adjust and construct context-appropriate responses" (p. 3) by utilising Reinforcement Learning from Human Feedback (RLHF). This can be particularly valuable in vocabulary acquisition, offering learners the opportunity to engage in contextualised, real-time conversations with AI tutors/peers/coaches (Kukulska-Hulme et al., 2023), which is hardly feasible in traditional, large-scale language classrooms. Yet, some words of caution are needed: (1) Learners will require careful guidance on making the best of chatbots, especially what kinds of prompts are constructive. (2) Though learners may advance their vocabulary acquisition through interactions with chatbots, they must develop metacognitive strategies to navigate encountered vocabulary, considering aspects like formality, tone, register, and style (Kim et al., 2022). (3) Despite the appearance of intelligence, chatbots lack genuine empathy. Therefore, learners should be careful when engaging with chatbots to mitigate potential risks of psychological harm brought about by chatbots.

Theme 3: Ethics and TEVL

Regardless of the technologies employed, ethical considerations must be upheld throughout the entire learning and teaching process. In particular, the advent of new technologies brings forth fresh ethical concerns. For example, the utilisation of generative AI in educational settings has prompted the development of governmental and institutional guidelines (e.g., UNESCO, n.d.). Nonetheless, Yang et al. (2024) underscore a gap in current university regulations, lacking clear and actionable directives for teachers and students. Based on this observation, they outline 16 concrete principles for educators, learners, and school administrators. This publication could serve as a valuable foundation for TEVL scholars in devising relevant principles for implementing generative AI in TEVL contexts.

In a similar vein, learners engaging with the Metaverse or XR technologies for vocabulary acquisition outside the classroom must contend with various challenges such as avatar-based harassment, educational inequity among different student populations, cyberbullying, privacy breaches, and mental health concerns like isolation and addiction (Mystakidis, 2022; Peña-Rios & Wu, 2023). Interestingly, an episode of *The Good*

Fight (season 6, episode 1) shed light on sexual harassment within the Metaverse, highlighting the societal attention drawn to such ethical dilemmas. However, these issues require more immediate and rigorous scholarly scrutiny in the realm of TEVL.

To conclude, despite the fact that L2 vocabulary acquisition has been extensively researched over the past decades, the continual emergence of innovative technologies has revolutionised this classic research field, offering novel learning experiences and instilling new pedagogical perspectives.

References

Hwang, G. J., & Chien, S. Y. (2022). Definition, roles, and potential research issues of the metaverse in education: An artificial intelligence perspective. *Computers and Education: Artificial Intelligence*, 3, 100082.

Kim, H., Yang, H., Shin, D., & Lee, J. H. (2022). Design principles and architecture of a second language learning chatbot. *Language Learning & Technology*, 26(1), 1–18. http://hdl.handle.net/10125/73463

Kohnke, L., Moorhouse, B. L., & Zou, D. (2023). ChatGPT for language teaching and learning. *RELC Journal*, 4(2), 537–550.

Korat, O. (2010). Reading electronic books as a support for vocabulary, story comprehension and word reading in kindergarten and first grade. *Computers & Education*, 55(1), 24–31.

Kukulska-Hulme, A., Bossu, C., Charitonos, K., Coughlan, T., Deacon, A., Deane, N., Ferguson, R., Herodotou, C., Huang, C-W., Mayisela, T., Rets, I., Sargent, J., Scanlon, E., Small, J., Walji, S., Weller, M., & Whitelock, D. (2023). *Innovating pedagogy 2023: Open university innovation report 11*. The Open University.

Kukulska-Hulme, A., & Lee, H. (2020). Intelligent assistants in language learning: An analysis of features and limitations. In K.-M. Frederiksen, S. Larsen, L. Bradley & S. Thouësny (Eds.), *CALL for widening participation: Short papers from EUROCALL 2020* (pp. 172–176). Research-publishing.net.

Lee, S., & Jeon, J. (2022). Visualizing a disembodied agent: Young EFL learners' perceptions of voice-controlled conversational agents as language partners. *Computer Assisted Language Learning*, 37(5–6), 1048–1073.

Lee, S. M., & Wu, J. G. (2023). Teaching with immersive virtual reality: Perceptions of Korean trainee teachers. *International Journal of Computer-Assisted Language Learning and Teaching*, 13(1), 1–14.

Lee, S. M., & Wu, J. G. (2024). Preparing teachers for the future: Microteaching in the immersive VR environment. *ReCALL*, 1–19. doi:10.1017/S0958344024000089

Liu, P. L. (2016). Mobile English vocabulary learning based on concept-mapping strategy. *Language Learning & Technology*, 20(3), 128–141.

Miller, L., & Wu, J. G. (Eds.). (2021). *Language learning with technology: Perspectives from Asia*. Springer.

Mishra, P., & Koehler, M. J. (2006). Technological pedagogical content knowledge: A framework for teacher knowledge. *Teachers College Record*, 108(6), 1017–1054.

Morgana, V., & Kukulska-Hulme, A. (Eds.). (2021). *Mobile assisted language learning across educational contexts*. Routledge.

Mystakidis, S. (2022). Metaverse. *Encyclopedia*, 2(1), 486–497.

Nation, I. S. P. (2007). The four strands. *Innovation in Language Learning and Teaching*, 1(1), 1–12.

Nation, I. S. P. (2022). *Learning vocabulary in another language* (3rd ed.). Cambridge University Press.

Nation, I. S. P., & Webb, S. (2011). *Researching and analyzing vocabulary*. Heinle, Cengage Learning.

Olinghouse, N. G., & Wilson, J. (2013). The relationship between vocabulary and writing quality in three genres. *Reading and Writing: An Interdisciplinary Journal*, 26, 45–65.

Pegrum, M., Hockly, N., & Dudeney, G. (2022). *Digital literacies*. Routledge.

Peña-Rios, A., & Wu, J. G. (2023). Guest Editorial: The metaverse and the future of education. *IEEE Transactions on Learning Technologies*, 16(6), 887–891.

Puentedura, R. R. (2006). Transformation, technology, and education [Web log post]. www.hippasus.com/rrpweblog/archives/2006_11.html

Qian, D. D. (2002). Investigating the relationship between vocabulary knowledge and academic reading performance: An assessment perspective. *Language Learning*, 52(3), 513–536.

Richards, J. C. (2015). The changing face of language learning: Learning beyond the classroom. *RELC Journal*, 46(1), 5–22.

Schmitt, N. (2010). *Researching vocabulary: A vocabulary research manual*. Palgrave Macmillan.

Stæhr, L. S. (2009). Vocabulary knowledge and advanced listening comprehension in English as a foreign language. *Studies in Second Language Acquisition*, 31(4), 577–607.

Teng, F. (2018). A learner-based approach of applying online reading to improve learner autonomy and lexical knowledge. *Revista Española de Lingüística Aplicada/Spanish Journal of Applied Linguistics*, 31(1), 104–134.

Teng, F. (2021). *Language learning through captioned videos: Incidental vocabulary acquisition*. Routledge.

Teng, F. (2022a). Vocabulary learning through videos: Captions, advance-organizer strategy, and their combination. *Computer Assisted Language Learning*, 35(3), 518–550. doi.org/10.1080/09588221.2020.1720253

Teng, F. (2022b). Incidental L2 vocabulary learning from viewing captioned videos: Effects of learner-related factors. *System*, 105, 102736. doi.org/10.1016/j.system.2022.102736

Teng, F. (2023a). Incidental vocabulary learning from captioned videos: Learners' prior vocabulary knowledge and working memory. *Journal of Computer Assisted Learning*, 39(2), 517–531. doi.org/10.1111/jcal.12756

Teng, F. (2023b). Effectiveness of captioned videos for incidental vocabulary learning and retention: The role of working memory. *Computer Assisted Language Learning*. doi.org/10.1080/09588221.2023.2173613

Teng, F. (2024). Incidental vocabulary learning from listening, reading, and viewing captioned videos: Frequency and prior vocabulary knowledge. *Applied Linguistics Review*. doi.org/10.1515/applirev-2023-0106

Uchihara, T., & Clenton, J. (2020). Investigating the role of vocabulary size in second language speaking ability. *Language Teaching Research*, 24(4), 540–556.

UNESCO. (n.d.). *AI: UNESCO mobilizes education ministers from around the world for a coordinated response to ChatGPT*. www.unesco.org/en/articles/ai-unesco-mobilizes-education-ministers-around-world-co-ordinated-response-chatgpt

Wang, M., Yu, H., Bell, Z., & Chu, X. (2022). Constructing an Edu-Metaverse ecosystem: A new and innovative framework. *IEEE Transactions on Learning Technologies*, 15(6), 685–696.

Webb, S. (Eds.). (2019). *The Routledge handbook of vocabulary studies*. Routledge.

Wu, J. G., & Miller, L. (2021). Raising native cultural awareness through WeChat: A case study with Chinese EFL students. *Computer Assisted Language Learning*, 34(4), 552–582.

Wu, J. G., Miller, L., Huang, Q., & Wang, M. (2021). Learning with immersive virtual reality: An exploratory study of Chinese college nursing students. *RELC Journal*. doi.org/10.1177/00336882211044860

Wu, J. G., Yang Z., Wu, S., & Zou, D. (2024a). Unveiling the synergy of peer feedback and the metaverse. *Computers & Education: X Reality*, 4, 100056.

Wu, J. G., Zhang, D., & Lee, S. M. (2024b). Into the brave new metaverse: Envisaging future language teaching and learning. *IEEE Transactions on Learning Technologies*, 17, 44–53.

Yang, Z., Wu, J. G., & Xie, H. (2024). Taming Frankenstein's monster: Ethical considerations relating to generative artificial intelligence in education. *Asia Pacific Journal of Education*, 1–14.

Zhang, D., Wang, M., & Wu, J. G. (2020). Design and implementation of augmented reality for English language education. In V. Geroimenko (Ed.), *Augmented reality in education: A new technology for teaching and learning* (pp. 217–234). Springer.

Zou, D., Huang, Y., & Xie, H. (2021). Digital game-based vocabulary learning: Where are we and where are we going? *Computer Assisted Language Learning*, 34(5–6), 751–777.

Zou, D., & Teng, F. (2023). Effects of tasks and multimedia annotations on vocabulary learning. *System*, 115, 103050. doi.org/10.1016/j.system.2023.103050

Part I
Theories and synthesis

2 Intentional vocabulary learning through captioned viewing

Comparing Vanderplank's 'cognitive-affective model' with Gesa and Miralpeix

Robert Vanderplank[1] and Mark Feng Teng[2]
[1]*Kellogg College, Oxford University*
[2]*Macao Polytechnic University*

Pre-reading questions

1. Can captioned viewing benefit second and foreign language learners' vocabulary learning?
2. What theories and models support captioned viewing in vocabulary learning?

Background

The idea that language learners might learn vocabulary from watching foreign language TV programs and films has a history stretching back to the 1980s (see, for example, Vanderplank, 1990 and Vanderplank, 2016, for summaries). However, as the sound and images are fleeting, and sound cannot be frozen only repeated, for many teachers, this medium was either a 'Friday afternoon treat', where little language learning was expected, or it was reduced to being a stimulus for tasks and other activities. Both inside and outside the classroom, learners and viewers often expected only to 'get the gist' of what they were watching unless translation subtitles were provided.

Vocabulary acts as the cornerstone of foreign language acquisition (Webb & Nation, 2017), forming the basis upon which learners construct their understanding and proficiency. The process of vocabulary acquisition presents considerable challenges. One such obstacle is that learners might struggle with attentional control, which is the ability to maintain focus on new vocabulary long enough to internalise it for future use (Koolstra & Beentjes, 1999). The task of committing a new word or phrase to memory demands significant mental focus and concentration, both of which may be lacking in some learners. Another potential hurdle in vocabulary acquisition is the difficulty learners might face in establishing a form-meaning link, that is, the process of associating a specific meaning with the orthographic representation of a word. Given these challenges, captioned media, which provide learners with text, sound, and images, would appear to offer potentially rich resources for EFL and second language (L2) vocabulary learning (Teng, 2021).

Much of the very extensive research on the benefits and limitations of captioned viewing for vocabulary learning in the last 20 years has been in the form of highly controlled studies, often bearing little resemblance to the technological and pedagogical realities of either the language classroom or the learner's behaviour when watching foreign language programmes in their free time. Many studies have drawn on various theories from cognitive psychology and language processing theory to understand how language learners make sense of the combination of sound, text, and images in order to better follow and process what they are viewing. However, there have been few attempts to design and test models, and identify specific operational conditions for learning a foreign language from watching captioned media in general and for learning vocabulary in particular.

This chapter looks at how the cognitive-affective model of language learning supported by captioned viewing proposed by Vanderplank (2016) can be applied to vocabulary learning, and the potential of captioned viewing as a targeted tool for vocabulary instruction. More precisely, we discuss (1) what captions are, (2) the frameworks, theories, or models that facilitate the use of captioned viewing, and (3) how the model fits a well-designed study of intentional vocabulary among EFL learners in a Spanish secondary school.

Understanding what captions are

Captions (or closed captions, same language subtitles, or intra-lingual subtitles) were originally developed in the 1970s, providing a means of accessing films and TV programmes for the deaf and hard-of-hearing community. They differ from 'traditional' subtitles, or interlingual subtitles, which typically carry the on-screen translated text accompanying a soundtrack in a different language within the video. In the United States, the captions were provided through closed caption decoders built into television sets; in other countries, such as the United Kingdom, they came through the Teletext system. From the start, the caption text was as close to verbatim as possible and had to follow strict rules such the number of lines on any screenshot, thus requiring skilled editing by captioners.

With advancements in technology, captions became more widely accessible, and it was noted that they could also provide crucial support for second language learners/viewers with normal hearing in both formal and informal settings. By providing a visual reinforcement of spoken language, captions have the potential to enhance the comprehension and retention of new vocabulary and structures.

In the last ten years, we have seen a transformative shift in the application of captioning as its use has broadened far beyond the deaf and hard-of-hearing community to foreign/second language learners/viewers and even to young native speakers. Captioning has also expanded beyond its English language borders, receiving support from the European Union (EU) for captioning in different languages, reinforcing the EU's commitment to its accessibility and equality agenda. Captions for many second language viewers have become the norm. In parallel, the amount of research literature on the value of captioned viewing has grown steadily (see Günter Burger's website: www.fremdsprache-und-spielfilm.de/Captions.htm), reflecting its unique position in the viewing of TV programmes and films worldwide.

Vanderplank (2016) proposed four principles underscoring the transformative potential of captioning: Captions transform films and programmes, such as documentaries and comedy series, into rich language resources for learners; captions may help to balance visual and verbal elements in a television programme; captions can have a liberating effect on both teachers and learners, enhancing choice, control, and responsibility; and captions may enable learners to watch programmes in a manner akin to that of native speakers. Martine Danan (2004) has also provided a comprehensive summary of the advantages and disadvantages of captioned and subtitled programmes. The benefits, as identified by research, include improvement in productive skills, the development of word recognition and vocabulary building, comprehension of details, and reducing learner-viewer anxiety. However, captions may not be suitable for lower-level learners or those with limited reading skills. Danan summarises the complementary explanations for how captions provide benefits rather than overloading the learner-viewer's faculties, the most commonly quoted being the notion of bimodal reinforcement of sound and text. This concept underscores the potential of captions as a tool for learning in our increasingly multilingual world.

Do multimedia learning theories help us better understand language learning from captioned viewing?

To date, there is no distinct set of theories of multimedia language learning with universally agreed-upon names. The various theories provide insights into how people learn and process information from multimedia sources, such as text, images, audio, and video. Below, we provide an overview of several educational theories and principles that are commonly applied to multimedia language learning. It is important to note that the field is evolving, and new theories may have already emerged.

1. Cognitive Load Theory:
   Cognitive Load Theory (CLT), proposed by John Sweller (2005), focuses on the cognitive load imposed on a learner's working memory. CLT attempts to explain how learners' cognitive resources are allocated and managed during the learning process. CLT emphasises the importance of managing the learner's cognitive load, which refers to the mental effort required to process and understand information. Recent literature on the theoretical underpinnings of watching captioned audiovisual material has focused on the notion of cognitive load as an important factor in enhancing or disrupting comprehension and learning gains (e.g. Frumuselu, 2018; Mayer, Lee & Peebles 2014; Sweller, 2005; Sweller et al., 2011).

   In the context of language learning, multimedia sources can be designed to reduce extraneous cognitive load by presenting information in a visually appealing and organised manner, using images, diagrams, and animations to illustrate concepts, and providing opportunities for active engagement and interaction. Obvious examples are using visuals to complement textual information to enhance understanding or providing accurate captions to enable viewers to follow unclear speech or foreign language programmes.

2. Dual Coding Theory:
   Dual Coding Theory (DCT), proposed by Alan Paivio (1986), posits that information is processed and stored in two forms: verbal and non-verbal. Information is better remembered when presented in both forms as while they are distinct forms, they are interconnected systems. In language learning, verbal information relates to the words, grammar, and syntax of the target language, while non-verbal information can include visual cues, gestures, and contextual information. Combining both verbal and non-verbal representations in multimedia materials can help to enhance learners' understanding and retention of language content.

   Martine Danan introduced the language learning world to DCT in her seminal article 'Captioning and subtitling: Undervalued language learning strategies' (2004), arguing that integrating visual elements, like images, diagrams, or, in her specific case, subtitle/caption text with speech in multimedia content can support language learning. Strictly speaking, DCT as originally proposed would not apply to caption-enhanced viewing, but the theory offers insights into the cognitive processes involved in viewing captioned material.

3. Cognitive Theory of Multimedia Learning:
   The Cognitive Theory of Multimedia Learning (CTML), as put forward in, for example, Mayer (2009, 2014) and Mayer, Lee and Peebles (2014) proposes that people learn better when information is presented using both words and relevant visuals, compared to using words alone. This principle of CTML highlights the importance of incorporating visual elements, such as images, videos, and diagrams, into language learning materials. Visuals can aid comprehension, facilitate the interpretation of meaning, and provide additional context for language learners. It was initially considered that subtitle/caption text would not fit into this principle as the cognitive load from the additional medium of text would be too heavy. However, more recent iterations have regarded the contribution of accurate captions in a more positive light, suggesting they provide enhanced understanding and actually reduce cognitive load.

   In many respects, as far as language learning with captioned viewing is concerned, the combining of textual information with relevant visuals (images, videos, and captions) to enhance comprehension might seem obvious, though issues have been frequently raised about whether the captions increase or decrease cognitive load. Nonetheless, researchers in the field of caption-enhanced language learning have frequently seized on CTML as a useful theoretical underpinning for their research.

4. Working Memory:
   Working Memory (WM, Baddeley, 1986; Baddeley & Hitch, 1974) is a key theory of language processing in cognitive psychology and is highly relevant to the process of multitasking required by watching captioned video. The model posits that WM is composed of several components, with the central executive functioning as the main controlling system, managing the overall system and problem-solving tasks. It oversees the allocation of information and tasks to its subsidiary systems, known as the visuo-spatial sketchpad and the phonological loop, which are integral elements within the WM structure. By assigning storage tasks and information flow to these subcomponents, the central executive frees up its capacity for additional tasks requiring cognitive processing. The visuo-spatial sketchpad, one of the subcomponents, controls the task of holding and manipulating visual and spatial information, while the phonological loop is concerned with handling and rehearsing verbal and auditory information.

   The WM model was further refined by Baddeley (2000), incorporating the sensory modalities that were previously overlooked and emphasising the crucial role of the episodic buffer in integrating these modalities. The episodic buffer integrates diverse forms of information and directly coordinates with the slave subsystems to fulfil the demands set by the central executive.

WM capacity influences the ability to process and understand the language presented in captions. Learners need to hold the new words in their memory while integrating them into their existing knowledge. In this respect, WM capacity affects the ability to learn and retain new vocabulary efficiently. Watching captioned videos requires simultaneous processing of visual and auditory information, and WM helps learners manage this dual task by holding and manipulating information from both modalities.

5. Moreno's Cognitive-Affective Theory of Learning with Media:
Research in cognitive psychology has expanded the theory of learning with media to include the affective domain, shedding light on factors that engage learner-viewers in watching captioned programmes attentively. Roxanna Moreno (2006; Moreno & Mayer, 2007) includes factors of self-regulation, self-efficacy, and motivation in her combined model 'integrating assumptions regarding the relationship between cognition, metacognition and motivation and affect' (Moreno & Mayer, 2007, p. 767).

The Cognitive-Affective Theory of Learning with Media (CATLM) focuses on cognitive and affective processes in multimedia learning. The model takes the theories outlined above and then incorporates a further affective component. Moreno makes four cognitive assumptions: firstly, the existence of verbal and non-verbal information processing channels that are relatively independent of one another; secondly, the limited capacity of WM, along with the virtually unlimited capacity of long-term memory; thirdly, enhanced learning through dual coding; and lastly, the need for learners to actively process information to construct meaning. The theory then adds three new assumptions: the affective mediation assumption, which suggests that motivational factors mediate learning by increasing or decreasing cognitive engagement; the metacognitive mediation assumption, which suggests that metacognitive factors mediate learning by regulating cognitive and affective processes; and thirdly, the individual differences assumption, which suggests that differences in learners' prior knowledge affect the efficiency of learning with methods and media.

A combined cognitive-affective learning theory has clear implications for how we should treat language learning from captioned TV programmes and films given that individual choice and preferences, motivation, purpose in watching, and levels of attention to visual, auditory, and textual input may vary greatly even within a single viewing of audiovisual material.

What is the value of all these theories for caption-enhanced language learning? Overall, the consensus in the literature appears to be that by understanding and applying multimedia learning theories, educators and language learners should be able to optimise the design and use of multimedia resources to enhance language learning experiences, promote comprehension, and improve retention of language knowledge and skills. Regarding the value of captions for language learning, applying the theoretical principles means ensuring certain criteria are met, such as minimum levels of foreign language knowledge and skills, well-selected, appropriately graded, and engaging viewing material, with accurate captions and a clear purpose in language-focused viewing.

Modelling language learning from captioned viewing

The very extensive literature on captioned viewing makes it clear that research is largely driven by empirical observation rather than by theory. From the earliest research, the value of watching with captions has been tested and compared against other formats such as translation subtitles and no captions. Findings from observations have been analysed and only then have researchers sought explanations and theoretical underpinnings to explain outcomes and behaviour. Attempting to capture and define the processes of language learning through captioned viewing is not new. Vanderplank (1990) attempted to do this in a staged model in which 'Attention' was a crucial factor (see Figure 2.1). From critical observations of his learners, Vanderplank concluded that these attention factors play a crucial role in determining if a learner-viewer will apply the necessary effort to watching a video or a programme with the goal of enhancing their language proficiency. This model sought to define 'Attention' as those factors that are most likely to encourage focused viewing. These factors are also significantly connected to the learner-viewer's perceived self-efficacy when watching. For the model to function effectively, it is crucial that learners also possess some degree of control over or purpose in what to focus their attention on. Crucially, Vanderplank noted that learners who engaged with captioned programmes needed to consciously extract language from the material to gain any tangible benefits. In Figure 2.1, the degree of attention paid – encompassing selection factors such as motivation and attitude, as well as grading factors like existing knowledge, current English skill level, language/information load, mode of presentation, and programme length – affects the learners' ability to assimilate comprehensible input and internalise the language into intake. This model also emphasises that the level of awareness learners possess about their own language learning is of importance for their experiences with captioned video viewing. In essence, the more conscious a learner is of their language learning, the more effective their captioned video viewing experiences are likely to be.

22 *Theory and Practice in Vocabulary Research in Digital Environments*

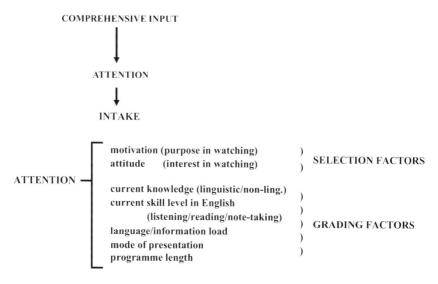

Figure 2.1 The model of attention with selection and grading factors
Source: Vanderplank, 1990, p. 228.

Vanderplank (1990) further refined the model, specifically the attention segment, to reflect the findings of the study and to accommodate how learners manage a substantial volume of comprehensible input. The initial attention factors did not fully capture the potential actions of learners when faced with abundant comprehensible input and the complexity of language acquisition. The resulting model is given in Figure 2.2.

In the model shown in Figure 2.2, learners pay attention to the extensive comprehensible input in a conscious, systematic, and reflective manner – each of these elements forming the essence of attentive viewing. Both the 'Attention' and 'Adaptation' stages are components of 'Taking out'. The learner may then proceed to 'adopt' what has been adapted by generating suitable spoken or written language. The model does not suggest that 'Adoption' corresponds to 'Taking in'. Adopting (or 'taking on') someone else's language does not imply that it has been 'taken in', in the sense of being absorbed or incorporated into one's linguistic proficiency. Only through regular, genuine usage can language truly be 'taken in'.

We mentioned earlier how technological changes, along with changes in language policies, have greatly contributed to the spread and acceptance of captioned media as valuable tools for language learning. It is, therefore, worth recording that, following further research in the mid-1990s,

Intentional vocabulary learning through captioned viewing 23

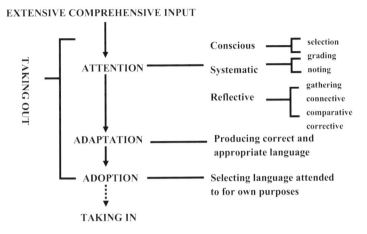

Figure 2.2 The model of 'Paying attention to the words'
Source: Vanderplank, 1990, p. 229; 2016, p. 64.

Vanderplank concluded that the operationalisation of the model might be too demanding to be feasible for most learners and in most classroom-based learning situations. The model, he suggested, might only be fully realised by independent learners outside the classroom. What he had found in his work with his own students over the years was that they were unlikely to give the attention and effort required to benefit greatly from watching with captions, if only due to the perceptions they brought to TV and film watching and the difficulty of exercising a degree of choice and control, a factor already identified as essential to the model operating successfully. There might be some autonomous learners who would be so motivated and strategic in their learning that they would exploit the opportunities offered by captioned viewing, but only in very small numbers.

What a difference 25 years can make. In 2016, following the findings of a study in which learners of French, German, Italian, and Spanish were provided with a wide selection of films on DVD with optional captions, Vanderplank published a fully revised model that included the iterative processes that allow learners to exercise choice and/or control. The revised model also sought to capture the perceptual and affective dimensions of captioned viewing noted in the project outcomes, drawing on the work of Roxanna Moreno (2006; Moreno & Mayer, 2007) and research on perceptual re-tuning by Mitterer and McQueen (2009). The revised model, the Cognitive-Affective Model, is shown in Figure 2.3.

24 *Theory and Practice in Vocabulary Research in Digital Environments*

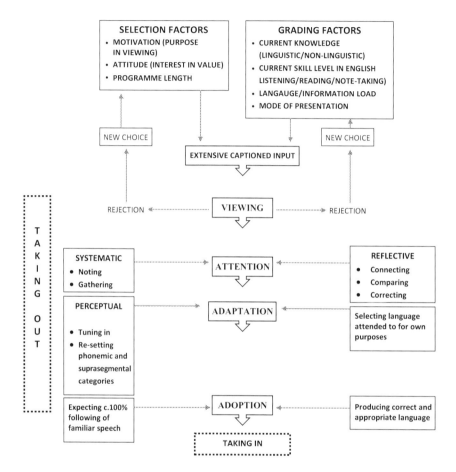

Figure 2.3 A cognitive-affective model of language learning through captioned viewing
Source: Vanderplank, 2016, p. 240.

As stated earlier, the process of learning language via captioned videos encompasses a wide range of variables, as shown in the cognitive-affective model (Figure 2.3). In the initial model (Figure 2.1), 'Attention' plays a pivotal role, acting as an element of the process rather than the final goal. This is also reflected in Figure 2.2, where 'Attention' and 'Adaptation' are integral components of the 'Taking out' phase. The main distinction between the models lies in the inclusion of additional aspects within the 'Attention' and 'Adaptation' stages in Figure 2.2. This revision takes into account motivation, attitude, and other affective factors.

Intentional vocabulary learning through captioned viewing 25

The implication of the updated model (Figure 2.3) is that simply watching a captioned programme does not guarantee effective language acquisition of any kind. The degree of engagement with the programme is greatly influenced by motivation and attitude as well as grading factors; extracting the target language requires conscious, systematic, and reflective attention – a significant task. Additional elements have been added to both the 'Adaptation' and 'Adoption' stages to account for perceptual tuning in, a concept supported by researchers such as Bravo (2008) and Mitterer and McQueen (2009). For language production, learners can adopt and utilise adapted language in spoken or written forms. However, adopting a language does not imply full absorption or assimilation into one's linguistic competence. It merely indicates the language's usefulness to the learner. On 'Taking in', consistent and genuine use is the only guarantee of fully internalising a new language.

In terms of vocabulary acquisition, Vanderplank's further work within the framework of the EURECAP project (2019) provided insights into the viability, opportunities, and limitations of both the model and its operationalisation. It was found that the model captured much of the feedback provided by EURECAP participants, in particular the choice and control with a loop for rejection, along with the attention, selection, and perception aspects of the model. Indeed, not only did participants sometimes reject films after watching for a short period, but they also adjusted their behaviour while watching, often because they had 'tuned in' to the voices, and new vocabulary had become familiar with frequent use. Most participants went no further than the 'Attention' stage of the model, gathering and noting words and phrases, pausing and rewinding to check, looking up new words and phrases. In itself, enhancing the process of vocabulary acquisition in this way may be considered a great benefit of watching with captions. However, it rather sells the potential of the medium short if watching with captions is to be reduced to simply gathering new words and phrases; the model encourages us to go much further and explore the full potential. In reality, while all participants appeared to be highly motivated to watch, understand, and enjoy the films, only a minority (10 out of 36) showed a strong, personal desire to exploit a rich language learning resource to the full and demonstrated the independent learning strategies necessary to fully exploit the captioned films.

Vanderplank argues that the key missing factor was the absence of guidance by an advisor and a lack of tasks designed to exploit the language and content of the films, which might have assisted participants through the essential 'Adaptation' and 'Adoption' stages. Only one participant specifically mentioned using what she had gained from watching a film in a presentation.

New understandings: How well does the cognitive-affective model fit Gesa and Miralpeix's article 'Extensive viewing as additional input for foreign language vocabulary learning: A longitudinal study in secondary school'?

In developing his model, Vanderplank explicitly focused on scenarios in which learners have choice and control as a consequence of his experiences with his learners in the 1990s. With technology offering teachers greater flexibility and a choice of materials and instruments, how would the model work with a well-designed and well-controlled trial in which learners were provided with tasks and activities, and their learning was monitored and tested over a substantial period? Although there are countless anecdotal accounts of how watching captioned media over a lengthy period can help spoken production (especially pronunciation), vocabulary acquisition, and listening comprehension, there have been relatively few well-controlled longitudinal studies reported in the literature on captioned media (Rodgers & Webb, 2017 and Bravo, 2008 are some exceptions).

The study of English vocabulary acquisition by teenage learners in a Spanish secondary school, reported by Ferran Gesa and Imma Miralpeix (2023), provides us with a meticulously well-designed, executed, and reported longitudinal study with which to test the operational performance of Vanderplank's model in a classroom setting. While the study does not provide participants with the autonomy and control that Vanderplank was seeking in developing his model, it appears to meet many of the criteria for language learning from captioned media given in the model, in particular the support and compelling reasons to encourage learners to pay attention to the language of the video material rather than watching for entertainment alone and possibly only getting 'the gist' of programmes.

Another reason for selecting the Gesa and Miralpeix study is that they provided a delayed post-viewing test a substantial amount of time (eight months!) after the intervention. The issue of how much language is retained by learners after an intervention has only been addressed to a very limited extent in the captioned viewing literature. Studies that have used delayed post-viewing tests have tended to re-test after only a relatively short period: Baltova (1999) tested retention after two weeks and found high rates of retention, Lertola (2012) after two weeks, and Peters and Webb (2018) after only one week (though the authors recognise the unreliability of the result).

The primary intention of the Gesa and Miralpeix study was to compare the relative effectiveness of intentional vocabulary learning enhanced by viewing a captioned TV series over a long period (one academic year) compared with vocabulary learning alone, and to test whether any gains were retained over the long term. The authors wished to test to what extent the teaching of target vocabulary prior to watching episodes of a captioned TV series over a period of one academic year could maximise vocabulary acquisition in English. Authentic audiovisual materials in the form of popular TV series were selected for the study, while other instruments, vocabulary tests, and language-focused activities were specially developed for the teaching intervention. Sixty-four grade 10 English learners were introduced to new target words each week through language-focused exercises. Thirty-three learners in the experimental group also watched an episode of a captioned TV series where these target words appeared. The control group did not watch the captioned programmes and continued to study with their usual textbook. The average age of participants was 15, and the number of boys and girls was roughly equal. All were in the last year of compulsory education. They had all received about 1,100 hours of instruction and were expected to have reached a B1 – so about (lower) intermediate – level of English on the Common European Framework of Reference (CEFR) scale. Further pre-viewing vocabulary tests showed that they had a receptive vocabulary of between 1,400 and 5,600 words (mean 3,376 words). They were not frequent viewers of original TV programmes, with or without captions.

All participants took pre-viewing and post-viewing tests on target word form and meaning recall at the beginning and end of each term, which included the target words for that term. A delayed post-viewing test at the end of the year, eight months after the intervention, measured vocabulary retention of the target words from the last term. Their results showed that while vocabulary was mainly learned intentionally, the additional viewing of the captioned TV series by the experimental group contributed significantly to higher lexical gains at different testing times.

A key aspect of the study for the purposes of the present chapter was that it focused on intentional vocabulary learning. It is often assumed that learner-viewers will 'pick up' words and phrases just by watching captioned programmes, as the captions provide access to audiovisual material that might otherwise be largely inaccessible or provide only 'gist watching'. The value of incidental vocabulary learning from captioned viewing has been shown to be largely marginal, with high numbers of viewing hours producing relatively limited amounts of new words and phrases acquired for the amount of time invested. It is the long-standing contention of the authors that captioned viewing requires both attention to the words and a definite language learning purpose (which might be related tasks and activities) if captioned viewing is to be successful in terms of language learning.

Our analysis below breaks down the cognitive-affective model, as shown in Figure 2.3, into its key components, and discusses how the approach taken by Gesa and Miralpeix follows or differs from the model in practice. In other words, is the model a good fit in practical terms in a well-designed and controlled study in a classroom context, one that led to significant gains in vocabulary acquisition by the participants?

Selection and grading

Firstly, are the selection and grading factors addressed in the intervention? The evidence from the 'Instruments' section indicates that selection and grading factors were taken into account reasonably comprehensively, as outlined below. However, no feedback is reported from learners on what they actually felt about the choices made by the researchers on their behalf.

SELECTION FACTORS

- MOTIVATION (PURPOSE IN VIEWING)
- ATTITUDE (INTEREST IN VIEWING)
- PROGRAMME LENGTH

Two old and much-loved American comedy series were chosen: *I Love Lucy* and *Seinfeld*. As Gesa and Miralpeix report, these two TV series were chosen because they had not been broadcast in Spain for many years and were not available on streaming services at the time of the intervention. *I Love Lucy* was also chosen as it had been used in a previous study with learners of a similar profile (Cokely & Muñoz, 2019), and *Seinfeld* had been piloted successfully in the same institution with a group of grade 11 learners. According to Gesa and Miralpeix, the results of this study showed that participants enjoyed watching *Seinfeld* and, as they found the series engaging, they were keen to watch more episodes. The 21 episodes selected were, therefore, considered appropriate in terms of content for the age group in the study. Each episode shown was about 22 minutes long and was shown uninterrupted (a pilot study had revealed that stopping the viewing in the middle to check attention levels was, in fact, disruptive to viewing – not surprising, perhaps, when one thinks about one's reaction to adverts in the middle of broadcasts).

When looking for series, (authors' communication) they had the choice of selecting programmes that were 20–25 minutes long or those that were about 40–45 minutes long. In Spanish high schools, English classes usually last for 50–55 minutes, so they opted for the shorter ones in order to have ample time for the pre- and post-viewing tasks. They also thought that more than 30 minutes would be too long (and perhaps overwhelming) for B1 level students.

In Term 1, students watched seven episodes from season five of *I Love Lucy*. In the next two terms, 14 episodes of *Seinfeld* from seasons four and

Intentional vocabulary learning through captioned viewing 29

five were viewed (seven in each term). In total, participants watched 21 episodes lasting an average of 22 minutes each, so they were exposed to 7 hours 54 minutes of original version TV.

In each of these sessions, and for the whole academic year, the experimental group started by doing the pre-viewing vocabulary task individually or in small groups. It was corrected immediately afterwards, and students could ask questions about the vocabulary presented, so all target words were presumably attended to well.

The group then watched the corresponding episode of the TV series, always presented in English with captions. The episode was projected onto the classroom whiteboard using an overhead projector. After that, the post-viewing vocabulary task was distributed, and the target words were played through a speaker. Students were given time to complete their answers. The task was corrected by the researcher to check if target words were learned immediately after being presented through language-focused instruction and encountered in the TV series. As expected, the scores on this task were always very high and reached a ceiling effect.

GRADING FACTORS

- CURRENT KNOWLEDGE
  (LINGUISTIC/NON-LINGUISTIC)
- CURRENT SKILL LEVEL IN ENGLISH
  (LISTENING/READING/NOTE-TAKING)
- LANGUAGE/INFORMATION LOAD
- MODE OF PRESENTATION

As mentioned above, the students had all received about 1,100 hours of instruction and were expected to have reached a B1 level of English (according to the CEFR scale). Pre-viewing vocabulary tests showed that they had a receptive vocabulary of between 1,400 and 5,600 words (mean 3,376 words). The authors report that they were not frequent viewers of original language TV programmes, with or without captions. In addition, comprehension tests administered to the caption-watching group participants showed that average comprehension was high.

In terms of vocabulary demands, through a corpus analysis and checking frequency lists, the two series were found to be very similar. In addition, the coverage level (information load in the model) in terms of three frequency bands up to the 3,000-word list was between 90% and 97% in the three terms. Taken together, the figures indicate that the two TV series were within the competence of the participants because they had a mean vocabulary size of 3,376 words and would be able to follow and understand most of what was happening.

At the start of each term, participants took a vocabulary listening test. Thirty-five target word items spoken twice by a native speaker were played via the overhead speakers of the classroom. Target words were presented in a quasi-randomised order, and four practice items were added at the beginning of the test to familiarise students with the format. The pre-viewing tests were used to assess participants' knowledge of the target words at the beginning of each academic term.

Time was given before and after to read and revise the questions and answers. The participants' task was to write down the English form of each word they heard and provide the Spanish or Catalan translation or definition if they knew it. Gesa and Miralpeix consider that this test format required participants to access target word meanings in their L1 through the L2 forms in order to be able to complete the task correctly, applying a process of translation.

The pre-viewing target word listening comprehension tests at the beginning of each term served not only to draw participants' attention to the sounds and potential meanings and forms of each word but also primed them for the TV series to follow. It was also a way of knowing if, by any chance, participants knew any of the target words already. In this way, gains would not be overestimated at the end, if that was the case.

Controlling for knowledge was also a way of being more precise in Gesa and Miralpeix's estimations of what could be actually learned from the input provided.

Extensive viewing with captions

The model then moves on to what happens while participants are viewing the extensive captioned input. Ideally, learner-viewers would be able to have control of their viewing and could stop, rewind, and replay as often as they wished, taking advantage of the ability to freeze-frame the caption text. In reality, in the language classroom, this level of control is rarely available. Teachers need, therefore, to devise means of ensuring that learners pay attention to the language of the programme through

Intentional vocabulary learning through captioned viewing 31

pre-viewing or in-viewing tasks and activities which provide a focus for attention. Vanderplank's prior research (for example, 1990, 2019) concluded that without compelling reasons to watch attentively and pay attention to the language of a captioned programme, most learner-viewers will tend to sit back and enjoy a programme as they would in their first language, particularly if it is a comedy show.

In each of the classes in the seven weeks following the vocabulary listening test, the experimental group began by doing the pre-viewing vocabulary task individually or in small groups. This task or activity centred on the five target words which had been selected from each episode (they were assumed to be unknown to the participants and were usually chosen from larger English corpora and higher frequency lists), making a total of 105 target words (35 each term). The task or activity was corrected immediately afterwards, and students could ask questions or share doubts about the vocabulary presented, so all target words could then be assumed to have been attended to. After that, the pre-viewing task was collected and retained for later analysis.

The group then watched the corresponding episode of the TV series. The episode was projected onto the classroom whiteboard using an overhead projector. After that, the post-viewing vocabulary task was distributed, and the audio of the target items was played via the overhead speakers of the classroom. Time was given before and after to read and revise the questions and answers.

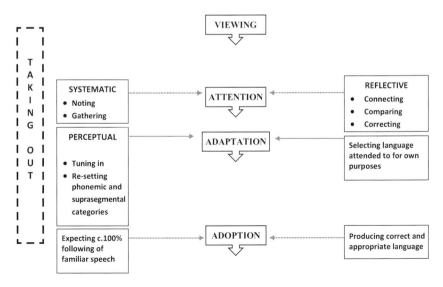

Figure 2.4 'Paying attention to the words' model

The Gesa and Miralpeix study contains no separate section on either Adaptation or Adoption so we can only infer from the descriptions of the pre- and post-viewing tests and tasks whether there was evidence of participants attending to language 'for own purposes', 'producing correct and appropriate language', 'tuning in', and 're-setting phonemic and suprasegmental categories'.

In all viewing sessions, participants did one pre-viewing vocabulary task and one post-viewing task specially devised for each episode. Pre-viewing tasks were designed to introduce the target vocabulary appearing in the episode (that is, the five target words), and the authors provide an example of an engaging word-matching task. They report that the task always consisted of one exercise following a focus-on-forms approach, and learners had to pay attention to the target words as they were needed in the activity. Different types of tasks were used throughout the year, such as fill-in-the-gaps, cloze tests, wordsearches, crosswords, and word–image matching exercises, as well as one exercise asking participants to match target words with their definitions.

In the post-viewing task at the end of each session, participants were asked to listen to the target words spoken twice, write down the forms in English, and select the best Spanish translation out of five different possibilities plus an 'I don't know' option.

According to Gesa and Miralpeix, the task drew on written form recall, prompted by the spoken form of the words, and meaning recognition. The task also provides evidence of students' receptive knowledge of the spoken forms of the target words, their productive knowledge of the written forms, and their recognition of the meanings of the words. The authors report that test scores were high, and reached a ceiling effect. On this basis, it is likely that the criterion of being able to follow the episodes fully was met to a large extent.

Thus, in terms of the model, the use of tasks, activities, and tests appears to meet its criteria for successful adaptation and adoption of the target words in each episode viewed, though again, there is no learner feedback to confirm this.

'Taking in' and the delayed vocabulary test

The nearest we come to evidence that the target words were taken in is through the outcome of the delayed test with a subset of the experimental group (24 out of 30) and control group (16 out of 27) to measure retention after eight months. The authors consider (personal communication) that, on reflection, they should have administered this test immediately after the summer holidays (2–3 months), as the participants would not then have taken any classes when the words might have occurred.

The delayed target word test assessed the 35 target words which were presented in Term 3, and it followed exactly the same format as the pre- and post-viewing tests for each term described above. This delayed test allowed the authors to measure how many target words learners had retained eight months after the intervention itself.

The delayed post-viewing test could be seen as acting as a guide as to whether a word had actually been fully taken in and internalised in long-term memory by a participant. Given the format of the test, we may reasonably assume that the participant would be able to use the word correctly and appropriately. As Gesa and Miralpeix report, the results of their study indicated that the target vocabulary was mainly learned intentionally (as a comparison with the control group who did not watch the captioned TV series was not significant), but that additional viewing of the captioned TV series significantly contributed to greater lexical gains at different testing times.

Although the experimental group remembered more word forms and more word meanings than the control (60.77% to 53.80% and 46.78% to 35.18% respectively), the differences were not significant. It is also worth remembering that as the experimental group had learned more in Term 3, they had more to lose, but, in fact, as a group, their retention was high. However, standard deviations were high for both groups at around 30% for both form and meaning. As Gesa and Miralpeix point out in their discussion of the retention findings, in addition to the long period of time between the intervention and the delayed test, there were other factors that may have influenced the results, such as uncontrolled exposure to target words and potential learning, and the natural consequences of participants' language learning development over the period. The large standard deviations also indicate the important role of individual differences. The authors suggest that the level of non-retention in the experimental group may be explained by one of the principles of the CTML (Mayer, 2009): While instruction through multimedia materials may facilitate learning, this learning is not likely to be retained by lower-level learners in the long run.

Where is WM in the model?

As noted in the description of WM, its processes and its applications, summarised earlier in this chapter, WM plays a key role in language development in the context of viewing captioned audiovisual material. Its role is pervasive, especially in situations where a learner-viewer has little or no control over the choice of material and actual viewing: in individual differences involved in selecting and grading materials by independent learners; in teachers selecting and grading materials taking into account the level of learners' language skills and knowledge; and in affecting levels of attention, focus, and effort displayed and deployed by learners. WM capacity also influences the ability to process and understand the language presented in the captions, while also enabling the storage and retrieval of new vocabulary encountered in captioned videos. If the language spoken and written in a captioned video is beyond the learner-viewer's WM capacity owing to limited language knowledge and/or skills, there will be little comprehension and even less acquisition. In situations where the learner-viewer cannot freeze-frame the caption text, they need to hold the new words in their memory while integrating them into their existing knowledge. Thus, WM capacity affects the ability to learn and retain new vocabulary efficiently and also the amount of language integrated, then fully acquired in long-term memory, ready for later retrieval and use.

Given its pervasiveness in viewing, Frumuselu's (2018) model (Figure 2.4), which puts WM at the heart of learning with media, captures its complexity and shares many characteristics with Vanderplank's operational model, while remaining at a more general and abstract level. If we were to incorporate WM into Vanderplank's (2016) model, it would have

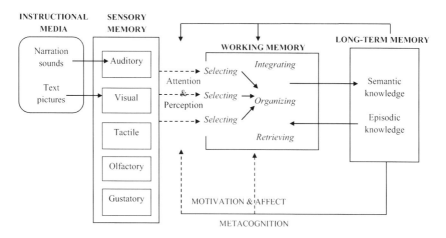

Figure 2.5 A cognitive-affective model of learning with media
Source: Frumuselu, 2018.

to be located below 'Viewing' and alongside 'Attention', 'Adaptation', and 'Adoption' to express how essential functioning WM capacity is in contexts where there is an absence of control by learner-viewers.

Implications for current and future research and teaching

One motive for developing a model, as Vanderplank (2016) reports, is to offer research 'spaces' for exploring new research questions which are appropriate for the new environment for language learning. Apart from questions testing the validity of the model as a whole, at each stage or level in the model there are possible questions related to the learner, the film or programme, and the technology. The 'Attention' space may also offer multiple research questions, particularly in classroom contexts where the teacher can set tasks to be completed outside class which may enhance learning supported by captions. Similarly, both 'Adaptation' and 'Adoption' lend themselves to task-based approaches where learners view captioned programmes or extensive clips and extract language that they can use in fulfilling tasks related to the programmes' themes or language. On the perceptual side, more research following up Mitterer and McQueen's (2009) findings is needed to test how much exposure to captioned viewing is needed and in what circumstances there is significant re-tuning of perceptual categories on more than a limited local level. Regarding 'Taking in', only longitudinal studies are able to show whether language has really been taken in for personal use.

Incorporating captioned viewing into language teaching can offer educators effective strategies that extend beyond the typical comprehension activities. However, in instructed second language acquisition contexts, where instructional time is often limited to two or three hours per week, providing extensive exposure to multimodal input can be challenging. Despite this, the use of short video clips can be a valuable tool to stimulate various facets of L2 vocabulary learning. The classroom use of captioned viewing could emphasise vocabulary knowledge training, engaging learners in both bottom-up (decoding) and top-down (conceptual understanding) processes. For instance, the presence of imagery and related storylines may stimulate top-down processes. On the other hand, audiovisual content with captions provides abundant opportunities for training in decoding skills. As Charles and Trenkic (2015) found, with regular exposure to captioned audiovisual input, learners' speech segmentation and decoding skills may improve greatly. Not only does this aid learners in processing the captioned input, but it also assists them in decoding new words in fresh contexts, ultimately decreasing cognitive processing load. Thus, the presence of captions may allow learners to process and interpret meaning more effectively, possibly leading to improved noticing of new words or enhancing the learning and retention of various aspects of vocabulary knowledge.

At an affective level, the presence of captions may help reduce learners' feelings of insecurity and anxiety when watching a film which not only has unfamiliar vocabulary, but also unclear and/or rapid speech and unfamiliar content. Paradoxically, it is the very presence of captions which, far from overloading the learner-viewer's ability to process the input, may actually increase both the level of attention to the language and the language learning effort.

Acknowledgement

We are grateful to John Benjamins Publishing Company for permission to use Figure 2.4. A cognitive-affective model of learning with media, originally published as Figure 2.4 on page 63 in: 'The implications of Cognitive Load Theory and exposure to subtitles in English Foreign Language (EFL)', Frumuselu, A. in *Audiovisual translation in applied linguistics: Educational perspectives. Special issue of Translation and Translanguaging in Multilingual Contexts* 4:1 (2018), Incalcaterra McLoughlin, L. et al. – TTMC 4:1 – 2018. John Benjamins Publishing Company. Amsterdam/Philadelphia.

Further reading

Teng, F. (2021). *Language learning through captioned videos: Incidental vocabulary acquisition*. New York: Routledge.
This book is a resource that delves into the role of captioned videos in fostering incidental vocabulary learning. The book provides empirical evidence and innovative strategies that can transform traditional language instruction, thereby equipping readers with practical knowledge on how to effectively integrate multimedia technology into their vocabulary teaching or learning process.

Vanderplank, R. (2016). *Captioned media in foreign language learning and teaching: Subtitles for the deaf and hard-of-hearing as tools for language learning*. Oxford: Palgrave Macmillan.
This book provides invaluable insights into how captioned media can be a powerful tool in foreign language acquisition, making it a must-read for educators and learners alike. Moreover, it expands the conversation to demonstrate the broad potential and inclusivity of using captions for language learning.

References

Baddeley, A. D. (1986). *Working memory*. New York: Oxford University Press.
Baddeley, A. (2000). The episodic buffer: A new component of working memory? *Trends in Cognitive Sciences*, 4 (11), 417–423.

Baddeley, A. and Hitch, G. (1974). Working memory. *Psychology of Learning and Motivation*, 8, 47–89.

Baltova, I. (1999). 'The effect of subtitled and staged video input on the learning and retention of. content and vocabulary in a second language'. Unpublished doctoral dissertation, University of Toronto. Ottawa: National Library of Canada. Available at www.collectionscanada.ca/obj/s4/f2/dsk3/ftp04/nq41096.pdf

Bravo, M.C.C. (2008). 'Putting the reader in the picture: Screen translation and foreign language learning'. Unpublished doctoral dissertation, Universitat Rovira I Virgili, Tarragona, Spain. Available at http://tdx.cat/handle/10803/8771

Cokely, M. and Muñoz, C. (2019). Captioned video, vocabulary and visual prompts: An exploratory study. In: C. Herrero and I. Vanderschelden (Eds.), *Using film and media in the language classroom: Reflections on research-led teaching* (pp. 61–75). Bristol: Multilingual Matters.

Danan, M. (2004). Captioning and subtitling: Undervalued language learning strategies. *Meta*, 49, 67–77.

Frumuselu, A. D. (2018). The implications of Cognitive Load Theory and exposure to subtitles in English Foreign Language (EFL). *Translation and Translanguaging in Multilingual Contexts*, 4 (1), 55–76.

Gesa, F. and Miralpeix, I. (2023). Extensive viewing as additional input for foreign language vocabulary learning: A longitudinal study in secondary school. *Language Teaching Research*, 1–34. https://journals.sagepub.com/doi/10.1177/13621688231169451

Koolstra, C. M. and Beentjes, J. W. (1999). Children's vocabulary acquisition in a foreign language through watching subtitled television programs at home. *Educational Technology Research & Development*, 47, 51–60.

Lertola, J. (2012). The effect of the subtitling task on vocabulary learning. In: A. Pym and D. Orrego-Carmona (Eds.), *Translation research projects* (pp. 61–70). Tarragona: Universitat Rovira i Virgili.

Mayer, R.E. (2009). *Multimedia learning, 2nd edition*. Cambridge: Cambridge University Press.

Mayer, R.E. (2014). *The Cambridge handbook of multimedia learning, 2nd Edition*. Cambridge: Cambridge University Press.

Mayer, R.E., Lee, H. and Peebles, A. (2014). Multimedia learning in a second language: A cognitive load perspective. *Applied Cognitive Psychology*, 28, 653–660.

Mitterer, H. and McQueen, J.M. (2009). Foreign subtitles help but native-language subtitles harm foreign speech perception. *PLOS ONE*, 4(11). e7785. https://doi:10.1371/journal.pone.0007785.

Moreno, R. (2006). Learning in high-tech and multimedia environments. *Current Directions in Psychological Science*, 15, 63–67.

Moreno, R. and Mayer, R.E. (2007). Interactive multimodal learning environments. *Educational Psychology Review*, 19, 309–326.

Paivio, A. (1986). *Mental representations: A dual coding approach*. Oxford: Oxford University Press.

Peters, E. and Webb, S. (2018). Incidental vocabulary acquisition through viewing L2 television: And factors that affect learning. *Studies in Second Language Acquisition*, 40 (3), 1–27.

Rodgers, M.P.H. and Webb, S. (2017). The effects of captions on EFL learners' comprehension of English-language television Programs. *CALICO Journal*, 34 (1), 20–38.

Sweller, J. (2005). Implications of cognitive load theory for multimedia learning. In: R.E. Mayer (Ed.), *The Cambridge handbook of multimedia learning* (pp. 19–30). Cambridge: Cambridge University Press.

Sweller, J., Ayres, P. and Kalyuga, S. (2011). *Cognitive load theory*. London: Springer.

Teng, F. (2021). *Language learning through captioned videos: Incidental vocabulary acquisition*. New York: Routledge.

Vanderplank, R. (1990). Paying attention to the words: Practical and theoretical problems in watching television programmes with uni-lingual (CEEFAX) subtitles. *System*, 18 (2), 221–234.

Vanderplank, R. (2016). *Captioned media in foreign language learning and teaching: Subtitles for the deaf and hard-of-hearing as tools for language learning*. Oxford: Palgrave Macmillan.

Vanderplank, R. (2019). Gist watching can only take you so far: attitudes, strategies and changes in behaviour in watching films with captions. *The Language Learning Journal*, 47 (4), 407–423.

Webb, S. and Nation, I. S. P. (2017). *How vocabulary is learned*. Oxford: Oxford University Press.

3 Mapping the digital game-based vocabulary learning landscape

A comprehensive bibliometric exploration

Zhaoyang Xiong[1], Junjie Gavin Wu[1], and Di Zou[2]

[1]*Faculty of Applied Sciences, Macao Polytechnic University, Macao*

[2]*Centre for English and Additional Languages, Lingnan University, Hong Kong*

Pre-reading questions

1. What are the current research trends and foci in digital game-based vocabulary learning studies?
2. Which countries/regions and institutions have been the most prolific in this research field?
3. What future developments can be anticipated in the realm of digital game-based vocabulary learning?

Background

Vocabulary is the cornerstone of language. For second language acquisition, vocabulary plays a significant role in affecting learners' proficiency across speaking, listening, writing, and reading (Webb & Nation, 2017). However, the process of acquiring L2 vocabulary learning can be challenging and daunting due to the complexities of spelling, pronunciation, meaning, and collocations (Nation, 2001). Conventional approaches to L2 vocabulary education predominantly rely on drills and memorization; over time, the waning effectiveness of memory retention leads to subpar learning outcomes despite numerous investments of time and effort (Teng, 2022, 2023). Moreover, restricted exposure to the target language in learners' linguistic environments and de-contextualized learning methods further hinder effective vocabulary acquisition (Lee et al., 2024).

To date, multiple studies have demonstrated the capacity of digital game-based vocabulary learning (DGBVL) to tackle these difficulties. DGBVL refers to the utilization of digital games to aid vocabulary learning (Li et al., 2019). From an affective standpoint, using digital games is often regarded as an effective means of increasing learning motivation (Hung et al., 2018; Zou et al., 2019). For example, Alawadhi and Abu-Ayyash (2021) used mixed methods to investigate students' perceptions of the Kahoot! platform. The results demonstrated its potential in piquing learning interest and enhancing the learning experience. In addition, digital games have been shown to be effective in vocabulary acquisition due to the provision of repeated exposure to ample linguistic input within immersive learning environments (Chen et al., 2016; Thompson & Von Gillern, 2020). For example, a quasi-experimental study conducted by Hung and Yeh (2023) assessed the effectiveness of augmented reality (AR)-enhanced game-based learning, observing positive results, with improvements in vocabulary acquisition.

Synthesis

Copious literature has explored the broader research domain of digital game-based language learning (DGBLL), without specifically focusing on vocabulary acquisition. For instance, Xu et al. (2019) performed a scoping study of 59 relevant publications from 2000 to 2018. The results underscored the use of both quantitative and qualitative methods, the prevalent adoption of digital games for vocabulary learning, and the preference for off-the-shelf games like massively multiplayer online role-playing games (MMORPGs) in DGBLL studies. Furthermore, several other scholarly inquiries have centered on more specific perspectives. For instance, Jabbari and Eslami (2018) reviewed the impact of MMORPGs on L2 learning and concluded that MMORPGs support target language learning by affording conducive learning environments and providing ample communicative opportunities. With respect to learner groups, Acquah and Katz (2020) explored the effectiveness of digital games in L2 learning, focusing on learners aged 6–18 years old. Following an examination of 26 selected studies, the authors reported on various aspects, including game genres, game platforms, study context, and the relationship between game features and learning outcomes.

More specifically in relation to vocabulary acquisition using digital games, though there have been several representative reviews on DGBVL, there is a scarcity of integrated and comprehensive reviews. Notable reviews include the meta-analysis by Chen et al. (2016), which scrutinized ten primary studies from 2003 to 2014. The findings suggested that game design could moderate the effects of digital game-based learning (DGBL) on vocabulary learning, while factors such as age and linguistic background did not demonstrate significant moderation effects. Moreover, adventure-based games demonstrated a larger effect size and were found to be more stimulating compared to non-adventure-based games. By adopting a four-condition framework to review 19 studies, Tsai and Tsai (2018) confirmed the efficacy of games in L2 vocabulary learning and the diverse learning outcomes resulting from various factors. Zou et al. (2019) conducted a systematic review of 21 research studies on DGBVL including aspects such as frameworks, research questions, outcomes, and implications. The results revealed ten key game types and their positive effects on vocabulary learning. In a more recent meta-analysis, Thompson and Von Gillern (2020) reviewed 19 studies, employing Bayesian methods to compare the effectiveness of video games and non-video games on English L2 acquisition, while also pondering various factors, including grade level, gender, type of hardware, and duration of intervention, among others.

While prior reviews have offered valuable insights into DGBVL, there remains a gap in the form of bibliometric reviews systematically analyzing research in this area. Therefore, this study utilizes CiteSpace to conduct a bibliometric analysis of DGBVL academic research. The objective is to provide a more in-depth understanding of the primary research area, current research conditions, and emerging trends, complementing traditional reviews and offering insights for future research. The research questions guiding this investigation are as follows:

RQ1: What is the annual publication trend for DGBVL?
RQ2: Which countries/regions and institutions are the primary contributors to DGBVL research?
RQ3: What are the main focal areas of DGBVL, and how have they evolved over time?
RQ4: What are the latest trends in the field?

Method

Bibliometric analysis was utilized to synthesize existing studies on digital DGBVL and attempt to forecast future trends in this field.

Data collection

The present study collected data from the Web of Science Core Collection and Scopus databases, covering articles published between 2008 and 2023. A topic search was performed to identify relevant literature within these databases. Search terms were derived from the definition of DGBVL and related reviews in this field. To ensure a comprehensive search, a range of alternative terms related to vocabulary learning and digital games were utilized. Three sets of search terms were generated and combined using Boolean operators, with the AND operator connecting the sets and the OR operator employed in each.

a. "game" OR "gaming" OR "gameplay" OR "game-based" OR "serious game" OR "educational game" OR "simulation game" OR "electronic game" OR "digital game" OR "computer game" OR "video game" OR "online game" OR "mobile game"
b. "word" OR "vocabulary" OR "lexical"
c. "learning" OR "acquisition"

Inclusion and exclusion criteria

To ensure the relevance of the publications included, specific inclusion and exclusion criteria were used.

Inclusion criteria:

1. scientific articles with original empirical research, including publications in journals and conference proceedings
2. articles published exclusively in English
3. publications released from January 2008 to December 2023

Exclusion criteria:

1. non-empirical articles, encompassing reviews, news items, book chapters, and editorials
2. publications in languages other than English
3. articles published before 2008

The initial search in Scopus yielded 531 results, which were subsequently refined to 413 articles after applying the exclusion criteria. In the Web of Science Core Collection, 803 publications were found in the initial search, with 760 remaining after applying the exclusion criteria. There is a non-overlap in publications between these two databases. Overall, a total of 1,335 initial results were identified, with 1,173 publications retained for further analysis.

Data analysis

In this study, the data analysis was conducted using CiteSpace, a bibliometric analysis tool developed by Professor Chaomei Chen from Drexel University. CiteSpace stands out as a multidimensional and dynamic

Mapping the digital game-based vocabulary learning landscape 43

information visualization tool that enables the exploration of trends and movement of specific research fields (Chen, 2016). By utilizing visualization techniques, CiteSpace facilitates the evaluation of research status, thematic evolution, and prediction of prospects. This study selected CiteSpace for its comprehensive and consistent analysis capabilities, distinguishing it from other measurement and analysis software such as VOSviewer and Bibiliometrix.

The following were the primary steps: first, to analyze the selected literature's temporal, geographical, and institutional attributes; second, several keyword analyses including co-occurrence, frequency, centrality, and cluster analyses were conducted to visually map the current state of DGBVL research. Then, by analyzing the keyword bursts, emerging trends and evolving frontiers were identified.

New understandings

RQ1: What is the annual publication trend for DGBVL?

Figure 3.1 visualizes the annual trend of DGBVL publications over the period 2008–2023, revealing a notable upward trajectory in the annual number of articles. The quantity surged from a mere 16 in 2008 to 102 in 2023, indicating a substantial growing interest in this area. Using four years as the unit of analysis, the evolution of this field can be further split into the following four phases, as shown in Figure 3.1b: during the first four years (2008–2011), the research area was still in its infancy with a total of 88 publications; during the second period (2012–2015), the number of publications increased to 161, showing that the field was beginning to take shape; the third period (2016–2020) witnessed a significant acceleration in the field's progression, characterized by 438 articles,

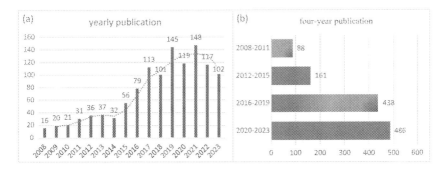

Figure 3.1 The annual scholarly output in DGBVL

44 *Theory and Practice in Vocabulary Research in Digital Environments*

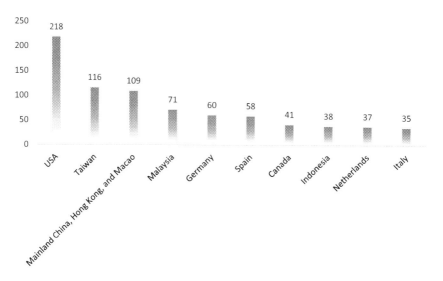

Figure 3.2 Top ten most prolific countries/regions in the field of DGBVL

potentially attributable to technological advancements and the demand for innovative learning methods; in the fourth period (2021–2023), the field entered a relatively stable phase, reaching a relatively high level of output. Despite a slight downward trend, these findings suggest that the field of DGBVL will persistently attract scholarly attention in the future.

RQ2: Which countries/regions and institutions are the primary contributors to DGBVL research?

Research on DGBVL has attracted interest from 88 different nations and regions. However, it is noteworthy that only 38.63% of them had more than ten publications, and the top ten most prolific ones, as depicted in Figure 3.2, accounted for nearly 67% of the total output. Leading the pack, the United States exhibited the highest productivity with 218 articles, followed by the Greater China area (including Taiwan (116), the region of Mainland China, Hong Kong, and Macao (109)), and Malaysia (71).

A total of 427 institutions have contributed to DGBVL research, with only nine contributing more than five publications. As illustrated in Figure 3.3, the National Taiwan Normal University emerged as the most prolific institution, making significant contributions with 23 articles. Other influential institutions include Carnegie Mellon University (eight articles), Radboud Universiteit Nijmegen (seven articles), and the Education University of Hong Kong (six articles). A closer examination

Mapping the digital game-based vocabulary learning landscape 45

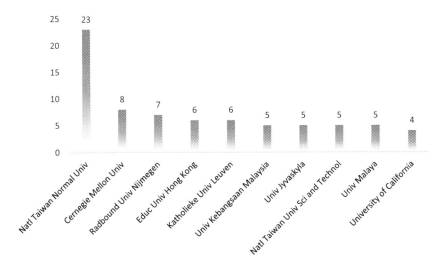

Figure 3.3 Top ten most prolific institutions in the field of DGBVL

of the institutional distribution reveals that half of the institutions were situated in Asia, three in Europe, and two in North America, indicating an unbalanced level of contributions in DGBVL research. This disparity in contributions can be attributed to several reasons. Firstly, it is worth noting that many European researchers do not publish in English. Secondly, diverse publishing cultures and varying incentives or pressures to publish globally exacerbate this imbalance.

RQ3: What are the main focal areas of DGBVL, and how have they evolved over time?

Keyword co-occurrence analysis

Figure 3.4 presents a knowledge mapping of keyword co-occurrence, where nodes represent keywords and their sizes reflect the frequency of occurrence. The interconnections between nodes are depicted by lines, with the thickness denoting the frequency of co-occurrence between terms (Chen, 2005). The network exhibits a density of 0.0221, consisting of 3,184 connections and 537 nodes, revealing the diverse research topics associated with DGBVL. However, the overall network density suggests significant potential for further improvement and more in-depth research in this field. Figure 3.4 highlights keywords such as "computer game," "student," "video game," "education," "game," "e-learning," "vocabulary,"

46 *Theory and Practice in Vocabulary Research in Digital Environments*

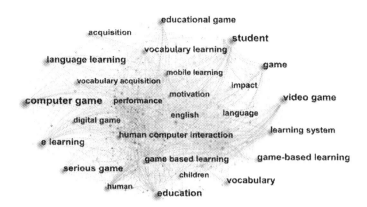

Figure 3.4 Visual mapping of keyword co-occurrence analysis

Table 3.1 Top ten keywords in terms of frequency and centrality

Number	Keyword	Frequency	Number	Keyword	Centrality
1	computer game	162	1	education	0.15
2	student	127	2	video game	0.13
3	video game	109	3	computer game	0.12
4	education	98	4	e-learning	0.12
5	game	89	5	learning system	0.12
6	e-learning	81	6	game	0.11
7	vocabulary	79	7	student	0.1
8	language learning	75	8	educational game	0.08
9	serious game	74	9	human-computer interaction	0.08
10	game-based learning	74	10	design	0.08

and "language learning," characterized by larger nodes and exhibiting a high degree of interconnectedness. These keywords partly indicate the shared research interests among scholars in the field.

In addition to visual mapping, frequency and centrality are used as metrics to assess the significance of keywords in CiteSpace. Keywords with higher frequency and centrality values are considered more influential. Table 3.1 lists the top ten keywords based on frequency and centrality. An examination of Table 3.1 reveals a convergence between high-frequency and high-centrality keywords. Notably, "computer game," "student,"

Mapping the digital game-based vocabulary learning landscape 47

"video games," "education game," and "e-learning" emerge as prominent keywords with high frequency and high centrality, suggesting researchers in DGBVL predominantly focus on these aspects when investigating their respective topics.

Keyword cluster analysis

Figure 3.5 presents a keyword cluster map for DGBVL research. Using the log-likelihood ratio (LLR) for labeling, each cluster is numbered, with the size of clusters gradually decreasing as the cluster number increases (Chen, 2016). Two metrics are utilized in CiteSpace to evaluate the clustering: modularity (Q) and silhouette (S). Q measures the level of network modularity, which refers to the degree of division of a network into distinct modules or clusters. Q values vary between -1 and 1, where values nearer to 1 imply a more pronounced clustering effect within the network (Chen et al., 2010). When the value exceeds 0.3, it indicates a substantial network structure. S is employed to assess the homogeneity or internal consistency of the network. A higher S value represents greater homogeneity within the network. Expressly, when the value approaches 1, it signifies a higher level of homogeneity. When S reaches 0.7, the clustering outcome is regarded as greatly trustworthy.

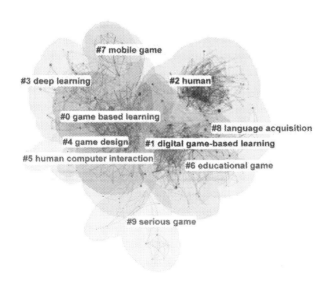

Figure 3.5 Visual mapping of keyword clustering in DGBVL research

Moreover, if the value of S surpasses 0.5, the clustering outcome could be deemed reasonable (Chen, 2016). As presented in Figure 3.5, the value of S at 0.5302 suggests the network has some degree of clustering, but there is room for further improvement in the division into distinct modules. On the other hand, the S of 0.7329 confirms a reasonably reliable clustering result.

CLUSTER #0: GAME-BASED LEARNING

This cluster, consisting of 110 articles published on average in 2014 (S = 0.53), focuses on enhancing students' learning outcomes through the integration of gamification and e-learning platforms. The primary themes explored within this cluster include game-based learning, e-learning, and learning systems, highlighting the significance of game-based learning in education and its close relationship with concepts such as learning systems and e-learning. The cluster emphasizes that through e-learning tools and platforms, learners can access games any time and anywhere, facilitating personalized vocabulary learning (Kukulska-Hulme, 2009). Furthermore, researchers can leverage data analysis techniques within e-learning environments to effectively monitor and assess learner progress and provide customized feedback (Wu & Miller, 2020).

CLUSTER #1: DIGITAL GAME-BASED LEARNING

With an average publication year of 2018 and an S value of 0.593, this cluster comprises 107 articles emphasizing engagement, interactive learning environments, teaching/learning strategies, and elementary education. Compared to Cluster #0, which focuses on integrating gamification and e-learning platforms, this cluster zooms in on the application of digital games and their impact on vocabulary acquisition. To clarify, DGBL is found to enhance learner engagement and vocabulary learning outcomes by providing engaging and interactive learning settings (Zhang et al., 2023). The cluster also underscores the significance of employing appropriate teaching and learning strategies to optimize the benefits of DGBL. Especially in the context of elementary education, DGBL demonstrates significant potential for enhancing vocabulary acquisition (e.g., Kazu & Kuvvetli, 2023).

CLUSTER #2: HUMAN

This cluster contains 92 articles with an average publication year of 2015 and an S value of 0.774. It comprises keywords related to human learning, such as gender and age. The findings emphasize the interest among researchers in examining gender and age differences to design games that specifically cater to the individual needs of learners (e.g., Yu, 2018).

CLUSTER #3: DEEP LEARNING

The S value of Cluster #3 is 0.866, with 56 articles published on average in 2016. The research in this cluster primarily focuses on deep learning and machine learning, involving terms such as convolutional neural networks, machine learning, and natural language processing. It implies that deep learning and machine learning have important applications in DGBVL, especially in language processing and learning algorithms. The emergence of deep learning highlights researchers' interest in the development of machine learning and artificial intelligence (AI). Integrating deep learning techniques into DGBVL can lead to a more intelligent and personalized learning experience, optimizing game content and assessing learning outcomes through automated feature extraction and model training (Chen et al., 2020).

CLUSTER #4: GAME DESIGN

Cluster #4 has an S value of 0.832, and the average publishing year for the 47 articles in this cluster is 2013. This cluster centers on exploring the interplay between game design and education, specifically highlighting the potential of DGBVL to stimulate active participation and enhance pedagogical practices by effectively integrating game design principles and educational approaches. It also suggests that researchers are interested in understanding how various elements of game design, such as game mechanics and feedback systems, can be used to create effective learning experiences (e.g., Li et al., 2019).

CLUSTER #5: HUMAN-COMPUTER INTERACTION

Cluster #5, with an S value of 0.846 and comprising 42 articles published around the average year of 2012, focuses on the utilization of human-computer interaction and the usability of digital games in educational settings, including in the context of autism. This cluster explores the intersection of terms such as computer software, autism, usability, and education. It suggests that when designing games, the usability of the game should be considered to provide a better learning experience. Specifically, the emergence of human-computer interaction indicates that researchers attach importance to the interactive experience between games and users (e.g., Ng et al., 2021). Optimizing human-computer interaction can improve learners' participation, motivation, and satisfaction, in turn improving the effect of DGBVL. Researchers explore designing intuitive, easy-to-use, and engaging game interfaces, controls, and interaction technologies for a better user experience (e.g., Chen et al., 2020).

CLUSTER #6: EDUCATIONAL GAME

With a high S value of 0.949, this cluster contains 20 articles published around the average year of 2018, indicating a recent focus on the exploration of educational games within DGBVL. This cluster delves into the extensive exploration of digital games within the educational domain, specifically focusing on areas such as phonological awareness and early identification (e.g., Krenca et al., 2019). It contributes valuable insights into the effective integration of digital games for educational purposes.

CLUSTER #7: MOBILE GAME

Cluster #7 covers 15 articles with an average publishing year of 2010. With an S value of 0.982, the members of this particular cluster appear to be very homogeneous. This cluster involves terms related to mobile games and Chinese education, including considerable attention to the Chinese language and Chinese literacy (e.g., Xiao & Li, 2022). Researchers have recognized the potential of mobile technology as a platform for delivering game-based vocabulary learning experiences. With the widespread adoption of smartphones and tablets, mobile games provide convenient and accessible tools for learners to engage with vocabulary learning content (e.g., Chen et al., 2019).

CLUSTER #8: LANGUAGE ACQUISITION

This cluster contains 14 publications with an average year of 2017. The S value is 0.946. Including keywords such as dialogue, cognitive development, language processing, and nonverbal, it focuses on language acquisition and cognitive development, especially in communicating and language processing. It shows the potential of DGBVL to enhance language acquisition and cognitive development. Researchers have explored how digital games provide opportunities for students to practice language skills in communicative contexts and how playing digital games can enhance cognitive processes such as attention, memory, and problem-solving (e.g., Lee, 2022).

CLUSTER #9: SERIOUS GAME

The S value of Cluster #9 is 0.958, with 14 articles and an average publication year of 2016. The main focus is on serious games, memorability, stems, fallback authentication, and security questions in the context of DGBVL. Researchers in this cluster have shown interest in exploring the effectiveness of game types that have a serious or educational purpose in vocabulary learning and investigating how game mechanics, such as repetition, feedback, and retrieval practice, enhance the memorability of vocabulary items and improve learning retention (e.g., Chen & Hsu, 2019). In addition, they may also have been exploring how word stems or lexical components can aid vocabulary acquisition, as well as investigating secure authentication methods and data protection measures within DGBVL platforms (e.g., Lee, 2022).

RQ4: What are the latest trends in the field?

To identify the evolving research frontiers in this field, this study utilized an integrated algorithm to detect keyword bursts, characterized by a substantial increase in citations for specific terms during a defined period. Figure 3.6 presents the top 20 burst terms in DGBVL research, together with corresponding burst intensity, beginning year, ending year, and length. Keywords that emerged prior to 2015 included "computer software," "teaching," "interactive computer graphics," "computer-aided instruction," "language learning," "online game," "learning system," "internet," "human-computer interaction," and "human." Notably, the keyword "computational linguistics" exhibited a vigorous intensity between 2011 and 2016, with a burst strength of 6.49, suggesting researchers were interested in using computer and natural language processing techniques to study and improve DGBVL. The keyword "teaching" has the longest duration, indicating that teaching practice is a significant focus within this area, and researchers have shown interest in exploring how digital games can be effectively utilized to enhance vocabulary learning and teaching practices.

Since 2016, terms such as "memory," "educational technology," and "deep learning" have emerged in the field of DGBVL, indicating a growing interest in the technological aspect of DGBVL. The duration of keyword bursts often signifies representative research frontiers and hotspots within a specific field. Figure 3.6 reveals that terms like "performance," "English," "acquisition," and "learners" have consistently appeared over time, suggesting that DGBVL research will continue to explore these areas. The burst of the keyword "performance" from 2018 to 2023 indicates researchers' focus on the impact of DGBVL on learners' performance and outcomes related to evaluating and improving learners' performance. The bursts of "English" and "acquisition" from 2021 to 2023 reflect research interests in applying digital games to English learning and language acquisition. The burst of "learner" from 2021 to 2023 points to researchers' attention to learners' characteristics in this field.

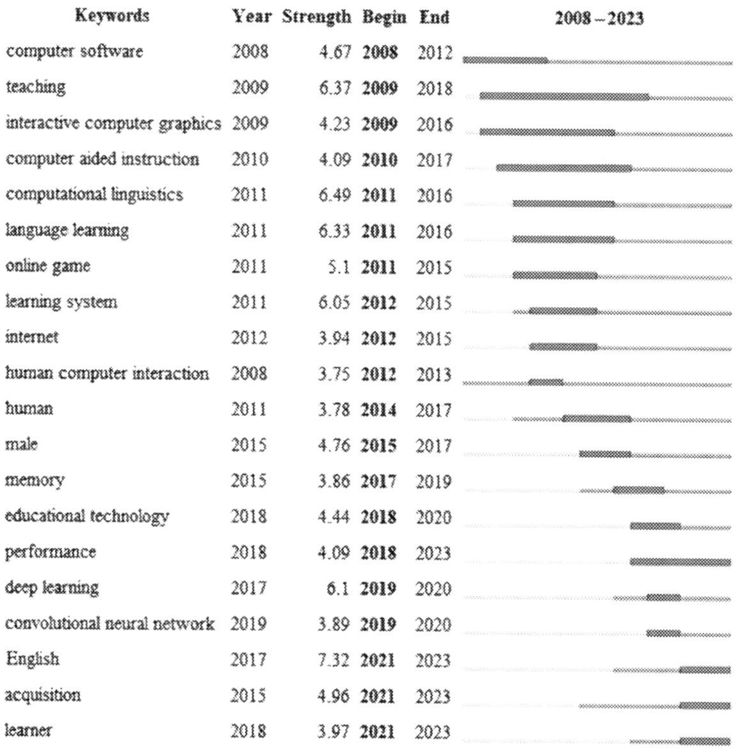

Keywords	Year	Strength	Begin	End	2008–2023
computer software	2008	4.67	2008	2012	
teaching	2009	6.37	2009	2018	
interactive computer graphics	2009	4.23	2009	2016	
computer aided instruction	2010	4.09	2010	2017	
computational linguistics	2011	6.49	2011	2016	
language learning	2011	6.33	2011	2016	
online game	2011	5.1	2011	2015	
learning system	2011	6.05	2012	2015	
internet	2012	3.94	2012	2015	
human computer interaction	2008	3.75	2012	2013	
human	2011	3.78	2014	2017	
male	2015	4.76	2015	2017	
memory	2015	3.86	2017	2019	
educational technology	2018	4.44	2018	2020	
performance	2018	4.09	2018	2023	
deep learning	2017	6.1	2019	2020	
convolutional neural network	2019	3.89	2019	2020	
English	2017	7.32	2021	2023	
acquisition	2015	4.96	2021	2023	
learner	2018	3.97	2021	2023	

Figure 3.6 Top 20 keywords with the strongest citation bursts

Implications for future research

This study conducted a bibliometric analysis on 1,173 publications from the Web of Science Core Database and Scopus from 2008 to 2023. Using CiteSpace, a visual map of DGBVL research was generated, providing valuable insights into the fundamental characteristics, research focal points, and emerging trends in this area. The analysis demonstrated a fluctuating yet growing trend in the literature on DGBVL, indicative of ongoing interest and expected continued growth in the foreseeable future. The United States and the Greater China area emerged as the most prolific contributors to DGBVL, with the National Taiwan Normal University standing out as a major contributor. Frequency and cluster analyses of keywords revealed a stable research topic structure in this field.

The study has confirmed that the impact of DGBVL has attracted prolonged attention and remains a topical issue in current research. Three conclusions can be drawn from this result. First, as prior research mentioned, the dynamic and evolving nature of the DGBVL field, driven by advancements in technology, has spurred researchers to explore cutting-edge technologies to enhance vocabulary learning experiences within games (Lai & Chen, 2021; Wen et al., 2023). Second, due to individual differences, researchers are keen to investigate how various game mechanics, features, and interface designs can cater to these differences to optimize learning outcomes (Denden et al., 2022; Yang & Quadir, 2018). Third, while research has illustrated the benefits of digital games in vocabulary learning, further empirical evidence is required to identify specific teaching strategies and game elements that boost the effectiveness of DGBVL. Studies have suggested the positive impact of competitive gaming scenarios and challenges on vocabulary acquisition (Wei et al., 2018; Yang et al., 2020).

Based on the current findings, we now suggest some areas that deserve more scholarly attention in future studies. First, serious games and educational games were found to be two frequently explored game types, consistent with the findings of the review by Acquah and Katz (2020). This emphasis might arise from the fact that, compared to other game types, these two genres focus more on achieving educational and learning goals (Chen & Hsu, 2019). These games provide targeted vocabulary learning content and activities, such as vocabulary exercises, memory tests, and contextual applications to facilitate the expansion of players' vocabulary. In light of this, it is advisable for educators to contemplate the integration of such games into L2 word instruction. Nevertheless, educators must carefully evaluate whether the vocabulary featured in these games aligns with intended learning objectives.

Second, similar to the impact of different game types on gameplay experience, the choice of hardware type can also influence the learning experience. As highlighted in a previous review (Hung et al., 2018), personal computers (PCs) have emerged as the predominant gaming platform due to their widespread adoption in modern educational practices. In addition, consistent with Elaish et al. (2017), this review confirms the popularity of digital games on mobile devices. In contrast to computer-based games, mobile games can take advantage of the portability and touchscreen capabilities of smartphones to provide interactive and tactile vocabulary learning activities (Kukulska-Hulme, 2021). More recently, the emergence of extended reality (XR) and generative AI in educational sectors is positioned to have significant impacts on the evolution of hardware and future student learning (Wu et al., 2024; Yang et al., 2024). Given the limitations and affordances of different hardware types, further research is needed to compare the efficacy of various hardware types in L2 vocabulary acquisition. Furthermore, educators should develop carefully crafted plans based on the availability of hardware types, educational objects, and student preferences to deliver an enriching vocabulary learning experience.

Third, through a close examination, it is evident that DGBVL has received considerable attention in Chinese and English language education, concurring with previous studies (Acquah & Katz, 2020; Hung et al., 2018). However, as demonstrated in the literature (James & Mayer, 2018; Kim et al., 2023; Shintaku, 2023), further investigation is warranted to explore its potential application in other, less commonly taught languages. Therefore, it is worthwhile to examine how DGBVL can bolster learners' vocabulary knowledge in various language learning contexts. Engaging activities, such as word spelling games, context-rich conversations, and word matching games, can be employed to develop an immersive and captivating learning environment (Teng, 2021). Moreover, the development of an interactive gaming platform, integrating multimedia resources and tailoring compelling game tasks and challenges, holds promise for enhancing students' engagement in the learning process (Hwang & Wang, 2016; Yang et al., 2020; Lee et al., 2024).

Fourth, in terms of technological advancements, the rapid progress in deep learning (DL) and machine learning (ML) has highlighted the potential of integrating AI with DGBVL as a future trend. The advancements in DL and ML have notably enhanced language processing and natural language comprehension. Aligning with the Zone of Proximal Development theory (Vygotsky, 1978), real-time adjustments to game difficulty can improve the learning experience by facilitating a seamless learning trajectory. As contended by Breien and Wasson (2020) and Huang et al. (2023), the utilization of DL and ML allows for the personalization and customization of games to meet the performance and requirements of individual players, providing targeted exercises and learning resources. For example, AI can assume diverse roles within digital games, such as a game coach, a learning companion, or an intelligent evaluator, delivering immediate feedback and suggestions to aid learners in error correction and skill enhancement (Hong et al., 2023; Polyzi & Moussiades, 2023). Furthermore, AI can dynamically adapt game difficulty levels and challenges based on learners' advancements and interests, thereby enhancing the overall learning experience (Shute & Rahimi, 2017). As Poole and Clarke-Midura (2023) pointed out, the integration of AI and DGBVL has great potential as a popular and effective learning tool in the future, facilitating vocabulary acquisition in an intriguing and interactive manner. However, the realization of such a system necessitates further research and technological advancements.

While this review provides a holistic analysis of DGBVL, future research could benefit from focusing on specific aspects. In particular, it would be valuable to explore the impact of distinct game elements or investigate the integration of advanced technologies like AI and XR within digital games for vocabulary learning (Lee et al., 2024; Lee & Wu, 2024).

Further reading

Franciosi, S. J. (2017). The effect of computer game-based learning on FL vocabulary transferability. *Educational Technology & Society*, 20(1), 123–133.
This research comprises two studies investigating the effectiveness of an online simulation game, *Energy City*, in enhancing vocabulary learning in English lessons. The findings underscore the transferability of acquired vocabulary from English courses using the game.

Tsai, Y. L., & Tsai, C. C. (2018). Digital game-based second-language vocabulary learning and conditions of research designs: A meta-analysis study. *Computers & Education*, 125, 345–357. https://doi.org/10.1016/j.compedu.2018.06.020
This meta-analysis study explored the effectiveness of digital games in second language vocabulary learning and proposed a four-condition framework to differentiate the empirical studies, which support the benefits of using digital games to enhance vocabulary acquisition.

Zou, D., Huang, Y., & Xie, H. (2019). Digital game-based vocabulary learning: Where are we and where are we going? *Computer Assisted Language Learning*, 34(5–6), 751–777. https://doi.org/10.1080/09588221.2019.1640745
This systematic review study reviewed studies on DGBVL from five perspectives: an overview of existing research, digital games for vocabulary learning, theoretical frameworks, research questions and results, and implications. Results illustrated ten predominant game types and their positive effects on vocabulary learning.

References

Acquah, E. O., & Katz, H. T. (2020). Digital game-based L2 learning outcomes for primary through high-school students: A systematic literature review. *Computers & Education*, 143, 103667. https://doi.org/10.1016/j.compedu.2019.103667

Alawadhi, A., & Abu-Ayyash, E. A. (2021). Students' perceptions of Kahoot!: An exploratory mixed-method study in EFL undergraduate classrooms in the UAE. *Education and Information Technologies*, 26(4), 3629–3658. https://doi.org/10.1007/s10639-020-10425-8

Breien, F., & Wasson, B. (2020). Narrative categorization in digital game-based learning: Engagement, motivation & learning. *British Journal of Educational Technology*, 52(1), 91–111. https://doi.org/10.1111/bjet.13004

Chen, C. (2005). CiteSpace II: Detecting and visualizing emerging trends and transient patterns in scientific literature. *Journal of the Association for Information Science and Technology*, 57(3), 359–377. https://doi.org/10.1002/asi.20317

Chen, C. (2016). *CiteSpace: A Practical Guide for Mapping Scientific Literature*. Nova Science Publishers.

Chen, C., Ibekwe-SanJuan, F., & Hou, J. (2010). The structure and dynamics of cocitation clusters: A multiple-perspective cocitation analysis. *Journal of the American Society for Information Science and Technology*, 61(7), 1386–1409. https://doi.org/10.1002/asi.21309

Chen, C., Liu, H., & Huang, H. (2019). Effects of a mobile game-based English vocabulary learning app on learners' perceptions and learning performance: A case study of Taiwanese EFL learners. *ReCALL*, 31(2), 170–188. https://doi.org/10.1017/s0958344018000228

Chen, H. H., & Hsu, H. L. (2019). The impact of a serious game on vocabulary and content learning. *Computer Assisted Language Learning*, 33(7), 811–832. https://doi.org/10.1080/09588221.2019.1593197

Chen, H. H., Hsu, H. L., & Chen, Z. H. (2020). A study on the effect of adding L1 glosses in the subtitle of an adventure game for vocabulary learning. *Interactive Learning Environments*, 31(4), 1889–1905. https://doi.org/10.1080/10494820.2020.1863233

Chen, M., Tseng, W., & Hsiao, T. (2016). The effectiveness of digital game-based vocabulary learning: A framework-based view of meta-analysis. *British Journal of Educational Technology*, 49(1), 69–77. https://doi.org/10.1111/bjet.12526

Chen, X., Xie, H., Zou, D., & Hwang, G. (2020). Application and theory gaps during the rise of Artificial Intelligence in Education. *Computers & Education: Artificial Intelligence*, 1, 100002. https://doi.org/10.1016/j.caeai.2020.100002

Denden, M., Tlili, A., Chen, N., Abed, M., Jemni, M., & Essalmi, F. (2022). The role of learners' characteristics in educational gamification systems: A systematic meta-review of the literature. *Interactive Learning Environments*, 32(3), 790–812. https://doi.org/10.1080/10494820.2022.2098777

Elaish, M. M., Shuib, L., Ghani, N. A., & Yadegaridehkordi, E. (2017). Mobile English Language Learning (MELL): A literature review. *Educational Review*, 71(2), 257–276. https://doi.org/10.1080/00131911.2017.1382445

Hong, J., Lin, C., & Juh, C. (2023). Using a Chatbot to learn English via Charades: The correlates between social presence, hedonic value, perceived value, and learning outcome. *Interactive Learning Environments*, 1–17. https://doi.org/10.1080/10494820.2023.2273485

Huang, X., Zou, D., Cheng, G., Chen, X., & Xie, H. (2023). Trends, research issues and applications of artificial intelligence in language education. *Educational Technology & Society*, 26(1), 112–131.

Hung, H. T., Yang, J. C., Hwang, G. J., Chu, H., & Wang, C. C. (2018). A scoping review of research on digital game-based language learning. *Computers & Education*, 126, 89–104. https://doi.org/10.1016/j.compedu.2018.07.001

Hung, H. T., & Yeh, H. C. (2023). Augmented-reality-enhanced game-based learning in flipped English classrooms: Effects on students' creative thinking and vocabulary acquisition. *Journal of Computer Assisted Learning*, 39(6), 1786–1800. https://doi.org/10.1111/jcal.12839

Hwang, G., & Wang, S. (2016). Single loop or double loop learning: English vocabulary learning performance and behavior of students in situated computer games with different guiding strategies. *Computers & Education*, 102, 188–201. https://doi.org/10.1016/j.compedu.2016.07.005

Jabbari, N., & Eslami, Z. R. (2018). Second language learning in the context of massively multiplayer online games: A scoping review. *ReCALL*, *31*(01), 92–113. https://doi.org/10.1017/s0958344018000058

James, K. K., & Mayer, R. E. (2018). Learning a second language by playing a game. *Applied Cognitive Psychology*, *33*(4), 669–674. https://doi.org/10.1002/acp.3492

Kazu, İ. Y., & Kuvvetli, M. (2023). A triangulation method on the effectiveness of digital game-based language learning for vocabulary acquisition. *Education and Information Technologies*, *28*(10), 13541–13567. https://doi.org/10.1007/s10639-023-11756-y

Kim, J. S., Kim, S. Y., Kim, S. M., Kim, H. J., & Han, D. H. (2023). Digital game-based Korean language learning for Russian immigrant children. *Games for Health Journal*, *12*(4), 280–287. https://doi.org/10.1089/g4h.2022.0031

Krenca, K., Segers, E., Chen, X., Shakory, S., Steele, J., & Verhoeven, L. (2019). Phonological specificity relates to phonological awareness and reading ability in English–French bilingual children. *Reading and Writing*, *33*(2), 267–291. https://doi.org/10.1007/s11145-019-09959-2

Kukulska-Hulme, A. (2009). Will mobile learning change language learning? *ReCALL*, *21*(2), 157–165. https://doi.org/10.1017/s0958344009000202

Kukulska-Hulme, A. (2021). Moving language teaching and learning from the known to the unknown. In L. Miller and J. G. Wu (Eds.), *Language Learning with Technology: Perspectives from Asia* (pp. 3–12). Springer.

Lai, K. W. K., & Chen, H. H. (2021). A comparative study on the effects of a VR and PC visual novel game on vocabulary learning. *Computer Assisted Language Learning*, *36*(3), 312–345. https://doi.org/10.1080/09588221.2021.1928226

Lee, S. (2022). Factors affecting incidental L2 vocabulary acquisition and retention in a game-enhanced learning environment. *ReCALL*, *35*(3), 274–289. https://doi.org/10.1017/s0958344022000209

Lee, S. M., & Wu, J. G. (2024). Preparing teachers for the future: Microteaching in the immersive VR environment. *ReCALL*, 1–19. https://doi.org/10.1017/s0958344024000089

Lee, S. M., Yang, Z., & Wu, J. G. (2024). Live, play, and learn: Language learner engagement in the immersive VR environment. *Education and Information Technologies*, *29*(9), 10529–10550. https://doi.org/10.1007/s10639-023-12215-4

Li, R., Meng, Z., Mi, T., Zhang, Z., & Wei, X. (2019). Modelling Chinese EFL learners' flow experiences in digital game-based vocabulary learning: the roles of learner and contextual factors. *Computer Assisted Language Learning*, *34*(4), 483–505. https://doi.org/10.1080/09588221.2019.1619585

Nation, I. S. P. (2001). *Learning Vocabulary in Another Language*. Cambridge University Press.

Ng, L. L., Azizie, R. S., & Chew, S. Y. (2021). Factors influencing ESL players' use of vocabulary learning strategies in massively multiplayer Online Role-Playing Games (MMORPG). *The Asia-Pacific Education Researcher*, *31*(4), 369–381. https://doi.org/10.1007/s40299-021-00578-6

Polyzi, P., & Moussiades, L. (2023). An artificial vocabulary learning assistant. *Education and Information Technologies*, 28(12), 16431–16455. https://doi.org/10.1007/s10639-023-11810-9

Poole, F. J., & Clarke-Midura, J. (2023). Applying educational data mining to explore individual experiences in digital games. *Language Learning and Technology*, 27(1), 1–26. https://doi.org/10.31219/osf.io/yzgac

Shintaku, K. (2023). Learning of L2 Japanese through video games. *Language Learning & Technology*, 27(1), 1–17. https://hdl.handle.net/10125/73540

Shute, V. J., & Rahimi, S. (2017). Review of computer-based assessment for learning in elementary and secondary education. *Journal of Computer Assisted Learning*, 33(1), 1–19. https://doi.org/10.1111/jcal.12172

Teng, M. F. (2021). *Language Learning through Captioned Videos: Incidental Vocabulary Acquisition*. Routledge.

Teng, M. F. (2022). Incidental L2 vocabulary learning from viewing captioned videos: Effects of learner-related factors. *System*, 105, 102736. https://doi.org/10.1016/j.system.2022.102736

Teng, M. F. (2023). Understanding incidental vocabulary learning in practice. *Asian Journal of English Language Teaching*, 32(1), 7–28.

Thompson, C. W., & Von Gillern, S. (2020). Video-game based instruction for vocabulary acquisition with English language learners: A Bayesian meta-analysis. *Educational Research Review*, 30, 100332. https://doi.org/10.1016/j.edurev.2020.100332

Tsai, Y. L., & Tsai, C. C. (2018). Digital game-based second-language vocabulary learning and conditions of research designs: A meta-analysis study. *Computers & Education*, 125, 345–357. https://doi.org/10.1016/j.compedu.2018.06.020

Vygotsky, L. S. (1978). *Mind in Society: The Development of Higher Psychological Processes*. Harvard University Press.

Webb, S. & Nation, I. S. P. (2017). *How Vocabulary Is Learned*. Oxford University Press.

Wei, C. W., Kao, H. Y., Lu, H. H., & Liu, Y. C. (2018). The effects of competitive gaming scenarios and personalized assistance strategies on English vocabulary learning. *Educational Technology & Society*, 21(3), 146–158. www.jstor.org/stable/26458514

Wen, J., Pack, A., Guan, Y., Zhang, L., & Zou, B. (2023). The influence of game-based learning media on academic English vocabulary learning in the EFL context. *Computer Assisted Language Learning*, 1–25. https://doi.org/10.1080/09588221.2023.2276800

Wu, J. G., & Miller, L. (2020). Improving English learners' speaking through mobile-assisted peer feedback. *RELC Journal*, 51(1), 168–178. https://doi.org/10.1177/0033688219895335

Wu, J. G., Zhang, D., & Lee, S. M. (2024). Into the brave new metaverse: Envisaging future language teaching and learning. *IEEE Transactions on Learning Technologies*, 17, 44–53.

Xiao, X., & Li, S. (2022). The use of flyswatter game to assist elementary learners' vocabulary learning: Gamification in TCSOL. *International Journal of Applied Linguistics*, 33(1), 3–17. https://doi.org/10.1111/ijal.12443

Xu, Z., Chen, Z., Eutsler, L., Geng, Z., & Kogut, A. (2019). A scoping review of digital game-based technology on English language learning. *Educational Technology Research and Development*, 68(3), 877–904. https://doi.org/10.1007/s11423-019-09702-2

Yang, J. C., & Quadir, B. (2018). Individual differences in an English learning achievement system: Gaming flow experience, gender differences and learning motivation. *Technology, Pedagogy and Education*, 27(3), 351–366. https://doi.org/10.1080/1475939x.2018.1460618

Yang, Q., Chang, S., Hwang, G., & Zou, D. (2020). Balancing cognitive complexity and gaming level: Effects of a cognitive complexity-based competition game on EFL students' English vocabulary learning performance, anxiety and behaviors. *Computers & Education*, 148, 103808. https://doi.org/10.1016/j.compedu.2020.103808

Yang, Z., Wu, J. G., & Xie, H. (2024). Taming Frankenstein's monster: Ethical considerations relating to generative artificial intelligence in education. *Asia Pacific Journal of Education*, 1–14. https://doi.org/10.1080/02188791.2023.2300137

Yu, Z. (2018). Differences in serious game-aided and traditional English vocabulary acquisition. *Computers & Education*, 127, 214–232. https://doi.org/10.1016/j.compedu.2018.07.014

Zhang, R., Zou, D., & Cheng, G. (2023). Learner engagement in digital game-based vocabulary learning and its effects on EFL vocabulary development. *System*, 119, 103173. https://doi.org/10.1016/j.system.2023.103173

Zou, D., Huang, Y., & Xie, H. (2019). Digital game-based vocabulary learning: Where are we and where are we going? *Computer Assisted Language Learning*, 34(5-6), 751–777. https://doi.org/10.1080/09588221.2019.1640745

4 Development of gloss studies in vocabulary learning research

Makoto Yoshii
Prefectural University of Kumamoto, Japan

Pre-reading questions

- What are effective glosses?
- Which language is better for glossing: L1 (learners' first language) or L2 (second language or target language)?
- Which format is better for glossing: single-mode glosses or multimodal glosses?
- What does the history of gloss research tell us?

Background

Glossing is useful for helping learners read and learn words through reading. A gloss here means a vocabulary gloss which explains what the glossed word means. Gloss research has been popular and important for vocabulary research. The recent increase in the volume of meta-analysis or review papers reminds us of how relevant it still is even today (Boers, 2022; Ramezanali et al., 2021; Yanagisawa et al., 2020). In this digital world, we continue to explore the potential of glosses. Looking at the development of gloss research helps us see the future and the direction we need to go from here.

The main goal of this chapter is to provide readers with an overview of gloss research and references with which they can investigate further. We will divide the development of gloss studies into three major periods: the 1990s, 2000s, and 2010s. We will use two major categories: single-mode glosses (SMGs) and multimodal glosses (MMGs). SMG means one type of gloss, particularly textual or verbal glosses. MMG means multiple modes of glosses which include text, picture, audio, video, or a combination of these. In this paper, we will identify the characteristics of each decade in the "Synthesis" section. We will summarize the development of gloss research in the "New understanding" section. We will then suggest what all these tell us about the future of gloss research and introduce some research ideas in the "Implications" section.

Synthesis

Resources: Seven review papers

We will utilize seven major review or meta-analysis papers to examine the development of gloss research (Abraham, 2008; Kim et al., 2020; Mohsen & Balakumar, 2011; Ramezanali et al., 2021; Vahedi et al., 2016; Yanagisawa et al., 2020; Zhang & Ma, 2021). These seven were chosen because they specifically focus on gloss research rather than multimedia or technology-enhanced language learning. They were also highly regarded by gloss researchers by being often cited. Each review paper examines gloss studies with its own interests and strict criteria for selecting them. The review papers cover various topics and provide us with a thorough view of gloss research. Detailed descriptions of the review papers can be found in Table 4.1. Here is a brief summary of each review paper in chronological order.

Abraham (2008) covered 14 years from 1994 to 2007 with 11 studies. The paper focused on computer-mediated glosses, reading comprehension, and vocabulary learning. This review dealt with moderating variables such as level of instruction, text type (genre), and type of assessment.

Mohsen and Balakumar (2011) covered 17 years from 1993 to 2009 and dealt with 18 studies. The objectives were to examine multimedia glosses, vocabulary learning, and comprehension through reading and listening. Their review included various topics: multimedia vs. printed, gloss modes (text, image, picture, video, etc.), multiple-choice vs. single translation, and L1 vs. L2.

Vahedi et al. (2016) looked at 34 studies over 14 years from 2001 to 2014. Their review specifically compared multiple glosses (text + visual) with single glosses (text only). The review dealt with the following moderating variables: proficiency levels, duration of the programs, contexts of learning, and publication years (2000s and 2010s).

Kim et al. (2020) specifically investigated the effects of L1 and L2 glosses with 26 studies covering 19 years from 2002 to 2020. Their review looked at reading comprehension, vocabulary learning, learner factors (learning contexts and proficiencies), and gloss features (format, location, and density).

Yanagisawa et al. (2020) were interested in the overall effect of glossing on L2 vocabulary learning through reading. Their review covered 42 studies over 24 years from 1994 to 2017 looking at variables such as glosses vs. no glosses, gloss formats (type, language, and mode), text characteristics, and learner factors.

Ramezanali et al. (2021) examined the effect of multimodal glossing on vocabulary, particularly comparing single vs. dual, and dual vs. triple

Table 4.1 List of review/meta-analysis papers on gloss research

Objectives	Period / # of articles	Topics or moderating variables	Theories	Main findings
Abraham (2008) - Computer-mediated glosses - Reading comprehension (RC) - Vocabulary learning (VL)	1994–2007 - 4 for RC - 7 for VL & RC	- Level of instruction - Text type (Genre) - Type of assessment		- Medium effect on reading comprehension - Large effect on vocabulary learning
Mohsen and Balakumar (2011) - Multimedia glosses - RC & listening comprehension (LC) - VL	1993–2009 - 13 for VL in reading - 5 for VL in listening	- Multimedia vs. printed - Mode (text, image, picture, video, etc.) - Multiple vs. single - L1 vs. L2	- Dual-coding hypothesis (Paivio, 1971, 1986) - Noticing hypothesis (Schmidt, 1990) - Mayer's generative theory of multimedia learning (1997, 2001) - Cognitive load theory (Chandler & Sweller, 1991)	- Multimedia glosses facilitate L2 vocabulary learning - Multimedia more effective than printed - Multiple more effective than single
Vahedi et al. (2016) - To compare multiple gloss (MG) and single gloss (SG) - It also looks at moderator variables	2001–2014 34 (actually from 30 papers which include 4 papers with 2 experiments)	- Proficiency level - Duration of the program - Context of learning - Publication year	- Noticing theory (Schmidt, 1995) - Cognitive load theory (Sweller & Chandler, 1991)	- MG (text + visual) was more effective than SG (text only), with large effect sizes - The intensity of the program and L2 proficiency were moderator variables - 2010s produced higher mean effect sizes than those in 2000s

Study	Period / Scope	Focus	Theoretical framework	Key findings
Kim et al. (2020) - To compare L1 and L2 - RC - VL	2002–2020 26 papers	- Outcome measures (RC, vocabulary tests – immediate & delayed) - Learner factors (English learning context & English proficiency level) - Instructional features (format, location, density)	- Revised hierarchical model (Kroll & Stewart, 1994) - Code-switching (Macaro, 2009)	- L1 was more effective than L2 - More evident in immediate vocabulary tests and RC test - L2 proficiency level was an influential moderator - L1 was particularly effective for beginners
Yanagisawa et al. (2020) - Overall effect of glossing on L2 VL through reading - Look at other moderating variables	1994–2017 42 studies	- Glossed vs. non-glossed - Gloss format (type, language, mode) - Text characteristics - Learner factors	- Noticing of unknown target language items (Bowles, 2004; Rott, 2005; Yanguas, 2009) - Form-meaning connections (Nation, 2013) - Mental effort hypothesis (Hulstijn, 1992) - Involvement load hypothesis (Laufer & Hulstijn, 2001)	- Glossed reading > non-glossed - MC = most effective; in-text and glossaries = least effective - No interaction between language (L1/L2) and proficiency (beginner/intermediate/advanced) - No significant difference among modes (textual, pictorial, auditory)
Ramezanali et al. (2021) - Effects of multimedia glossing - Dual vs. single - Dual vs. triple - 11 moderating variables	1999–2019 22 studies	- Dual vs. single - Dual vs. triple - Quality of data sample	- The cognitive theory of multimedia learning (Mayer, 2014) - Dual-coding hypothesis (Mayer, 2014)	- Overall effect of additional gloss: medium (immediate), small (delayed)

(Continued)

Table 4.1 (Continued)

Objectives	Period / # of articles	Topics or moderating variables	Theories	Main findings
		- Learner factors (proficiency) - Gloss language - Text type (narrative vs. expository) - Test format	- Limited cognitive capacity / overloaded information (Sakar & Ercetin, 2005) - Split attention (Mayer & Moreno, 1998)	- Influential moderator variables: learner (e.g., proficiency), gloss language, text type (narrative vs. expository) and research design (e.g., test format) - Dual > single - No difference between dual and triple
Zhang and Ma (2021) - Effects of textual glosses - Media (paper vs. hypermedia) - Academic status (college vs. high school) - Outcome measures (receptive vs. productive) - Language (L1 vs. L2) - Proximity (in-text, margin, pop-up)	1994–2018 20 studies	- Language (L1 vs. L2) - Location (in-text, margin, pop-up) - Mode (single vs. multiple-choice) - L2 proficiency - Outcome measures (receptive vs. productive)	- Involvement load hypothesis (Laufer & Hulstijn, 2001) - Input hypothesis	- Medium effect of textual glosses on L2 vocabulary learning - Effects persist over time - Location and mode influence effects - Language does not influence effects - Outcome measures also matter

glosses. Their review dealt with 22 studies over 21 years from 1999 to 2019. The moderating variables of the review included proficiency, gloss language, text type (narrative vs. expository), and test format.

Zhang and Ma (2021) focused on the effect of textual glosses on vocabulary learning. Their review looked at 20 studies over 25 years from 1994 to 2018 with various topics: media (paper vs. computer), academic status (college or high school), outcome measures (receptive vs. productive), language (L1 vs. L2), and location (in-text, margin, pop-up).

Processes of analyses

We use the term "review" paper to represent a review or meta-analysis article. We use the term "study" to represent an individual gloss article. All the studies mentioned in each review were compiled into one list, totaling 173 studies. Then, they were rearranged by decade: the 1990s with 12 studies (Table 4.2), the 2000s with 29 studies (Table 4.3), and the 2010s with 48 studies (Table 4.4), totaling 89 studies. The number of studies was reduced from 173 to 89 because 32 studies were quoted in the reviews multiple times. For example, Jacobs et al. (1994) in Table 4.2 appeared in three reviews (Mohsen & Balakumar, 2011; Yanagisawa et al., 2020; Zhang & Ma, 2021). The number was also reduced by excluding MA theses, dissertations, proceedings, and book chapters. This list represents journal articles, and it was important to unify the quantity and quality of the studies.

The studies are divided into two main categories: One is SMGs, and the other is MMGs. These categories were chosen by examining the review papers and their topics or issues. SMGs mainly focus on text or verbal glosses while MMGs deal with text, picture, audio, video, and combinations. Sub-headings were also provided to group similar studies: L1 and L2, single-choice gloss vs. multiple-choice gloss in SMG; comparison of MMG and SMG in MMG.

In the list, main findings are drawn from immediate effects or results, excluding delayed results. This was because timings of delayed tests differed, and what learners did or were exposed to between immediate and delayed tests was not clear.

Each table shows the main categories (SMG or MMG), author(s) and publishing years, main findings, and review paper(s) in which they appeared. Readers who are interested in individual studies in these tables are encouraged to consult the review papers in which they appear and find the details.

Gloss research in the 1990s

Table 4.2 provides a summary of gloss studies in the 1990s collected and compiled from the seven review papers. The table shows the main

Table 4.2 List of gloss studies in the 1990s

Single-mode gloss (SMG): mainly verbal or textual gloss

Author(s), year	Main findings	Found in
Inferencing, guessing, dictionary, and gloss		
Knight (1994)	Computerized dictionary > no dictionary	①
Hulstijn et al. (1996)	Marginal > dictionary or NG, few dictionary lookups	⑤
Aizawa (1998)	Guessing ≈ marginal glosses > dictionary, NG	⑤
L1 and L2		
Jacobs et al. (1994)	L1 ≈ L2 > NG	②, ⑤, ⑦
Ko (1995)	Intentional vs. incidental, L1 > L2 > NG	④, ⑤
Single-choice gloss (SCG) vs. multiple-choice gloss (MCG)		
Hulstijn (1992)	Inferencing, mental effort, Inferring (high mental effort) > given (low mental effort), Danger of incorrect guessing for NG and MCG	⑦
Watanabe (1997)	Format, locations, SCG, MCG > appositive, NG. SCG ≈ MCG, appositive ≈ NG, no effect of translation activity	⑤
Nagata (1999)	Computerized gloss, feedback, SCG < MCG	⑤
Mitarai and Aizawa (1999)	L1 > L2, L1 SCG ≈ L1 MCG, L2 SCG < L2 MCG	④

Multimodal gloss (MMG):
Text, picture, auditory, video, or combination glosses

Author(s), year	Main findings	Found in
Multimodal gloss (MMG) vs. single-mode gloss (SMG)		
Chun and Plass (1996)	Dual coding, T+P > T+V, T	②
Plass et al. (1998)	Visual and verbal, preference, T+P > T+V > T	②
Kost et al. (1999)	Visual and verbal, T+P > P > T	⑥

List of abbreviations
NG = No gloss, L1 = First language text gloss, L2 = Second language text gloss, T = Text, P = Picture, V = Video, A = Audio, SCG = Single-choice gloss, MCG = Multiple-choice gloss, SMG = Single-mode gloss, MMG = Multimodal gloss, > greater than, < less than, ≈ almost the same

List of review papers (number corresponds to each paper)
① Abraham (2008); ② Mohsen and Balakumar (2011); ③ Vahedi et al. (2016); ④ Kim et al. (2020); ⑤ Yanagisawa et al. (2020); ⑥ Ramezanali et al. (2021); and ⑦ Zhang and Ma (2021)

Table 4.3 List of gloss studies in the 2000s

Single-mode gloss (SMG): mainly verbal or textual gloss

Author(s), year	Main findings	Found in
Lookups		
De Ridder (2002)	More lookups with visible, visible ≈ invisible Reading task: general > specific	③
Locations		
Cheng and Good (2009)	Locations, gloss > NG, L1+L2 sentence > L1 in text > L1 marginal > NG	⑤

Single-choice gloss (SCG) vs. multiple-choice gloss (MCG)

Rott et al. (2002)	Mental effort, noticing, L2 writing, MCG, combination > L2 text construction	⑤
Miyasako (2002)	Mental effort, L2 MCG effective, L2: effective for higher proficiency, L1: effective for lower proficiency	④, ⑤, ⑦
Rott (2005)	Think-aloud, SCG < MCG	⑤
Shiki (2008)	L1 MCG > L1 SCG or L2 SCG or L2 MCG	④, ⑤
Lin and Huang (2008)	SCG (given) < MCG (inferred)	⑤
Martínez-Fernández (2008)	Think-aloud, involvement hypothesis not supported Word form: fill-in > NG, Meaning: fill-in > NG, MCG, MCG ≈ NG, SCG	⑤
Other topics		
Bowles (2004)	Think-aloud, noticing words: paper ≈ computer > NG	①, ⑤

Multimodal gloss (MMG): text, picture, auditory, video, or combination glosses

Author(s), year	Main findings	Found in
Multimodal gloss (MMG) > single-mode gloss (SMG)		
Al-Seghayer (2001)	T + V > T+P, T, video builds a mental image better	②, ③
Jones and Plass (2002)	Mayer's Generative Theory (1997, 2001) T+P > T, P, NG	②
Yoshii and Flaitz (2002)	Addition of picture T+P > P, T	②, ⑤, ⑥
Jones (2003)	Listening, generative theory, students' views T+P > T, P, NG, interview data support the above	②
Yeh and Wang (2003)	T+P > T, T+P+A, Perceptual learning styles: no significant effect	②, ⑥
Jones (2004)	Listening, glosses > NG T, T+P > P	②
Jones (2006)	Listening, working in pairs ≈ working alone, glosses > NG	②

(Continued)

68 *Theory and Practice in Vocabulary Research in Digital Environments*

Table 4.3 (Continued)

Single-mode gloss (SMG): mainly verbal or textual gloss

Author(s), year	Main findings	Found in
Yoshii (2006)	L1 ≈ L2, MMG > SMG L2+P slightly better retention than others	②, ③, ④, ⑤, ⑥
Akbulut (2007)	T+P, T+V > T	②, ⑥
Kim and Gilman (2008)	Addition of picture = helpful T+P, T+A+P = helpful, no effect of reduced text	③
Jones (2009)	Listening, spatial and Verbal abilities, T+P > P, T Working with P: high verbal > low verbal Working with T+P: high ≈ low	②
Shahrokni (2009)	Dual coding, T+P > T, P	③, ⑤, ⑥
Lin (2009)	Action verbs, T + animation ≈ T+P > T	⑥

SMG ≈ MMG

| Yanguas (2009) | Noticing, attention, gloss > NG, T ≈ P ≈ T+P | ②, ③, ⑤,
⑥, ⑦ |

SMG > MMG

| Acha (2009) | Children, cognitive load, T > T+P, P | ②, ⑥ |

Other topics

Nikolova (2002)	Authoring > using, authoring ≈ using when time is controlled T+A+P > A, T	②
Plass et al. (2003)	Cognitive load, generative theory With P: high verbal and spatial > low verbal and spatial With T: high ≈ low	①, ⑥
Chun and Payne (2004)	More lookups for lower WM learners	②
Al-Musallam et al. (2005)	Animated > still	③
Abraham (2007)	Verbal (L1, L2), visual (videos, images), gloss > no gloss Choice ≈ forced	①

List of abbreviations
NG = No gloss, L1 = First language text gloss, L2 = Second language text gloss, T = Text, P = Picture, V = Video, A = Audio, SCG = Single-choice gloss, MCG = Multiple-choice gloss, SMG = Single-mode gloss, MMG = Multimodal gloss, > greater than, < less than, ≈ almost the same

List of the review papers (Number corresponds to each paper)
① Abraham (2008); ② Mohsen and Balakumar (2011); ③ Vahedi et al. (2016); ④ Kim et al. (2020); ⑤ Yanagisawa et al. (2020); ⑥ Ramezanali et al. (2021); and ⑦ Zhang and Ma (2021)

categories of the studies, author(s) and publishing years, main findings, and review paper(s) in which they appeared. Studies are divided into two main categories: One is SMGs, which mainly focus on text or verbal glosses; and the other is MMGs, with text, picture, audio, video, and combinations.

The 1990s can be characterized as a foundational period for gloss studies. Most of the studies were on SMGs, with the main topics being guessing, inferences, intentional vs. incidental, mental effort, location, single-choice gloss (SCG) vs. multiple-choice gloss (MCG), among others. An SCG is a usual gloss with a single translation. This term is used here to contrast with MCGs, which contain a multiple-choice format, asking learners to choose the most appropriate meaning of a word out of a few choices. The idea of MCGs was introduced in Hulstijn (1992) to promote more mental effort from learners having to infer or guess the meaning of a word. This idea and its effectiveness were tested in Watanabe (1997) using printed materials, followed by Mitarai and Aizawa (1999) with the inclusion of gloss languages (L1 vs. L2). MCGs were further investigated with computers by Nagata (1999) providing immediate feedback on learners' choices on MCGs. The findings of these studies indicated that MCGs were better than SCGs. This topic was carried over to the next decade. The topic of gloss language appeared in this period (Jacobs et al., 1994; Ko, 1995; Mitarai & Aizawa, 1999) and favored L1 overall. Vigorous investigation did not occur till the 2010s.

It was also the dawn of MMGs, with three studies (Chun & Plass, 1996; Kost et al., 1999; and Plass et al., 1998). Chun and Plass (1996) and Plass et al. (1998) were computer-based studies, took advantage of multimedia, and utilized video clips along with texts and pictures. Their project was one of the pioneering works in MMG research and opened a new era for gloss study. Kost et al. (1999) were unique in that their study examined the effect of picture glosses using printed texts. The theoretical backbone of MMGs was dual-coding theory (Paivio, 1986). Learners process information better when it is coded both verbally with texts and visually with pictures than when it is coded verbally or visually alone. The results of these early studies showed that glosses with text plus pictures were more effective than glosses with text alone or pictures alone, thus supporting the dual-coding theory. The introduction of MMGs brought greater excitement and interest in gloss studies, and we see these in the expansions of study in the next decade.

The 1990s was a foundational time for gloss research. The studies in this period introduced important topics and issues and paved the way for gloss research to follow.

Gloss research in the 2000s

This decade was a flourishing time for gloss studies. Table 4.3 presents a list of both SMG and MMG studies in the 2000s. The total number of studies increased from 12 in the 1990s to 29 in the 2000s. First, we will look at the development in SMG studies and then in MMG studies.

This decade marks steady progress in SMG studies. There were similar issues as those in the 1990s such as lookups (visible or invisible links), locations, and SCGs and MCGs. We particularly see an increase in MCG studies. MCGs were considered to be a tool for promoting guessing and inferring. Researchers were interested in how they could help learners put in more mental effort or get involved in working with glosses. All six MCG studies were conducted with printed materials (see SCG vs. MCG in the SMG section of Table 4.3). Even though the idea of implementing MCGs using computers was introduced in Nagata (1999), actual digital implementation did not occur till the 2010s. Most of the MCG studies pointed to the advantage of MCGs; however, toward the end of the 2000s, a different result started appearing. For instance, Martínez-Fernández (2008) showed that MCGs, SCGs, and no glosses were equally effective.

Table 4.3 shows a drastic increase in MMG studies from just three in the 1990s to 20 in the 2000s. Much research was devoted to the comparison of SMGs and MMGs. Researchers were excited about glosses in the digital world and wanted to show how multimodal glossing was effective in comparison with single-mode. They also explored different issues including listening materials, individual factors (proficiencies, learning styles, and working memory), different L1s and L2s, and MMGs (text, audio, picture, animation, video, etc.). Researchers wanted to explore which modes or combinations of them were effective for vocabulary learning. As can be seen in Table 4.3, the majority of studies support the dual-coding hypothesis. However, at the end of this period, studies started showing different results (Acha, 2009; Yanguas, 2009). It was an indication that there might be cases where SMGs work better than MMGs for certain learners. We will revisit this issue in the "New understanding" section. Regarding theories, the cognitive load hypothesis started to play a more important role than in the previous decade (Acha, 2009; Plass et al., 1998). The theory points out that learners have limited capacity to take in information at a given time. Going beyond the limit causes cognitive overload and results in ineffective learning.

This decade saw major growth in gloss studies, especially in MMG studies. It was a flourishing time for gloss research dealing with a variety of issues such as cognitive load, mental effort, and working memory, besides the dual-coding hypothesis. They continued to grow in the next

Development of gloss studies in vocabulary learning research 71

decade; however, we will see different patterns for developments in SMG and MMG studies.

Gloss research in the 2010s

We now come to the last decade of the development of gloss research covered in this chapter. The 2010s can be characterized as a time for further exploration and maturation. The number of gloss studies jumped from 29 in the 2000s to 48 in the 2010s. SMG research and MMG research showed different patterns of change. It was almost a reversal of the pattern seen from the 1990s to the 2000s. In the 2000s, we saw a steady increase of SMG and a drastic increase of MMG research. In the 2010s, we see a jump in SMG and a decrease in MMG research. As Table 4.4 shows, the majority of SMG papers were on L1 vs. L2, which was a remarkable change of research interests. As seen in Table 4.2, we had three earlier studies which examined this issue. In the next decade, this topic did not attract much interest, and no particular study which focused on this issue can be found in Table 4.3. We had L1 and L2 related studies, such as the study by Cheng and Good (2009) which had a group of L1 glosses plus L2 sample sentences in their experiment, and Miyasako (2002) and Shiki (2008) examined SCGs and MCGs combined with L1 and L2. However, none of these studies solely focused on L1 vs. L2. Now we see a drastic increase of 15 studies on language issues, and the results also varied in the 2010s. We will look at this research on gloss languages in more detail in the next section.

Besides the gloss languages, five studies were conducted on SCG and MCG issues. In the previous decade, we saw signs of increasing interest in this topic. Computers allow us to implement MCGs with immediate feedback on learners' choices confirming their answers or pointing out wrong inferences. We would have expected more studies on MCGs specifically utilizing digital glosses. However, the number of studies on the topic decreased from the 2000s, and the results are also not conclusive. Some favored MCGs (Farvadin & Biria, 2012; Gan, 2014), while others favored SCGs (Pishghadam & Ghahari, 2011; and Yoshii, 2013), and one study did not see any differences (Hsu, 2011).

SMG research also explored various other topics, looking at locations, concordance, dictionary styles, implicit vs. explicit, computer vs. paper, assessment methods, grammar, and working memory, to name a few.

In the 2000s, we saw a drastic jump in MMG research, and we might expect that the trend would continue in the 2010s. However, the number slightly decreased, and the results of the studies varied. We will look at the details in the next section. The use of new tools such as eye-tracking opened a new door for analyzing the phenomenon (Warren et al., 2018),

Table 4.4 List of gloss studies in the 2010s

Single-mode gloss (SMG): mainly verbal or textual gloss

Author(s), year	Main findings	Found in
L1 > L2		
Arpacı (2016)	L1 > L2, L1 preferred	④, ⑤
Ertürk (2016)	L1 > L2, NG > L2, preference on L1	④, ⑤, ⑦
Öztürk and Yorgancı (2017)	L1 > L2	④
Kongtawee and Sappapan (2018)	L1 > L2	④
Huang (2018)	L1 MCG > L1 SCG or L2 MCG or L2 SCG or NG	⑦
L1 ≈ L2		
Ko (2012)	Glosses >NG, L1 ≈ L2, learners preferred L2	④, ⑤, ⑦
Rouhi and Mohebbi (2012)	Glosses >NG, L1 ≈ L2 (L1 slightly better), noticing, input enhancement	④
Sadeghi and Ahmadi (2012)	A + L2 > marginal, L1 ≈ L2	⑤
Salehi and Naserieh (2013)	Glosses > NG, L1 ≈ L2, L1 preferred, mixed best (1st time with L1 & L2, 2nd time with the previous sentence)	④, ⑤
Choi (2016)	L1 ≈ L2	④, ⑤, ⑦
Kim and Choi (2017)	L1 ≈ L2, high intermediate: L1 > L2, L1 preferred (those who experienced L2, preference not extreme)	④
Barabadi et al. (2018)	L1 + pronunciation, L2 + pronunciation > L1, L2 L1 ≈ L2	④
Kang et al. (2020)	Both L1 and L2 good for form-meaning, eye-tracking	④
L1 < L2		
Taheri and Zade (2014)	L1 < L2, Concrete > abstract	④
L1 and L2 with proficiency		
Ko (2017)	Low level: L1, L1+L2 > L2, NG High level: L2, L1+L2 > L1, NG The most preferred: L1 + L2	④, ⑤
Proficiency and frequency		
Zhao and Ren (2017)	Glosses > NG (recall and recognition) Higher proficiency: higher freq ≈ lower freq Lower proficiency: higher freq > lower freq	⑤
SCG and MCG		
Hsu (2011)	SCG ≈ MCG	③
Pishghadam and Ghahari (2011)	G > N L1 SCG > among other groups (NG, L2 SCG, L1 MCG, and L2 MCG)	④

Table 4.4 (Continued)

Single-mode gloss (SMG): mainly verbal or textual gloss

Author(s), year	Main findings	Found in
Farvardin and Biria (2012)	L2 MCG > L1 SCG, L2 SCG	④, ⑤
Yoshii (2013)	SCG > MCG	③, ⑤
Gan (2014)	G > NG MCG > SCG > NG	③, ⑤
Other topics with SMG (text-focused)		
Zarei and Hasani (2011)	L1 and L2, location, L2: no significant differences, L1: for recognition, pre-text, marginal > post-text, for recall, in-text > post-text	④, ⑤
Poole (2012)	Concordance > dictionary	③
Shabani (2014)	G > NG, explicit > implicit	③
Chen (2014)	Assessment methods: different methods with different outcomes Locations, in-text: best of all, pop-up: lowest on all	⑦
Lee et al. (2016)	Cognitive load, electronic > paper, NG	⑤, ⑦
Jung (2016)	Grammar and Vocabulary: glosses > NG	⑤, ⑦
Samian et al. (2016)	G > NG, giving (write definition) > receiving (just look)	⑤
Varol and Erçetin (2016)	Regardless of conditions (lexical or topical information) Glosses > NG, WM	⑤
Multimodal glosses / textual, pictorial, auditory, video		
MMG > SMG		
Tabatabaei and Shams (2011)	Glosses > NG, T+P > T, P	③, ⑤, ⑥
Lin and Tseng (2012)	T+V > T+P, T	③, ⑥
Moazzeni et al. (2014)	T+V > other groups (SCG, MCG, T+P+A, and NG)	③, ⑤, ⑥
Faramarzi et al. (2014)	T+P > T, P	③
Moradan and Vafaei (2016)	T+P > T, P	⑤, ⑥
Boers et al. (2017a)	Dual coding vs. amount of attention, eye-tracking, T+P > T T+P: more & longer attention	⑤, ⑦
Ramezanali and Faez (2019)	Overall T+V, T+A > T T also effective on certain occasions, cognitive theory, perceptions	⑥
MMG ≑ SMG		
Ahangari and Abdollahpour (2010)	G > NG, no differences among the groups (still picture; dynamic picture; and text)	③

(*Continued*)

Table 4.4 (Continued)

Single-mode gloss (SMG): mainly verbal or textual gloss

Author(s), year	Main findings	Found in
Tabatabaei and Mirzaei (2014)	Idiom: glosses > NG T+P ≈ T, P	③
Zarei and Mahmoodzadeh (2014)	G > NG No significant differences among the groups (T, P, T+P, and NG)	③, ⑥
Çakmak and Erçetin (2018)	Glosses > NG, T+P ≈ T ≈ P, mobile-assisted L2 listening Low proficiency	⑦
MMG < SMG		
Boers et al. (2017b)	T+P < P, meaning and form	⑤, ⑥, ⑦
Warren et al. (2018)	Eye-tracking, time fixed and vocabulary learning: close relationship Picture gloss: smallest fixed time, yet most effective among the groups (T, P, and T+P)	⑥
Other topics with SMG and MMG		
AbuSeileek (2011)	Glosses > NG After the word location was the best among the groups (in the margin, at the bottom of the screen, in a pop-up window, and after glossed word)	⑦
Abidin et al. (2011)	Computer (T, P, A) > paper (T)	③
Yousefzadeh (2011)	Computer (T+P) > paper (T)	③
Türk and Erçetin (2014)	Simultaneous (T+P) > interactive (select T, P, or both), T+P simultaneously presented reduce cognitive load and result in better learning	⑥
Sadeghi et al. (2016)	T+P+A > T+P, intentional vs. incidental	⑥
Rassaei (2018)	Text vs. audio, perceptual style (visual vs. verbal) L1 glosses, A > T > NG, moderating role of perceptual style Auditory learners with audio: highest rate of VL	⑤

List of abbreviations
NG = No gloss, L1 = First language text gloss, L2 = Second language text gloss, T = Text, P = Picture, V = Video, A = Audio, SCG = Single-choice gloss, MCG = Multiple-choice gloss, SMG = Single-mode gloss, MMG = Multimodal gloss, > greater than, < less than, ≈ almost the same

List of review papers (Number corresponds to each paper)
① Abraham (2008); ② Mohsen and Balakumar (2011); ③ Vahedi et al. (2016); ④ Kim et al. (2020); ⑤ Yanagisawa et al. (2020); ⑥ Ramezanali et al. (2021); and ⑦ Zhang and Ma (2021)

and the cognitive load hypothesis became more important in understanding SMGs and MMGs (Boers et al., 2017a; Ramezanali & Faez, 2019; Türk & Erçetin, 2014).

This decade marked a time of further exploration. SMG research flourished, with a particular interest in L1 vs. L2. MMG research, although it did not show a rapid increase, continued to explore the use of new tools such as eye-tracking. The results of SMG and MMG research showed more variety, which would require further inquiry. It was also a maturing time for gloss research because we saw a number of review papers trying to make sense of what had been learned so far in the field. This chapter is in the same vein. We need this kind of review to reflect on what we have learned and see what we still need to learn.

New understanding

Summary of gloss research from the 1990s to the 2010s

We have looked at the development of gloss research from the 1990s to the 2010s. Now, we will look at the overall picture of gloss research development. Figure 4.1 shows the changes in the numbers of studies of SMGs and MMGs. It shows that the "total" number of gloss studies almost tripled from the 1990s to the 2000s, and doubled from the 2000s to the

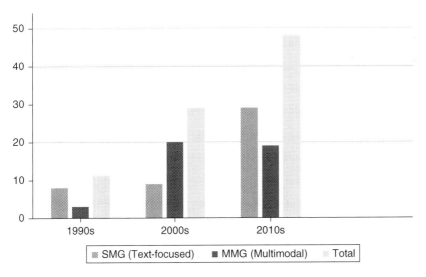

Figure 4.1 Changes in the numbers of SMG, MMG, and total gloss papers from the 1990s to the 2010s

2010s. Gloss research has enjoyed a fourfold increase from the 1990s to the 2010s. As we have seen in "Synthesis" section, the patterns of change differed between SMG and MMG research. SMG research maintained the same number of gloss studies from the 1990s to the 2000s, and then it had a threefold increase in the 2010s. MMG research showed an initial sudden jump, an almost sevenfold increase, from the 1990s to the 2000s, and then it plateaued in the 2010s. It was as if the interest in MMGs had shifted to SMGs. Glossing in the past with printed materials was confined by limited space and gloss mode, mainly limited to text, sometimes with pictorial information. Computerized glossing brought a whole new world to gloss research with almost unlimited digital space and a variety of multimodal tools. This inspired researchers and was connected to the blossoming of MMG studies. While MMG studies started settling down, the importance and value of SMG (especially textual) studies were reevaluated and sparked renewed interest. As a way to a new understanding of gloss research, we will revisit the language of glosses (L1 vs. L2) and compare SMG and MMG research.

L1 glosses vs. L2 glosses

Now, we will revisit L1 vs. L2 studies. This was the main topic in SMG research, especially in the 2010s. Half of the studies at that time were devoted to this topic (16 out of 29 studies). Figure 4.2 shows how the findings for L1 vs. L2 changed over three decades. In the figure, "L1" stands for those studies which favored L1 over L2. "L2" stands for studies favoring L2. "NoD" stands for those which showed no differences between L1 and L2.

As we have seen in the "Synthesis" section, we started with three studies in the 1990s and had no specific study on this topic during the 2000s, and then, all of a sudden, 14 studies appeared. The results of these studies are not conclusive. Figure 4.2 shows more results indicating "no difference (NoD)" than advantages of L1. "NoD" means we did not see any significant differences between L1 and L2. Previously, it was reported that L1 seemed to be more effective than L2 (Kim et al., 2020; Yanagisawa et al., 2020). That is true in one sense when we compare the studies favoring one language or the other, because only one study favored L2 (Taheri & Zade, 2014). However, the fact that the majority showed no significant differences calls for further careful investigation. No differences mean the results could turn to favor L1 or L2, either way, depending on other factors. One of the major factors is L2 proficiency, and this is a somewhat problematic issue. The first problem is that we do not know the extent to which proficiency interacts with choice of gloss language. While Kim et al. (2020) found L2 proficiency was a significant moderator, Yanagisawa et al.

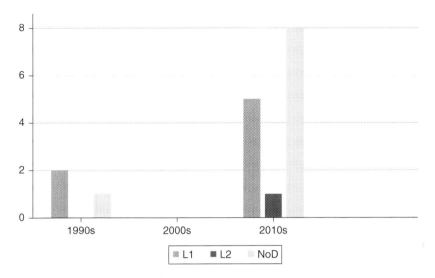

Figure 4.2 Changes of results favoring L1, L2, and showing no differences

(2020) did not. A sensible way to handle the proficiency issue appears to be to select the language according to learners' proficiency. Kim et al. (2020) and Ko (2017) suggested that we could use L1 for beginners and L2 for intermediate or higher learners. Another problem with proficiency is that it is difficult to measure. In fact, previous studies used different measurements, which makes it difficult to compare the results. It is also interesting to note that there seems to be the potential for L1 plus L2 glossing. L1 plus L2 together might be preferred by learners and more effective than L1 or L2 alone (Ko, 2017; Yanagisawa et al., 2020). Because it is difficult to ascertain learners' proficiency, it is advisable for us to give learners a choice of gloss languages according to their proficiency and preference. Giving choices of L1, L2, or both may facilitate learners' preferred learning and bring better results. We will see the specific research ideas on this issue in the next section.

Single-mode glosses vs. multimodal glosses

Figure 4.1 showed a drastic increase in MMG studies (20 studies) in the 2000s, and the number of the studies stayed almost the same (19 studies) in the 2010s. Researchers continued to look at the effects of MMGs and compared them with SMGs in these two decades. Although the number of MMG studies and the topics stayed the same, the results changed

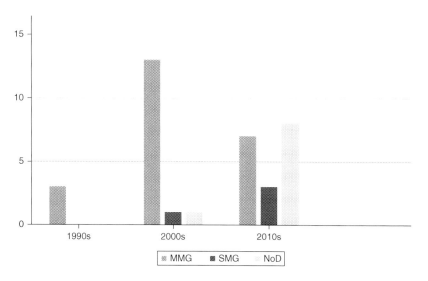

Figure 4.3 Changes of results favoring MMGs, SMGs, and showing no differences

remarkably. Figure 4.3 displays the changes of the results favoring MMGs, SMGs, or resulting in no differences ("NoD"). As seen in Figure 4.3, almost all the studies (13 out of 15) favored MMGs, leaving only one case with similar results between MMGs and SMGs (Yanguas, 2009) and one case favoring SMGs (Acha, 2009) in the 2000s. However, this picture changed in the 2010s. MMGs lost their dominance and other results started manifesting: Seven studies favored MMGs, four showed similar benefits, and two favored SMGs in the 2010s (Boers et al., 2017b; Warren et al., 2018). These changes lead us to reexamine the effectiveness of MMGs and reevaluate the dual-coding theory.

Dual coding is a long-standing theory behind the benefits of MMGs, and many studies have supported the theory. The new findings (Boers et al., 2017a, 2017b; Warren et al., 2018) challenge us to look at other reasons why dual-coded information works.

Boers et al. (2017b) was a paper-based study and examined two conditions. One group read a text with textual glosses provided in the margin; the other group read it with the same textual glosses with the addition of pictures. Their study did not show any advantage of adding pictures to glosses. We saw a similar case in Acha (2009). In this study, the participants were children, and they did better on recall of word translations when glosses were presented in text only rather than text plus picture. The children paid more attention to pictures than expected, which caused their attention to be split between text and picture. It was surprising to see similar results with university students who did not retain words better with the addition of pictures to glosses compared to those students who had no pictures (Boers et al., 2017b). This was a reminder that, regardless of age, amount or allocation of attention might play as important a role as dual processes play.

Warren et al. (2018) compared three conditions: text only, text plus picture, and picture only. They used an eye-tracking tool to record learners' eye movements. Their study found that picture only was the best of the three options, even though the total time of attention was the smallest.

The notion of attention was introduced into other recent studies (Boers et al., 2017a; Boers, 2022). Boers et al. (2017a) compared text only with text plus picture using an eye-tracker. The study found that the learners gave longer attention to text and picture glosses than text-only or picture-only glosses. Boers (2022) pointed out that the advantage of MMGs might be related to accessing glosses more than once or paying more attention to them. Future studies can look at these issues. Some ideas and suggestions will be presented in the next section.

New understanding of gloss research

What does this journey through gloss research tell us? First, it reminds us of a cycle of research. When a certain topic is introduced, it takes time to grow. Some topics may enjoy a rapid increase in interest, as we saw in multimodal studies in the 2000s in Figure 4.1. Some may have to wait for some time to flourish; such was the case for single-mode studies in the 2010s. The cycle also includes times during which research attention appears to have plateaued. We see that in single-mode studies from the 1990s to the 2000s and in multimodal studies from the 2000s to 2010s in Figure 4.1. It does not mean that nothing is happening. Contrastingly, we may see a pattern of steady growth or maturation. This can be observed in the multimodal studies from the 2000s to the 2010s. The number of the studies plateaued, as shown in Figure 4.1; however, the contents of the findings tell a different story, as seen in Figure 4.3. We saw more variety in the results which made us rethink and reevaluate what we know about MMGs. Reflection on what we have accumulated in a research field comes through review or meta-analysis papers. Reflection is needed to go on to the next level in the field. Gloss research, with a number of such review papers, including this chapter, is ready to move on to the next stage.

What are effective glosses? We have seen that L1 tends to be better than L2 and that MMGs are better than SMGs. We have also seen that L2 proficiency might be one of the keys to determine glosses' effectiveness. Because it is difficult to measure learners' proficiency, it might be a good

80 *Theory and Practice in Vocabulary Research in Digital Environments*

idea to provide choices for the languages or modes they prefer. However, when learners are given choices, it may be important to limit the options; otherwise, the cognitive load may be too great.

Implications

This section contains some ideas for further gloss studies on L1 vs. L2 and SMGs vs. MMGs. We will look at an example on gloss languages. Presenting L1 and L2 together was mentioned as better than L1 or L2 (Ko, 2017; Yanagisawa et al., 2020) even though this is contrary to the split attention or redundancy effect. We investigate if simultaneous presentation of L1 and L2 is really better than L1 (with further access to L2) or L2 (with further access to L1). We also investigate the effectiveness of looking at a gloss twice, L1 and L2 one at a time, and compare that with the simultaneous presentation of L1 and L2. Figure 4.4 shows three different conditions for glosses: L1 (Japanese) plus L2 (English) on the word "scribble" on the left; the example in the middle has L1 and a choice of L2 by clicking on the L2 button; and the one on the right has L2 with further access to L1.

Interesting questions can be raised. Which of these options is the best and why? Do learners in either L1 or L2 conditions click on the button to have access to the other language? For how long do learners pay attention in each condition? If eye-tracking is available, we can obtain further information on fixed time or total amount of time focused on each gloss and which part. Think-aloud methods also shed light on what learners actually do and why in these conditions. We have seen that L2 proficiency might be an important factor in determining the effectiveness of the language of glossing. Do learners with different proficiencies behave differently in these conditions? How does their performance on vocabulary learning differ in relation to proficiency and lookup behavior?

We will now move on to research ideas for MMGs. We could implement a study on MMGs to compare dual coding and the frequency of access to

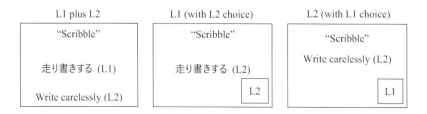

Figure 4.4 Three conditions for L1 vs. L2

Development of gloss studies in vocabulary learning research 81

Figure 4.5 Three conditions for text and picture

glosses. We prepare three different conditions of glosses. One is text plus picture presented together (simultaneous presentation); and the other two are either text-only or picture-only conditions. They contain an option to look further at another gloss (interactional presentation): a picture gloss for text only and a text gloss for picture only, as seen in Figure 4.5. In this example, L1 (Japanese) was used for the text gloss. We could certainly replace L1 with L2 and see if the results would differ.

Similar questions as those in the L1 vs. L2 study can be raised. Which option is the best and why? Do learners in either text-only or picture-only conditions click further to have access to the other mode? For how long do learners pay attention in each condition? Eye-tracking would give us further information on fixed time or total amount of time focused on each gloss and which part. Think-aloud methods can give us more qualitative data on what learners actually do and why with these conditions. We may see L2 proficiency play an important role in determining the effectiveness of the gloss modes. Do learners with different proficiencies behave differently in these conditions? How does their performance on vocabulary learning differ in relation to proficiency and lookup behavior? Answers to these questions may shed more light on MMGs. We need to see which plays a more important role in influencing MMGs: either the dual-coding hypothesis or amount of attention.

The last suggestion is a long-term study on glossing. We saw L2 proficiency may play an important role in the choice of gloss language. This may also affect the effectiveness of MMGs. Gloss research so far has focused on one-shot studies, and there is a lack of long-term investigation of how learners' behavior with glossing changes over time. We could implement studies with the conditions represented in Figures 4.4 and 4.5 with the same learners at different times. We do need to come up with multiple texts to use at multiple times. The findings of long-term investigation at different times would help us understand how learners change their gloss lookup behavior as their proficiency improves. Data at different times with the same learners would help us better understand gloss language issues and the effectiveness of multimodal approaches. This chapter will hopefully generate interest in further gloss studies and vocabulary learning in the 2020s.

Further reading

Three articles are recommended for readers:

Boers, F., Warren, P., He, L., & Deconinck, J. (2017b). Does adding pictures to glosses enhance vocabulary uptake from reading? *System*, *66*, 113–129. https://doi.org/10.1016/j.system.2017.03.017

This study helps readers understand how gloss research may be conducted. This was a pen-and-paper study and examined the effectiveness of the addition of pictures. The study is unique in that it featured three experiments with three different groups of participants, and the results favored the text-only group over the text-plus-picture group.

Warren, P., Boers, F., Grimshaw, G., & Siyanova-Chanturia, A. (2018). The effect of gloss type on learners' intake of new words during reading: Evidence from eye-tracking. *Studies in Second Language Acquisition*, *40*, 883–906. https://doi.org/10.1017/S0272263118000177

This study gives readers an idea of how eye-tracking data can shed new light on gloss research. It challenges us to rethink why multimodal presentations are effective. Amount of attention was introduced as a possible factor influencing learning besides dual-coding effects.

Yanagisawa, A., Webb, S., & Uchihara, T. (2020). How do different forms of glossing contribute to L2 vocabulary learning from reading?: A meta-regression analysis. *Studies in Second Language Acquisition*, *42*(2), 411–438.

This is one of the recent meta-analysis papers on glossing. The study covers various issues regarding glosses including gloss format (type, language, mode), text characteristics, and learner characteristics. The study gives readers a good understanding of gloss research and how a meta-analysis may be conducted.

References

Abidin, M. J. Z., Pour-Mohammadi, M., Shoar, N. S., See, T. H. C., & Jafre, A. M. (2011). A comparative study of using multimedia annotation and printed textual glossary in learning vocabulary. *International Journal of Learning and Development*, *1*(1), 82–90.

Abraham, L. B. (2007). Second language reading comprehension and vocabulary learning with multimedia. *Hispania*, *90*, 98–109.

Abraham, L. B. (2008). Computer-mediated glosses in second language reading comprehension and vocabulary learning: A meta-analysis. *Computer Assisted Language Learning*, *21*, 199–226. https://doi.org/10.1080/09588220802090246

AbuSeileek, A. F. (2011). Hypermedia annotation presentation: The effect of location and type on the EFL learners' achievement in reading comprehension and vocabulary acquisition. *Computers & Education*, 57, 1281–1291.

Acha, J. (2009) The effectiveness of multimedia programmes in children's vocabulary learning. *British Journal of Educational Technology*, 40(1), 23–31.

Ahangari, S., & Abdollahpour, Z. (2010). The effect of multimedia annotations on Iranian EFL learners' L2 vocabulary acquisition. *The Journal of Applied Linguistics*, 3(1), 1–18.

Aizawa, K. (1998). Incidental vocabulary learning through reading: Guessing exercises, glossing or accessing dictionaries? *The Bulletin of the Kanto-Koshin-Etsu English Language Education Society*, 12, 79–94. https://doi.org/10.20806/katejo.12.0_79

Akbulut, Y. (2007). Effects of multimedia annotations on incidental vocabulary learning and reading comprehension of advanced learners of English as a foreign language. *Instructional Science: An International Journal of the Learning Sciences*, 35(6), 499–517.

Al-Musallam, E., Al-Twairesh, N., & Al-Shubaily, S. (2005). Acquisition of vocabulary items through multimedia vs. still pictures: A comparative study. *Language Learning*, 6(2), 56–68.

Al-Seghayer, K. (2001). The effect of multimedia annotations modes on L2 vocabulary acquisition: A comparative study. *Language Learning & Technology*, 5(1), 202–232. http://llt.msu.edu/vol5num1/alseghayer/default.html

Arpacı, D. (2016). The effects of accessing L1 versus L2 definitional glosses on L2 learners' reading comprehension and vocabulary learning. *Eurasian Journal of Applied Linguistics*, 2(1), 15–29.

Barabadi, E., Asma, A., & Panahi, A. (2018). The relative impact of L1 and L2 glosses along with computer-generated phonological guidance on EFL learners' vocabulary learning. *Cogent Education*, 5, 1–13.

Boers, F. (2022). Glossing and vocabulary learning. *Language Teaching*, 55(1), 1–23.

Boers, F., Warren, P., Grimshaw, G., & Siyanova-Chanturia, A. (2017a). On the benefits of multimodal annotations for vocabulary uptake from reading. *Computer Assisted Language Learning*, 30, 709–725. https://doi.org/10.1080/09588221.2017.1356335

Bowles, M. A. (2004). L2 glossing: To CALL or not to CALL. *Hispania*, 87, 541. https://doi.org/10.2307/20063060

Çakmak, F., & Erçetin, G. (2018). Effects of gloss type on text recall and incidental vocabulary learning in mobile-assisted L2 listening. *ReCALL*, 30, 24–47.

Chandler, P. and Sweller, J. (1991). Cognitive load theory and the format of instruction. *Cognition and Instruction*, 8, 293–332.

Chen, I.-J. (2014). Hypertext glosses for foreign language reading comprehension and vocabulary acquisition: Effects of assessment methods. *Computer Assisted Language Learning*, 29, 413–426.

Cheng, Y.-H., & Good, R. L. (2009). L1 glosses: Effects on EFL learners' reading comprehension and vocabulary retention. *Reading in a Foreign Language*, 21(2), 119–142.

Choi, S. (2016). Effects of L1 and L2 glosses on incidental vocabulary acquisition and lexical representations. *Learning and Individual Differences*, 45, 137–143.

Chun, D. & Payne, J. S. (2004). What makes learners click: Working memory and look-up behavior. *System*, 32, 481–503.

Chun, D. M., & Plass, J. L. (1996). Effects of multimedia annotations on vocabulary acquisition. *The Modern Language Journal*, 80, 183–198. https://doi.org/10.2307/328635

De Ridder, I. (2002). Visible or invisible links: Does highlighting of hyperlinks affect incidental vocabulary acquisition, text comprehension, and the reading process? *Language Learning & Technology*, 6(1), 123–146.

Ertürk, Z. ÿzdem. (2016). The effect of glossing on EFL learners' incidental vocabulary learning in reading. *Procedia – Social and Behavioral Sciences*, 232, 373–381. https://doi.org/10.1016/j.sbspro.2016.10.052

Faramarzi, S., Elekaei, A., & Koosha, M. (2014). On the impact of multimedia glosses on reading comprehension, vocabulary gain and vocabulary retention. *International Journal of Language Learning and Applied Linguistics World*, 6(4), 623–634.

Farvardin, M. T., & Biria, R. (2012). The impact of gloss types on Iranian EFL students' reading comprehension and lexical retention. *International Journal of Instruction*, 5(1), 99–114.

Gan, X. (2014). Study on the effects of gloss type on Chinese EFL learners' incidental vocabulary acquisition. *Theory and Practice in Language Studies*, 4(6), 1251–1256. https://doi.org/10.4304/tpls.4.6.1251-1256

Hsu, M-H. (2011). The effect of first language gloss on reading comprehension, lexical acquisition and retention: Single gloss and multiple-choice gloss. *WHAMPOA – An Interdisciplinary Journal*, 61, 33–52.

Huang, H. (2018). Computer multimedia aided word annotation for incidental vocabulary acquisition in English Reading. *Educational Sciences: Theory & Practice*, 18, 3417–3427.

Hulstijn, J. H. (1992). Retention of inferred and given word meanings: Experiments in incidental vocabulary learning. In P. J. L. Arnaud & H. Béjoint (Eds.), *Vocabulary and applied linguistics* (pp. 113–125). London, UK: Palgrave Macmillan UK. https://doi.org/10.1007/978-1-349-12396-4_11

Hulstijn, J. H., Hollander, M., & Greidanus, T. (1996). Incidental vocabulary learning by advanced foreign language students: The influence of marginal glosses, dictionary use, and reoccurrence of unknown words. *The Modern Language Journal*, 80, 327–339. https://doi.org/10.2307/329439

Jacobs, G. M., Dufon, P., & Hong, F. C. (1994). L1 and L2 vocabulary glosses in L2 reading passages: Their effectiveness for increasing comprehension and vocabulary knowledge. *Journal of Research in Reading*, 17(1), 19–28. https://doi.org/10.1111/j.1467-9817.1994.tb00049.x

Jones, L. C. (2003). Supporting listening comprehension and vocabulary acquisition with multimedia annotations: The students' voice. *CALICO Journal*, 21(1), 41–65.

Jones, L. (2004). Testing L2 vocabulary recognition and recall using pictorial and written test items. *Language Learning and Technology*, 8(3), 122–143. http://llt.msu.edu/vol8num3/jones/default.html

Jones, L. (2006). Effects of collaboration and multimedia annotations on vocabulary learning and listening comprehension. *CALICO Journal*, 24(1), 33–58.
Jones, L. (2009). Supporting student differences in listening comprehension and vocabulary learning with multimedia annotations. *CALICO Journal*, 26(2), 267–289.
Jones, L., & Plass, J. (2002). Supporting listening comprehension and vocabulary acquisition in French with multimedia annotations. *The Modern Language Journal*, 86(4), 546–561.
Jung, J. (2016). Effects of glosses on learning of L2 grammar and vocabulary. *Language Teaching Research*, 20(1), 92–112. https://doi.org/10.1177/1362168815571151
Kang, H., Kweon, S.-O., & Choi, S. (2020). Using eye-tracking to examine the role of first and second language glosses. *Language Teaching Research*. 26, https://doi.org/10.1177/1362168820928567.
Kim, D., & Gilman, D. A. (2008). Effects of text, audio, and graphic aids in multimedia instruction for vocabulary acquisition. *Educational Technology & Society*, 11(3), 114–126.
Kim, H.-S., & Choi, U.-Y. (2017). L1 vs. L2 glosses, learner perceptions, and L2 vocabulary learning. *Modern English Education*, 18, 67–89.
Kim, H. S., Lee, J. H., & Lee, H. (2020). The relative effects of L1 and L2 glosses on L2 learning: A meta-analysis. *Language Teaching Research*, 28(1), https://doi.org/10.1177/1362168820981394.
Ko, M. H. (1995). Glossing in incidental and intentional learning of foreign language vocabulary and reading. *University of Hawai'i Working Papers in ESL*, 13(2), 49–94.
Ko, M. H. (2012). Glossing and second language vocabulary learning. *TESOL Quarterly*, 46, 56–79.
Ko, M. H. (2017). The relationship between gloss type and L2 proficiency in incidental vocabulary learning. *The Modern English Society*, 18(3), 47–69. https://doi.org/10.18095/meeso.2017.18.3.03
Kongtawee, P., & Sappapan, P. (2018). The effects of L1 and L2 hypertext glosses on reading comprehension and vocabulary retention among Thai secondary school students. *Arab World English Journal*, 9, 367–380.
Kost, C. R., Foss, P., & Lenzini, J. J. (1999). Textual and pictorial glosses: Effectiveness on incidental vocabulary growth when reading in a foreign language. *Foreign Language Annals*, 32, 89–97. https://doi.org/10.1111/j.1944-9720.1999.tb02378.x
Kroll, J. F., & Stewart, E. (1994). Category interference in translation and picture naming: Evidence for asymmetric connections between bilingual memory representations. *Journal of Memory and Language*, 33, 149–174.
Laufer, B., & Hulstijn, J. H. (2001). Incidental vocabulary acquisition in a second language: The construct of task-induced involvement. *Applied Linguistics*, 22, 1–26. https://doi.org/10.1093/applin/22.1.1
Lee, H., Lee, H., & Lee, J. H. (2016). Evaluation of electronic and paper textual glosses on second language vocabulary learning and reading comprehension. *The Asia-Pacific Education Researcher*, 25, 499–507.

Lin, C. (2009). Learning action verbs with animation. *The JALT CALL Journal, 5*(3), 23–40.

Lin, C., & Huang, H. (2008). Meaning-inferred gloss and meaning-given gloss on incidental vocabulary learning. *Journal of National Taiwan Normal University: Humanities & Social Sciences, 53*(2), 87–116.

Lin, C., & Tseng, Y. (2012). Videos and animations for vocabulary learning: A study on difficult words. *TOJET: The Turkish Online Journal of Educational Technology, 11*(4), 346–355.

Macaro, E. (2009). Teacher use of codeswitching in the second language classroom: Exploring 'optimal' use. In Turnbull, M., & J. Dailey-O'Cain (Eds.), *First language use in second and foreign language learning* (pp. 35–49). Tonawanda, NY: Multilingual Matters.

Martínez-Fernández, A. (2008). Revisiting the involvement load hypothesis: Awareness, type of task and type of item. In M. A. Bowles, R. Foote, S. Perpiñán, & R. Bhatt (Eds.), *Selected proceedings of the 2007 Second Language Research Forum* (pp. 210–228). Somerville, MA: Cascadilla Proceedings Project.

Mayer, R. E. (1997). Multimedia learning: Are we asking the right questions? *Educational Psychologist, 32*(1), 1–19.

Mayer, R. E. (2001). *Multimedia learning*. New York: Cambridge University Press.

Mayer, R. E. (Ed.). (2014). *The Cambridge handbook of multimedia learning*. New York, NY: Cambridge University Press.

Mayer, R. E., & Moreno, R. (1998). A split-attention effect in multimedia learning: Evidence for dual processing systems in working memory. *Journal of Educational Psychology, 90*(2), 312–320. http://dx.doi.org/10.1037/0022-0663.90.2.312

Mitarai, Y., & Aizawa, K. (1999). The effects of different types of glosses in vocabulary learning and reading comprehension. ARELE: *Annual Review of English Language Education in Japan, 10*, 73–82.

Miyasako, N. (2002). Does text-glossing have any effects on incidental vocabulary learning through reading for Japanese senior high school students? *Language Education & Technology, 39*, 1–20. https://doi.org/10.24539/let.39.0_1

Moazzeni, Z., Bagheri, M. S., Sadighi, F., & Zamanian, M. (2014). The effect of different gloss types on incidental vocabulary retention of Iranian EFL students. *International Journal of Language Learning and Applied Linguistics World, 5*(2), 396–415.

Mohsen, M. A., & Balakumar, M. (2011). A review of multimedia glosses and their effects on L2 vocabulary acquisition in CALL literature. *ReCALL, 23*, 135–159. https://doi.org/10.1017/S095834401100005X

Moradan, A., & Vafaei, M. (2016). The effect of glosses on incidental vocabulary learning of Iranian EFL learners. *International Journal of Applied Linguistics and English Literature, 5*(6), 34–42. https://doi.org/10.7575/aiac.ijalel.v.5n.6p.34

Nagata, N. (1999). The effectiveness of computer-assisted interactive glosses. *Foreign Language Annals, 32*(4), 469–479. https://doi.org/10.1111/j.1944-9720.1999.tb00876.x

Nation, I. S. P. (2013). *Learning vocabulary in another language* (2nd ed.). New York, NY: Cambridge University Press.

Nikolova, O. (2002). Effects of learners' participation in authoring of multimedia materials on student acquisition of vocabulary. *Language Learning & Technology*, 6(1), 100–122. http://llt.msu.edu/vol6num1/nikolova/default.html

Öztürk M.S., & Yorgancı, M. (2017). Effects of L1 and L2 glosses on incidental vocabulary learning of EFL prep students. *International Periodical for the Languages, Literature and History of Turkish or Turkic*, 12, 635–656.

Paivio, A. (1971). *Imagery and verbal processes*. New York: Holt, Rinehart, & Winston. (Reprinted 1979, Hillsdale, NJ: Lawrence Erlbaum Associate).

Paivio, A. (1986). *Mental representations: A dual coding approach*. New York: Oxford University Press.

Pishghadam, R., & Ghahari, S. (2011). The impact of glossing on incidental vocabulary learning: A comparative study. *Iranian EFL Journal*, 7, 8–29.

Plass, J. L., Chun, D. M., Mayer, R. E., & Leutner, D. (2003). Cognitive load in reading a foreign language text with multimedia aids and the influence of verbal and spatial abilities. *Computers in Human Behavior*, 19, 221–243. https://doi.org/10.1016/S0747-5632(02)00015-8

Plass, J. L., Chun, D. M., Mayer, R. E., & Leutner, D. (1998). Supporting visual and verbal learning preferences in a second-language multimedia learning environment. *Journal of Educational Psychology*, 90, 25–36.

Poole, R. (2012). Concordance- based glosses for vocabulary acquisition. *CALICO Journal*, 29(4), 679–693.

Ramezanali, N., & Faez, F. (2019). Vocabulary learning and retention through multimedia glossing. *Language Learning and Technology*, 23(2), 105–124.

Ramezanali, N., Uchihara, T., & Faez, F. (2021). Efficacy of multimodal glossing on second language vocabulary learning: A meta-analysis. *TESOL Quarterly*, 55(1), 105–133.

Rassaei, E. (2018). Computer-mediated textual and audio glosses, perceptual style and L2 vocabulary learning. *Language Teaching Research*, 22(6), 657–675.

Rott, S. (2005). Processing glosses: A qualitative exploration of how form-meaning connections are established and strengthened. *Reading in a Foreign Language*, 17, 95–124.

Rott, S., Williams, J., & Cameron, R. (2002). The effect of multiple-choice L1 glosses and input-output cycles on lexical acquisition and retention. *Language Teaching Research*, 6(3), 183–222. https://doi.org/10.1191/1362168802lr108oa

Rouhi, A., & Mohebbi, H. (2012). The effect of computer assisted L1 and L2 glosses on L2 vocabulary learning. *The Journal of Asia TEFL*, 9, 1–19.

Sadeghi, K., & Ahmadi, N. (2012). The effect of gloss type and mode on Iranian EFL learners' vocabulary acquisition. *Issues in Language Teaching*, 1, 159–188.

Sadeghi, K., Khezrlou, S., & Modirkhameneh, S. (2016). Calling Iranian learners of L2 English: Effect of gloss type on lexical retention and reading performance under different learning conditions. *Journal of Research in Reading*, 39(1), 1–21. https://doi.org/10.1111/1467-9817.12088

Sakar, A., & Erçetin, G. (2005). Effectiveness of hypermedia annotation for foreign language reading. *Journal of Computer Assisted Learning*, 21, 28–38. https://doi.org/10.1111/j.1365-2729.2005.00108.x

Salehi, V., & Naserieh, F. (2013). The effects of verbal glosses on vocabulary learning and reading comprehension. *Asian EFL Journal*, 15, 24–64.

Samian, H. V., Foo, T. C. V., & Mohebbi, H. (2016). The effects of giving and receiving marginal L1 glosses on L2 vocabulary learning by upper secondary learners. *English Language Teaching*, 9(2), 66–76.

Schmidt, R. (1990). The role of consciousness in second language learning. *Applied Linguistics*, 11, 129–158.

Schmidt, R. (1995). Consciousness and foreign language learning. In R. Schmidt, (Ed.), *Attention and Awareness in Foreign Language Learning* (pp. 1–63). University of Hawai'i at Manoa: Second Language Teaching and Curriculum Center.

Shabani, K. (2014). The effects of computerized instruction of vocabulary through hypertexts on L2 learners' cognitive functioning. *Procedia- Social and Behavioral Sciences*, 149(2014), 868–873.

Shahrokni, S. A. (2009). Second language incidental vocabulary acquisition: the effect of on-line textual, pictorial, and textual pictorial glosses. *Electronic Journal for English as a Second Language*, 13(3), 25–35.

Shiki, O. (2008). Effects of glosses on incidental vocabulary learning: Which gloss-type works better, L1, L2, single choice, or multiple choices for Japanese university students? *Journal of Inquiry and Research*, 87, 39–56.

Sweller, J., & Chandler, P. (1991). Evidence for cognitive load theory. *Cognition and Instruction*, 8, 23–34.

Tabatabaei, O., & Mirzaei, M. (2014). Comprehension and idiom learning of Iranian EFL learners. *Journal of Educational and Social Research*, 4(1), 45–56.

Tabatabaei, O., & Shams, N. (2011). The effect of multimedia glosses on online computerized L2 text comprehension and vocabulary learning of Iranian EFL learners. *Journal of Language Teaching and Research*, 2(3), 714–725. https://doi.org/10.4304/jltr.2.3.714-725

Taheri, P., & Zade, M.H. (2014). On the incidental learning of abstract and concrete vocabulary items in L1 gloss and L2 gloss. *English Language Teaching*, 1, 77–91.

Türk, E., & Erçetin, G. (2014). Effects of interactive versus simultaneous display of multimedia glosses on L2 reading comprehension and incidental vocabulary learning. *Computer Assisted Language Learning*, 27(1), 1–25.

Vahedi, V. S., Ghonsooly, B., & Pishghadam, R. (2016). Vocabulary glossing: A meta-analysis of the relative effectiveness of different gloss types on L2 vocabulary acquisition. *Teaching English with Technology*, 16, 3–25.

Varol, B., & Erçetin, G. (2016). Effects of working memory and gloss type on L2 text comprehension and incidental vocabulary learning in computer-based reading. *Procedia - Social and Behavioral Sciences*, 232, 759–768. https://doi.org/10.1016/j.sbspro.2016.10.103

Warren, P., Boers, F., Grimshaw, G., & Siyanova-Chanturia, A. (2018). The effect of gloss type on learners' intake of new words during reading: Evidence from eye-tracking. *Studies in Second Language Acquisition*, 40, 883–906. https://doi.org/10.1017/S0272263118000177

Watanabe, Y. (1997). Input, intake, and retention: Effects of increased processing on incidental learning of foreign language vocabulary. *Studies in Second Language Acquisition*, 19(3), 287–307. https://doi.org/10.1017/S027226319700301X

Yanguas, I. (2009). Multimedia glosses and their effect on L2 text comprehension and vocabulary learning. *Language Learning & Technology*, 13(2), 48–67.

Yeh, Y., & Wang, C. (2003). Effects of multimedia vocabulary annotations and learning styles on vocabulary learning. *CALICO Journal*, 21(1), 131–144.

Yoshii, M. (2006). L1 and L2 glosses: Their effects on incidental vocabulary learning. *Language Learning & Technology*, 10(3), 85–101. http://llt.msu.edu/vol10num3/yoshii/default.html

Yoshii, M. (2013). Effects of gloss types on vocabulary learning through reading: Comparison of single translation and multiple-choice gloss types. *CALICO Journal*, 30, 203–229.

Yoshii, M., & Flaitz, J. (2002). Second language incidental vocabulary retention: The effect of picture and annotation types. *CALICO Journal*, 20(1), 33–58.110.

Yousefzadeh, M. (2011). Computer-based glosses vs. traditional paper-based glosses and L2 learners vocabulary acquisition. *International Journal on New Trends in Education and Their Implications*, 2(3), 99–102.

Zarei, A. A., & Hasani, S. (2011). The effects of glossing conventions on L2 vocabulary recognition and production. *The Journal of Teaching Language Skills*, 3, 209–233.

Zarei, A., & Mahmoodzadeh, P. (2014). The effect of multimedia glosses on L2 reading comprehension and vocabulary production. *Journal of English Language and Literature*, 1(1), 1–7. https://doi.org/10.17722/jell.v1i1.6.

Zhang, C., & Ma, R. (2021). The effect of textual glosses on L2 vocabulary acquisition: A meta-analysis. *Language Teaching Research*, 28(3), https://doi.org/10.1177/13621688211011511

Zhao, T., & Ren, J. (2017). Incidental L2 lexical acquisition in reading: The role of L2-gloss frequency and learner proficiency. *The Language Learning Journal*, 47, 608–624. https://doi.org/10.1080/09571736.2017.1349168

Part II
Pedagogical practices

5 A corpus-based study of learners' language learning trajectories with captioned viewing

Implications for vocabulary learning practices

Mark Feng Teng[1] and Jesse W. C. Yip[2]

[1]Faculty of Languages and Translation, Macao Polytechnic University, Macau SAR, China

[2]Department of Linguistics and Modern Language Studies, The Education University of Hong Kong, Hong Kong SAR, China

Pre-reading question

Can learners' language learning trajectories be understood through an analysis of captioned viewing?

Background

Initially conceived to aid the deaf and hard of hearing, captioning has a history dating back to the 1970s, with a predominant focus on the English language, but only in the past ten years has there been a proliferation of multilingual audiovisual content supported by cost-efficient technologies that facilitate comprehensive engagement with these resources. A substantial number of research over the past 35 years robustly affirms the pedagogical benefits of utilizing captions—subtitles in the language of the video intended for the deaf or hard of hearing—as a tool for enhancing language comprehension and acquisition among second or foreign language learners. This is extensively documented in two monographs (Teng, 2021; Vanderplank, 2016a), which conclude that captions significantly augment access to, and comprehension of, televised media and films for individuals with competent reading abilities in the captioned language.

Vanderplank (2016b) explains the efficacy of captions, amalgamating pivotal findings from foundational studies and offering a holistic view of the existing scholarly terrain while pinpointing lacunae for future inquiry.

DOI: 10.4324/9781003367543-7

This work also casts light on emergent and promising modalities for language learning, particularly for learners navigating foreign language content on the internet, now more approachable due to the ubiquity of captions. In their interactions with video content, study participants demonstrated a propensity to consult embedded texts to elucidate unfamiliar vocabulary promptly, thereby reducing the time and effort traditionally associated with dictionary-based word retrieval methods. The immediate availability of textual representations of unknown lexemes within videos thus confers a significant pedagogical advantage.

The amalgamation of accessible multilingual audiovisual content with the technological apparatus to harness it presents expansive opportunities for linguistic acculturation. The integration of captioning within language learning platforms can significantly enhance linguistic comprehension, facilitate vocabulary acquisition, and improve overall language comprehension (Teng, 2023). A meta-analysis study by Montero Perez et al. (2013) backs up the idea that the presence of captions markedly elevates access to and understanding of television programming and films for second or foreign language learners, thereby advancing lexical learning. The study suggests that the strategic use of captions offers a dual-channel approach to language learning and combines visual and auditory sensory inputs synergistically to reinforce comprehension and retention (Montero Perez et al., 2013). This multimodal integration is particularly beneficial for learners who possess a foundational level of literacy in the target language, allowing them to contextualize and internalize new vocabulary effectively.

Notwithstanding the substantial body of research elucidating the immediate advantages of captioned media consumption, the longitudinal impact on learners' trajectories in foreign language acquisition remains inadequately explored. Learners engaging with foreign language content via captions may gain a more nuanced understanding of certain lexicons and phrases, particularly with consistent exposure. However, the field has not yet achieved sufficient attention in understanding the full scope of how regular engagement with captioned media can bolster foreign language proficiency. Moreover, there exists a dearth of comprehensive insight into the ideal conditions that amplify the pedagogical value of captions in language learning. The characteristics of learner-viewers who can effectively leverage the potential of captions for language acquisition are not fully understood. This chapter aims to broaden our comprehension of how foreign language learners interact with captions. By probing into their experiences and engagement with captioned videos, this research endeavors to unearth insights that will deepen our grasp of the pedagogical merits of captioned viewing.

Captioned audiovisual input and language learning

Sweller's Cognitive Load Theory (2011) posits the notion of the limited capacity of working memory and suggests that cognitive overload can occur when attempting to process substantial amounts of information through verbal and visual channels simultaneously. The use of captioned videos in technological learning tools, where audio, visual, and textual captions are present, aligns with this theory. These elements work together to distribute cognitive load, thereby facilitating learning rather than hindering it (Vanderplank, 2016). Dual Coding Theory (Paivio, 2007), which suggests that verbal and imagery systems can operate independently and reinforce each other, further explains the benefits of captions for foreign language learning The theory posits that the activation of both systems enhances information retrieval.

Captioned videos engage both the nonverbal and verbal systems, enabling effective language recall, dynamic speech comprehension, and the development of vocabulary and language skills (Teng, 2021). Cognitive and affective models support the idea that captioned videos, as audiovisual input, do not exceed viewers' cognitive capacities but instead aid learning by balancing the processing loads from multiple sources.

Vanderplank (1990) delved into the long-term effects of captioned viewing on English language comprehension over periods ranging from eight to ten weeks. The results indicated that participants were able to surpass mere comprehension enhancement and basic vocabulary gains by actively interacting with the language presented in captions. Strategies such as note-taking and concentrated attention to the captions during viewing were found to be advantageous. In a subsequent study, Vanderplank (2016b) identified challenges in directing participants—exchange students with English proficiency levels from B2 to C1—to approach popular television programs as a medium for language learning, rather than solely for entertainment. A tendency to treat viewing such media as a leisure activity posed a substantial obstacle to maximizing the educational potential of captions.

Montero Perez et al. (2013) synthesized the outcomes of existing research through a meta-analysis to assess the effects of captions on video comprehension and vocabulary learning. This comprehensive review, which included 15 studies on comprehension and ten on vocabulary acquisition, yielded overwhelmingly positive results, demonstrating that captions significantly enhance both content understanding and vocabulary acquisition, as reflected by the large effect sizes.

Teng (2022, 2023) has further reinforced the evidence supporting captions as a facilitator of vocabulary learning. The studies not only confirm the beneficial impact of captions, but also draw attention to the critical role of individual learner differences in the language acquisition process. Teng's investigations emphasize the importance of proficiency level, innate language aptitude, and working memory capacity in determining the success of caption use for vocabulary learning. In a recent study, Teng and Cui (2023) scrutinized captions for incidental vocabulary learning, comparing the effects on single words and collocations. Their research shed light on the differential impacts that full versus keyword-specific captions have on learning various linguistic elements, offering insight into how different captioning techniques influence language acquisition.

In addition to the demonstrated benefits of captioned videos for language acquisition, a limited number of studies have explored learners' experiences with these educational tools. Maria da Conceição Condinho Bravo's (2010) longitudinal research examined the effects of viewing captioned versus uncaptioned programs across different genres and languages, including English and Portuguese. The initial phase of the study involved 32 adult learners of varying linguistic backgrounds and proficiency levels in Portuguese, who were exposed to six video clips in a classroom setting. The results indicated a general difficulty in comprehending uncaptioned content. Advanced learners, in particular, expressed a preference for viewing these clips independently and at their own pace. Initially perceived as leisure activities, these audiovisual sessions gradually took on an educational dimension as participants started to actively note down unfamiliar words and phrases. Vanderplank (2019) undertook a qualitative investigation with 36 intermediate to advanced learners of French, German, Italian, and Spanish at a UK university. These learners had the flexibility to watch DVDs of a curated selection of films with optional captions at their leisure. Through detailed viewing diaries, the study identified diverse patterns in viewing practices, attitudes towards captioned content, and strategies for using captions to support language learning. Participants were classified into three distinct groups according to their approach: minimal users, who engaged with the films primarily for enjoyment; evolving users, who showed progressive changes in their viewing habits; and maximal users, who adeptly incorporated films into their language learning regimen.

While prior research has illuminated various aspects of language learning through captioned videos, there remains a lack of insight into a possible longitudinal language learning trajectory. To bridge this knowledge gap, the present study aims to explore the following research questions:

1. In what manner do students' language learning trajectories unfold when they engage with captioned viewing over time?

2. What are the key benefits and obstacles encountered by learners as they endeavor to learn vocabulary through captioned viewing?

Method

Participants

To recruit participants for the study, requests for volunteers were distributed among students enrolled in courses at an education university in China that featured a self-access language learning center. The eligibility criteria required the participants to have achieved a minimum score of 110 out of 150 points in the English subject upon admission to the university. The participants' baseline language levels were also determined through a self-assessment questionnaire, which indicated that all participants reported an intermediate level or higher level. A total of 30 participants (16 females and 14 males) voluntarily participated in the study. Each participant expressed their interest in joining on their own initiative. The questionnaires revealed that while all participants possessed confidence in their reading skills in English, they were unconfident when it came to watching TV programs and films in that language. Furthermore, they all shared a common goal of wanting to enhance their ability to watch English films with confidence. The dataset included 20 participants (11 females and 9 males) who provided reflective diaries to us for no less than ten weeks. Those who provided only a few lines during this process were not included. In the results section of this chapter, comments provided by the participants in their online or hard-copy diaries are presented using participant numbers to maintain anonymity. These diary entries serve as valuable qualitative data to gain insights into the participants' experiences and perceptions of captioned videos for language learning.

Captioned videos

Captioned videos from YouTube and Netflix were selected for the study. These videos were specifically chosen to ensure a diverse representation of genres, encompassing comedies, documentaries, thrillers, dramas, modern settings, historical settings, and more. The aim was to include a broad selection of videos that would expose the participants to a variety of storytelling styles, contexts, and language usage. This approach allowed for a comprehensive exploration of the effects of captions across different genres and film types, enabling a more robust analysis of the participants' language learning experiences.

Data collection

The data collection took place during an existing 16-week course on listening comprehension. This time frame allowed for a comprehensive investigation into learners' experiences and perceptions of using captions for language learning. As part of the course requirements, participants were required to watch at least one video per week, following the comprehension exercises provided to them. This ensured that participants had consistent exposure to the materials and created standardized conditions for data collection.

To gather qualitative data and insights from the participants, a diary methodology was employed. The diary entries prompted participants to reflect on emotional changes they experienced while watching captioned videos. This aspect aimed to capture the affective dimensions of using captions, such as the participants' engagement, motivation, and enjoyment while interacting with the materials. Moreover, participants were encouraged to report any observed behavioral and cognitive changes in their language learning during and after watching captioned videos. This allowed researchers to gain insights into potential cognitive benefits and learning strategies associated with caption use. To ensure inclusivity and accommodate the participants' language preferences, they were given the option to submit their diary entries either as hard copies or online, using English. Eventually, we collected 307 diary entries, compiling a 100,000-word corpus of learners' experiences in language learning with captioned videos.

In addition to the diary entries, we conducted focus-group interviews, which provide supplementary data to the corpus-based analysis of the diary entries. The 30 participants were divided into five focus groups (six participants per group) for the interviews. The interviews, which were semi-structured and lasted approximately 1.5 hours, were conducted in an interview room at the university, guided by several interview questions, including the following: (1) Could you describe the development or changes in your language learning experience through captioned videos? (2) What were the major challenges you encountered in the process? (3) After weeks of learning, what do you conclude from your experience of language learning through captioned viewing? The authors, who were the interviewers, asked follow-up questions to elicit relevant information from the participants, using the interview guide. Each interview session was audio-recorded and transcribed into text for further analysis.

Data analysis

The present study adopts a corpus-based approach to discourse analysis. This method, commonly called corpus-based discourse analysis, combines corpus linguistics and discourse analysis, involving quantitative analysis of linguistic patterns that frequently occur in the discourse, and qualitative interpretation analysis of their meanings (Yip, 2024). Corpus linguistics refers to a variety of techniques for analyzing linguistic patterns in collections of digitized, naturally occurring language (Cheng, 2012; McEnery & Wilson, 2001), and the analysis is processed using corpus analysis tools. Advantages of employing corpus-based discourse analysis include reducing research bias and revealing particular hegemonic discourses and the incremental effect of discourse (Baker, 2006). Thus, this approach has been used to investigate various types of discourse, such as the examination scripts of English language learners (Chung et al., 2023), interactions between psychotherapist and client (Yip, 2022), and business brand construction (Lam, 2018).

The self-compiled corpus of learners' experiences in learning language with captioned videos was divided into three sub-corpora, representing three stages of the participants' learning experience based on the time of submitting the diary entries: Initial Stage (Weeks 1–5), Middle Stage (Weeks 6–10), and Final Stage (Weeks 11–16). The sub-corpora were then analyzed separately using the corpus analysis tool AntConc 4.2.3. The analysis focused on lexical items using two techniques from corpus linguistics, namely word frequency lists and concordance analysis. This is because 'lexical words are the main carriers of information and contribute more to the semantic construction and communication' (Lam, 2018, p. 200). In addition, concordance analysis was conducted to examine lexical items in their sentential context, providing qualitative analysis that enhances understanding of how a specific word or phrase functions and its meaning. Concordance lines of the generated high-frequency words and high-frequency collocates will be examined and used as examples to instantiate and explain the arguments. In the interpretation of the concordance analysis, the notions of semantic preference and semantic prosody (Sinclair, 1991) were employed. Semantic preference of a lexical item is defined as 'the restriction of regular co-occurrence to items which share a semantic feature' (Sinclair, 2004, p. 142), such as illness and suffering. Semantic prosody is related to the discourse function of a unit of meaning (Hunston, 2007), referring to whether the collocates of a word tend to be positive or negative (Handford, 2010). This series of corpus analyses enabled us to capture the motifs of the learners' experiences at different stages through statistical analysis of word occurrences and qualitative analysis of word meanings.

The focus-group interview transcripts were also analyzed based on the three-stage approach (i.e., Initial, Middle, and Final Stage). The authors iteratively read the transcripts to obtain a general understanding of the development of the participants' language learning experiences with captioned videos. Subsequently, common themes in each stage of their learning were identified and compared with the results obtained from the corpus-based analysis of the diary entries. To conduct an inter-reliability check, the authors independently analyzed and identified the themes, and then compared and discussed them to generalize the common themes of each stage. The authors eventually reached agreement on all the general themes presented in this chapter.

Results

Initial Stage

Table 5.1 displays the 20 most frequently used words in the sub-corpus consisting of diary entries submitted by participants during the Initial Stage of the study (Weeks 1–5).

Table 5.1 presents the high-frequency words categorized into two semantic domains: (1) learning experience with captioned videos, and (2) moods and emotions. It was observed that many students perceived learning English with captioned videos as a journey and considered it to be a novel learning approach. Consequently, nearly half of the high-frequency words in Table 5.1, such as 'language,' 'caption(s),' 'learning,' 'captioned,' 'videos,' 'films,' 'journey,' and 'experience,' were associated with the domain of learning experience with captioned videos. The domain of moods and emotions played a significant role in reflecting the main themes of the participants' Initial Stage. Words such as 'feel/felt/feeling,' 'emotional,' 'emotions,' and 'sense' indicated that the participants experienced various emotions while learning with captioned videos. The word 'excitement,' which was one of the top 20 most frequently occurring words, was prominently present in the corpus. The following examples provide further clarification:

> Excerpt 1
> It's a positive emotional journey in which I feel more connected to the content and confident in my language learning abilities.
> (Participant 1)
>
> Excerpt 2
> Initially, I felt a mix of excitement and apprehension, as I wanted to fully engage with the film while also focusing on language acquisition.
> (Participant 6)

In addition to excitement, the concordance analysis reveals that participants also experienced anxiety while utilizing captioned videos for English learning. Consequently, participants describe the learning process

Table 5.1 Frequency and dispersion of top 20 lexical words at Initial Stage

Rank	Words	Frequency	Normalized frequency	Dispersion	Rank	Words	Frequency	Normalized frequency	Dispersion
1	language	91	2.533	0.932	11	understand(ing)	21	0.585	0.841
2	caption(s)	65	1.810	0.779	12	watching	20	0.557	0.633
3	learning	56	1.559	0.903	13	emotion(s)	17	0.473	0.703
4	captioned	39	1.086	0.479	14	sense	17	0.473	0.74
5	emotional	33	0.919	0.795	15	moment(s)	15	0.418	0.62
6	video(s)	30	0.835	0.462	16	experience	15	0.418	0.79
7	more	26	0.724	0.804	17	myself	15	0.418	0.751
8	feel/felt/feeling	25	0.696	0.33	18	dialogue	14	0.390	0.751
9	journey	23	0.640	0.877	19	noticed	13	0.362	0.571
10	film(s)	23	0.640	0.820	20	excitement	11	0.306	0.236

as 'emotional' due to the presence of both positive and negative emotions during the Initial Stage. The words 'understand(ing)' and 'noticed' provide further insight into the participants' emotional state, as shown in the following excerpts:

> Excerpt 3
> The challenge of <u>understanding</u> the <u>language</u> and keeping up with the <u>dialogue</u> led to moments of distraction and reduced focus.
> (Participant 3)
>
> Excerpt 4
> I <u>noticed</u> an improvement in my cognitive processing speed as I became more adept at quickly reading the <u>captions</u> and comprehending the <u>dialogue</u>.
> (Participant 20)
>
> Excerpt 5
> For instance, if I <u>felt</u> stressed or tired before watching a <u>film</u>, I <u>noticed</u> a decline in my ability to concentrate and absorb the <u>language</u> content.
> (Participant 29)

The concordances revealed a strong connection between the participants' emotions and their ability to comprehend the dialogue or captions in the videos. Some participants found the process of understanding the dialogue challenging, as they struggled to concentrate on the content. These difficulties resulted in stress and apprehension.

Interview data from participants in the study revealed a complex array of emotions, predominantly characterized by a combination of excitement and anxiety, during their exposure to captioned viewing. This emotional duality appears to be indicative of the Initial Stage of the participants' interactions with the captioned content.

> Interview 1
> I was actually quite <u>excited</u> about it. The captions made it <u>easier</u> for me to understand what the speaker was saying, especially with complex terms.
> (Participant 19)
>
> Interview 2
> Well, I <u>liked</u> having the captions, but it was a bit <u>overwhelming</u>. I was trying to read and listen at the same time, and I <u>worried</u> about missing important information.
> (Participant 17)

It appears that the participants expressed a palpable sense of excitement, possibly stemming from the novelty and heightened engagement facilitated by the addition of captions. The presence of captions seemed to introduce a new layer of interaction, enriching their viewing experience and enhancing their comprehension of the content. However, intertwined with this excitement was a discernible undercurrent of anxiety among the participants. This anxiety could be attributed to their unfamiliarity with the captioned format or potential concerns about being able to effectively engage with the content while simultaneously processing textual information. This is why participants articulated feelings of apprehension, expressing concerns about the potential cognitive load associated with dual processing—simultaneously watching and reading.

Middle Stage

Following a five-week period of learning English with captioned videos, it was expected that the participants would have undergone changes. Table 5.2 presents the high-frequency words derived from the sub-corpus consisting of diary entries submitted for Weeks 6–10 of their learning journey.

We expected to find words such as 'language,' 'caption(s),' 'learning,' 'film(s),' 'captioned,' 'video(s),' 'journey,' and 'watch(ing)' among the top high-frequency lexical items in the corpus, as the participants were actively engaged in a learning journey that involved watching captioned videos to learn English. However, what distinguishes the characteristics of the participants' learning experience during the Middle Stage are the lexical words that depict more than the theme of the event. While the words 'emotional' and 'sense' appear in both the Initial and Middle Stage corpora, they demonstrate different semantic preferences. Specifically, the participants experienced a combination of positive and negative emotions during the Initial Stage, whereas negative emotions were more prevalent during the Middle Stage. The following concordances provide further elaboration:

Excerpt 6
I experienced moments of <u>emotional fatigue</u> accompanied by <u>frustration and decreased enthusiasm</u>.

(Participant 5)

Excerpt 7
There were specific techniques that helped me overcome <u>emotional setbacks</u>.

(Participant 18)

Excerpt 8
There were instances when I found myself getting distracted by unrelated tasks or losing focus on the language learning process. These

Table 5.2 Frequency and dispersion of top 20 lexical words at Middle Stage

Rank	Words	Frequency	Normalized frequency	Dispersion	Rank	Words	Frequency	Normalized frequency	Dispersion
1	language	181	2.622	0.923	11	journey	31	0.449	0.845
2	caption(s)	117	1.695	0.802	12	watch(ing)	29	0.420	0.783
3	learning	115	1.666	0.946	13	vocabulary	28	0.406	0.842
4	film(s)	57	0.826	0.623	14	skills	27	0.391	0.786
5	more	46	0.666	0.792	15	help(ed)	27	0.391	0.637
6	emotional	45	0.652	0.703	16	frustration/frustrated	26	0.377	0.424
7	captioned	42	0.608	0.66	17	approach	24	0.348	0.682
8	video(s)	40	0.579	0.611	18	culture/cultural	23	0.333	0.76
9	understand(ing)	40	0.579	0.864	19	moment(s)	23	0.333	0.664
10	sense	33	0.478	0.788	20	spoken	21	0.304	0.74

moments of distraction led to a sense of frustration and a feeling of wasting valuable learning opportunities.

(Participant 25)

The excerpts highlight that participants encountered frustration and discouragement when they realized their weak comprehension of video dialogue and faced difficulties with listening exercises. As a result, the lexical item 'frustration/frustrated' emerges as one of the top 20 highest-frequency words in the corpus. Feeling excited at the beginning, participants gradually faced growing challenges in their learning journey, leading to feelings of frustration. The lexical items 'vocabulary,' 'skills,' and 'spoken' are associated with the language skills and vocabulary that participants aimed to develop through the spoken discourse in captioned videos.

Excerpt 9
Whenever I came across unfamiliar words or expressions, I would pause the film, make note of those words, and later incorporate them into my vocabulary practice.

(Participant 22)

Excerpt 10
It was an invaluable opportunity to further refine my language skills and connect with native speakers on a deeper level.

(Participant 13)

Excerpt 11
This approach helped me develop greater fluency and adaptability in understanding spoken language without the support of written text.

(Participant 7)

The excerpts indicate that, at this stage, participants were able to identify specific linguistic aspects that they could improve through captioned videos after six weeks of practice. In addition to the potential improvement in linguistic competence, the presence of the lexical item 'culture/cultural' suggests that participants were also aware of how their learning journey enhanced their cultural sensitivity:

Excerpt 12
I approached French films with a critical mindset, appreciating their artistic and cultural aspects while actively analyzing the language.

(Participant 20)

Excerpt 13
Experienced a renewed surge of motivation as I discovered the joy of connecting with the <u>language</u> and <u>culture</u> through <u>captioned videos</u>.
(Participant 21)

Through the captioned videos, participants were exposed to diverse cultures, and these cultural exposures were intertwined with the language learning process. Some participants experienced frustration during the Middle Stage of their learning journey, but they also began to recognize more specific benefits brought about by the practice, such as an improved vocabulary repertoire, spoken language proficiency, and increased cultural awareness. This is further evidenced in the following interview data:

Interview 1
Honestly, I found it a bit discouraging. As I pushed through the frustration, I started seeing real benefits. My vocabulary expanded significantly, and I became more <u>confident</u> in comprehension.
(Participant 16)

Interview 2
I began to understand cultural nuances better, which added <u>a whole new dimension</u> to my language skills.
(Participant 18)

The interview data seemed to illustrate a positive trajectory for the Middle Stage. Despite the challenges, participants recognized substantial benefits from the learning. Perseverance through frustration resulted in an expanded vocabulary repertoire, increased comprehension, and heightened cultural awareness. This shift in perception suggests that, over time, learners began to appreciate the cumulative advantages of learning through captioned viewing, highlighting the importance of a long-term perspective in language acquisition.

Final Stage
After completing at least ten weeks of learning English with captioned videos, the participants reached the Final Stage of their learning journey. The diary entries submitted by the participants in Weeks 11–16 of the project were included in the sub-corpus representing the Final Stage. Table 5.3 shows the top 20 highest-frequency lexical items extracted from this sub-corpus.

By excluding the high-frequency words related to the theme of language learning through captioned videos, we identified the lexical words that

Table 5.3 Frequency and dispersion of top 20 lexical words at Final Stage

Rank	Words	Frequency	Normalized frequency	Dispersion	Rank	Words	Frequency	Normalized frequency	Dispersion
1	language	284	0.0347	0.932	11	captioned	37	0.0045	0.479
2	learning	157	0.0192	0.903	12	experience	37	0.0045	0.79
3	captions	124	0.0152	0.779	13	film(s)	35	0.0043	0.901
4	emotional	69	0.0084	0.795	14	use/using	33	0.0040	0.721
5	film(s)	62	0.0076	0.711	15	comprehension	33	0.0040	0.809
6	culture/cultural	54	0.0066	0.722	16	allowed	31	0.0038	0.783
7	more	47	0.0057	0.804	17	overall	30	0.0037	0.851
8	understand(ing)	47	0.0057	0.83	18	cognitive	28	0.0034	0.463
9	journey	38	0.0046	0.877	19	deep(er)	26	0.0032	0.839
10	video(s)	38	0.0046	0.452	20	nuance(s)	25	0.0031	0.851

characterize the participants' experience during the Final Stage of their learning journey. These words can be grouped into three main semantic domains: emotions ('emotional'), cultural awareness ('culture/cultural'), and language proficiency ('understanding,' 'comprehension,' and 'cognitive'). To uncover the semantic preferences and prosodies of these domains, we conducted a concordance analysis of the words. In terms of the domain of emotions, unlike the previous stages, the frequency list does not reveal specific emotions, such as excitement and frustration, occurring frequently in the corpora. However, the concordance analysis demonstrates that most participants expressed satisfaction upon concluding their learning experience with captioned videos:

> Excerpt 14
> By experiencing the <u>emotional</u> depth of the films, I gained a heightened appreciation for the language as a powerful tool for storytelling and communication.
> (Participant 3)
>
> Excerpt 15
> Optimizing my <u>emotional</u> state positively influenced my concentration, <u>comprehension</u>, and overall engagement with the captioned films.
> (Participant 19)

The excerpts indicate that despite recognizing negative emotions during the previous stage of the learning process, the participants believed and appreciated that the emotional journey contributed to their language learning. Furthermore, the ranking of the lexical item 'culture/cultural' rises from 18 in the Middle Stage to 6 in the Final Stage, suggesting that more participants emphasized the cultural aspect in their learning with captioned videos over time.

> Excerpt 16
> I actively sought out supplementary resources to gain a better <u>understanding</u> of the <u>cultural</u> elements depicted in the videos.
> (Participant 23)
>
> Excerpt 17
> It expanded my worldview and nurtured a sense of empathy, which is vital for effective language communication and cross-<u>cultural</u> interactions.
> (Participant 25)

The excerpts reveal that the participants found value in the videos that showcased cultural contexts and believed that these cultural elements enhanced their understanding of language within specific cultures and their proficiency in intercultural communication. Moreover, the participants highlighted their cognitive improvements resulting from the learning process.

> Excerpt 18
> The cognitive benefits of using captions in language learning are remarkable. One of the most noticeable changes I've experienced is improved memory retention.
> (Participant 5)
>
> Excerpt 19
> Captions have become a catalyst for cognitive development, sharpening my critical thinking, problem-solving, and language acquisition abilities.
> (Participant 27)

After engaging in at least ten weeks of learning with captioned videos, the participants acknowledged the benefits of this learning method in enhancing their cognitive abilities, including memory and vocabulary retention, comprehension skills, and critical thinking skills. Notably, two comparative lexical words, 'more' and 'deeper,' frequently appear in the corpus. These words indicate and summarize the participants' progress after more than ten weeks of learning.

> Excerpt 20
> By managing and maintaining a balanced emotional state, I was able to engage with the films more effectively, stay focused, and absorb the language content more efficiently.
> (Participant 11)
>
> Excerpt 21
> It not only accelerated my language acquisition but also fostered a deeper connection and appreciation for the language.
> (Participant 6)

The semantic preferences of the high-frequency lexical words at this stage shift towards positive expressions. At the Final Stage, the participants demonstrate the ability to recognize the overall improvements resulting from language learning with captioned videos. These improvements encompass cognitive development, cultural sensitivity, intercultural communication, comprehension skills, and vocabulary acquisition. This is also supported in the following interview data:

Interview 1
I can see a significant <u>boost</u> in my cognitive abilities. I process information faster.
(Participant 11)

Interview 2
My understanding of different cultures has deepened, and I find it <u>easier</u> to communicate across <u>cultural boundaries</u>.
(Participant 23)

Interview 3
My comprehension skills have shot up, and my vocabulary is far <u>more extensive</u> than before.
(Participant 1)

Interview 4
The repetition of words that used to bother me initially turned out to be a <u>blessing</u>.
(Participant 9)

Interview 5
It's not just about the language anymore; it's about understanding the context and nuances. Captioned videos exposed me to diverse cultural expressions, and that's made <u>a huge difference</u>.
(Participant 24)

In the Final Stage of their language learning trajectories with captioned viewing, participants exhibited a profound recognition of multifaceted improvements across various domains. Benefits included cognitive development, intercultural understanding, comprehension, and vocabulary acquisition. It appears that the dual sensory input of audio and text in captioned videos can enhance cognitive functions, contributing to improved comprehension and vocabulary learning outcomes. The data reflect the adaptive nature of learners who, over time, recognized the strategic importance of repetition in reinforcing and expanding their language skills. This also points to the broader impact of language learning beyond linguistic proficiency, encompassing cultural sensitivity and effective cross-cultural communication.

New understandings

By summarizing and integrating the findings of the corpus-based analysis, we have developed a comprehensive model that illustrates the progression

Learners' language learning trajectories with captioned viewing 111

Figure 5.1 Proposed model of the trajectory of language learning with captioned viewing

of the participants' learning trajectories with captioned viewing (see Figure 5.1). This model serves as a valuable tool in addressing the two research questions.

As depicted in Figure 5.1, the participants in this study, who were university students with an intermediate level or higher proficiency in English, experienced a range of emotions at different stages of utilizing captioned videos for English language learning. Initially, they demonstrated a blend of enthusiasm and trepidation, welcoming the novel method but also recognizing the challenges in grasping the captions and film dialogue. This partially supports the findings from Conceição Condinho Bravo (2010), and Vanderplank (2019). In our study, participants were cognizant of both the appeal and the potential complexities of using captioned videos. We observed a notable shift in learners' sentiments. Participants' attitudes veered towards the negative as they grappled with hurdles such as sustaining concentration and deciphering dialogues. Notwithstanding these challenges, the participants identified a broader spectrum of specific advantages from captioned viewing. Beyond general language skill enhancement, they emphasized vocabulary enrichment and increased cultural awareness as they unraveled video narratives. In the last stage, the overall assessment of their learning experience was affirmative. Participants acknowledged that engaging with captioned viewing is beneficial for their language proficiency and communication skills, encompassing cognitive growth and intercultural communicative competence.

To bridge research gaps, we propose a corpus-based model of learning trajectories that outlines a phased progression consisting of three distinct stages, each elucidating the nuanced dynamics inherent in the integration of captioned viewing for language learning. In the Initial Stage, learners navigate a spectrum of affective states, encompassing both positive and negative emotions, alongside an optimistic outlook on linguistic advancement. Concurrently, they manifest an early awareness of the challenges inherent in utilizing captioned videos, thus establishing a foundation for a nuanced understanding of potential impediments. Transitioning to the Middle Stage, learners encounter setbacks and experience negative emotions along their learning trajectory, alongside discernible advancements in vocabulary acquisition and spoken language proficiency. This phase also fosters the cultivation of cultural awareness as learners engage with captioned content, leading to a deeper understanding of the cultural dimensions intertwined with the language being studied. Ultimately, the Final Stage culminates in a positive evaluation of the instructional modality, transcending the initial fluctuations in emotional disposition. To conclude, learners articulate an acknowledgment of comprehensive advancements in language proficiency, cognitive faculties, communication skills, and cultural knowledge, underscoring the holistic pedagogical benefits derived from sustained engagement with captioned videos in the realm of language learning.

Implications

Addressing the existing research gap, the present study contributes by elucidating the emotional trajectory and introspective processes experienced by participants who embraced the captioned video learning approach. The nuanced findings underscore that learners traversed a spectrum of emotional states, commencing with a blend of positive and negative emotions. Subsequently, there was a predominant shift towards negative emotions before a culmination in a positive overall evaluation of their learning experience. Moreover, the reflective insights gleaned from participants illuminate an evolving awareness throughout the learning journey. Learners demonstrated an increasing recognition of the extent of their linguistic progress and a discernment of specific domains in which their proficiency had developed. The corpus-based model of language learning trajectories through captioned viewing reinforces the understandings proposed by Vanderplank and Teng in this volume, as well as the cognitive and affective model put forward by Teng (2024).

These revelations provide valuable implications for vocabulary learning in the context of captioned video utilization. Strategies that encourage positive emotions may contribute to more effective vocabulary acquisition through captioned viewing. Targeted interventions or support mechanisms should be developed to guide learners in their vocabulary learning through captioned viewing. Designing instructional materials that incorporate cultural elements may contribute to a more comprehensive and meaningful vocabulary learning experience. Encouraging learners to reflect on their progress, identify areas of improvement, and set personalized language goals can foster autonomy and self-directed vocabulary learning. These insights carry significance for educators and curriculum designers aiming to optimize vocabulary instruction by strategically integrating captioned videos into language learning programs.

Further reading

Teng, F. (2021). *Language learning through captioned videos: Incidental vocabulary acquisition*. Routledge.
This book delves into critical considerations in the design of research pertaining to vocabulary studies within the framework of captioned viewing. Readers will find comprehensive insights into the impact of captioned videos on vocabulary learning, encompassing not only the cognitive aspects but also examining learners' perceptions of this educational approach. Additionally, the book explores the intricate interplay of individual differences among learners and how these factors may influence the process of vocabulary learning through captioned viewing.

Vanderplank, R. (2016). *Captioned media in foreign language learning and teaching*. Palgrave.
This book encompasses both theoretical and empirical research focused on the out-of-class use of captioned videos for language learning. Within its pages, readers can gain valuable insights into cognitive and affective models associated with language acquisition through captioned viewing. The exploration within the book extends to the implications of such learning methodologies, offering a comprehensive examination of the broader impact on language education.

References

Baker, P. (2006). Using *corpora in discourse analysis*. Continuum.
Bravo, C. (2010). Text on screen and text on air: a useful tool for foreign language teachers and learners. In J. Díaz Cintas, A. Matamala, & J. Neves (Eds.), *New insights into audiovisual translation and media accessibility: Media for all* (pp. 269–283). Rodopi.
Cheng, W. (2012). *Exploring corpus linguistics: Language in action*. Routledge.
Chung, E., Crosthewaite, P. R., & Lee, C. (2023). The use of metadiscourse by secondary-level Chinese learners of English in examination scripts: Insights from a corpus-based study. *International Review of Applied Linguistics in Language Teaching*. https://doi.org/10.1515/iral-2022-0155
Handford, M. (2010). What can a corpus tell us about specialist genres? In A. O'Keeffe & M. McCarthy (Eds.), *The Routledge handbook of corpus linguistics* (pp. 255–269). Routledge.
Hunston, S. (2007). Semantic prosody revisited. *International Journal of Corpus Linguistics*, *122*(2), 249–268.

Lam, P. W. Y. (2018). The discursive construction and realization of the Hong Kong brand: A corpus-informed study. *Text & Talk*, *38*(2), 191–216.

McEnery, T., & Wilson, A. (2001). *Corpus linguistics: An introduction*. Edinburgh University Press.

Montero Perez, M., Van Den Noortgate, W., & Desmet, P. (2013). Captioned video for L2 listening and vocabulary learning: A meta-analysis. *System*, *41*, 720–739.

Paivio, A. (2007). *Mind and its evolution: A dual coding theoretical approach*. Erlbaum.

Sinclair, J. (1991). *Corpus, concordance, collocation*. Oxford University Press.

Sinclair, J. (2004). *Trust the text: Language, corpus and discourse*. Routledge.

Sweller, J. (2011). Cognitive load theory. In J. P. Mestre, & B. H. Ross (Eds.), *Psychology of learning and motivation* (vol. 55, pp. 37–76). Academic Press.

Teng, F. (2021). *Language learning through captioned videos: Incidental vocabulary acquisition*. Routledge.

Teng, F. (2022). Incidental L2 vocabulary learning from viewing captioned videos: Effects of learner-related factors. *System*, *105*, 102736.

Teng, F. (2023). Incidental vocabulary learning from captioned video genres: Vocabulary knowledge, comprehension, repetition, and working memory. *Computer Assisted Language Learning*, 1–40. https://doi.org/10.1080/09588221.2023.2275158

Teng, F. (2024). Captioned viewing for language learning: A cognitive and affective model. In H. P. Bui & E. Namaziandost (Eds.), *Innovations in technologies for language teaching and learning*. Springer.

Teng, F., & Cui, Y. (2023). Comparing incidental learning of single words and collocations from different captioning conditions: The role of vocabulary knowledge and working memory. *Journal of Computer Assisted Learning 40*(3). https://doi.org/10.1111/jcal.12910

Vanderplank, R. (1990). Paying attention to the words: Practical and theoretical problems in watching television programmes with uni-lingual (CEEFAX) subtitles. *System*, *18*(2), 221–234.

Vanderplank, R. (2016a). *Captioned media in foreign language learning and teaching*. Palgrave.

Vanderplank, R. (2016b). 'Effects of' and 'effects with' captions: How exactly does watching a TV programme with same-language subtitles make a difference to language learners? *Language Teaching*, *49*(2), 235–250.

Vanderplank, R. (2019). 'Gist watching can only take you so far': attitudes, strategies and changes in behaviour in watching films with captions. *The Language Learning Journal*, *47*(1). https://doi.org/10.1080/09571736.2019.1610033

Yip, J. W. C. (2022). Management of therapist directiveness in integrative psychotherapy: A corpus-assisted discourse study. *Discourse and Interaction*, *15*, 132–151.

Yip, J. W. C. (2024). *Discourse of online social support: A Study of online self-help groups for anxiety and depression*. Springer.

6 L2 vocabulary learning with an AI chatbot
From linguistic, affective, and cognitive perspectives

Sangmin-Michelle Lee
School of Global Communication, Kyung Hee University, Korea

Pre-reading questions

1. What are some obstacles that EFL students face in terms of L2 vocabulary learning?
2. What are some instructional methods and strategies which can cultivate students' productive skills in L2?
3. What are the characteristics of a chatbot? How can we utilize a chatbot to promote students' productive vocabulary knowledge?

Introduction

Vocabulary learning is essential to second language (L2) learning, and vocabulary knowledge can be an indicator of L2 development (Chen et al., 2019). However, vocabulary learning is often a tedious and daunting task for English as a foreign language (EFL) students because it requires considerable memorization, repetition, and regurgitation, mainly due to a lack of authentic and meaningful opportunities to learn and use words within a specific context (Lee, 2023). In recent years, the advancement of technology has offered new opportunities for vocabulary learning. Chatbots, in particular, have been gaining popularity owing to their capacity to understand human language and communicate with users in L2 (Fryer et al., 2020; Huang et al., 2021). This capacity enables L2 students to engage in more authentic communicative tasks. Particularly in the EFL context, chatbots can serve as a useful communicative interlocutor (Jeong & Choi, 2021) and help students learn vocabulary in a natural and meaningful way (Kim, 2018; Kim et al., 2022). Chatbots can facilitate L2 vocabulary learning by responding to students' inquiries, providing feedback, and offering more personalized intervention (Jeon, 2023; Kim, 2016, 2018; Xu et al., 2021). From the technological affordance perspective, chatbots are easy to use and convenient without time and space limitations (Fryer et al.,

2020; Kim & Lee, 2023). However, weaknesses of chatbots have been also reported, such as language errors, misunderstanding, and inability to read users' intention or recognize their speech (Huang et al., 2021; Lee & Jeon, 2024). As it is still in the developing stage, more evidence-based research on the pedagogical use of chatbots is required. The present study utilized a chatbot to facilitate L2 vocabulary learning and investigated its effectiveness and the students' perceptions of their experience with it.

Literature review

L2 vocabulary learning approaches

Because vocabulary learning has long been emphasized in L2 learning, a significant number of discussions on effective approaches to L2 vocabulary learning have circulated in the L2 teaching community (Lee, 2023). One of these is the discussion of incidental vs. intentional vocabulary learning. One group of scholars has advocated incidental vocabulary learning because it allows learners to learn vocabulary more naturally from the context or through interaction with others (Zheng et al., 2015), which makes vocabulary learning more effective and motivating (Sundqvist & Sylvén, 2016). Others have advocated intentional vocabulary learning because learners' conscious awareness of and attention to the target words is crucial to successful vocabulary learning (Schmitt, 2008). These scholars have claimed that intentional vocabulary learning takes less time than incidental vocabulary learning, results in less attrition, and thus is more effective (Schmitt, 2008; Teng, 2020).

Another well-known dichotomy is receptive vs. productive vocabulary knowledge. With receptive vocabulary knowledge, learners can recognize the meaning of a word but rarely use it appropriately, while productive vocabulary knowledge enables learners to use the word in the appropriate context. Productive knowledge is known to be more difficult to acquire because it requires more and deeper knowledge of a word, such as its grammatical function and associations in terms of orthography (in writing) and pronunciation (in speaking) (Teng & Xu, 2022). This argument is consistent with Involvement Load Theory. According to this theory, a task with a higher load, which demands a need for, search for, and evaluation of a word, can contribute significantly more to vocabulary learning, as it requires more attention to and awareness of the word from the learner (Laufer & Hulstijn, 2001; Lee, 2023). Prior studies have maintained that productive vocabulary tasks can cultivate vocabulary learning more effectively than receptive vocabulary tasks (Bao, 2019; Kim & Kim, 2022; Webb, 2008) and that vocabulary teaching should push word knowledge beyond receptive knowledge to productive mastery

(González-Fernández & Schmitt, 2020, Kim & Kim, 2022; Teng & Xu, 2022). However, vocabulary learning tasks often focus on receptive knowledge (e.g., listening, reading), which results in a significant gap between learners' receptive and productive vocabulary knowledge (Webb, 2008; Teng & Xu, 2022).

In addition, prior studies have emphasized the critical role of human emotion in stimulating and sustaining cognition, especially memory, in vocabulary learning (Amran & Baker, 2020; Lee, 2023). Learners' feelings and experiences are strongly associated with learning, and not only interlocutors' verbal expression but also their facial expressions and gestures influence learners' emotions, and thus memory, in the learning process (Baixauli, 2017; Sandi & Haller, 2015). According to Amran and Baker (2020), learners' positive emotions, such as enjoyment, hope, and pride, led to positive learning outcomes, while their negative emotions, such as shame, anxiety, and boredom, decreased the achievement of learning outcomes. Particularly in L2 learning, emotions play a significant role because learners are often engaged with other people during tasks (Kim, 2016; Kim et al., 2022). Therefore, to enhance L2 learning outcomes, diverse aspects of learning, including cognitive and emotional aspects, should be considered in learning tasks.

L2 vocabulary learning with chatbots

Traditional surface vocabulary learning approaches, such as rote memorization, drills, and practice, often result in students becoming demotivated and bored, and reaching learning outcomes can be frustrating despite learners' efforts (Lee, 2023; Teng, 2020). To mitigate this problem, chatbots, along with other diverse technologies, have been integrated into vocabulary learning in recent years. A chatbot is "a conversational user interface, which allows potential users to engage in a meaningful verbal exchange with a computer program" (Kim et al., 2022). Previous studies have explained the pedagogical benefits of using a chatbot in L2 classes. Most importantly, due to its capability of communicating in both oral and written modes and mimicking human conversations, a chatbot offers opportunities for meaningful verbal exchanges in L2 (Kim et al., 2022). In EFL classrooms in which opportunities for productive skills, such as speaking and writing, are limited, learners have insufficient opportunities to use the language they are learning. In this situation, a chatbot can serve as an alternative pedagogical tool for learners to practice the target language. From a language learning perspective, using a chatbot has a positive impact on oral language skills (Ayedoun et al., 2019; Kim, 2016; Kim et al., 2022) and written language skills (Lin & Chang, 2020). A chatbot can facilitate vocabulary learning by providing glosses, thus preventing high cognitive load (Jeon, 2023); by providing a one-on-one environment and feedback to learners, thus individualizing the learning situation (Chen et al., 2020; Lee & Jeon, 2024); or by cultivating a positive attitude toward vocabulary learning (Kim, 2018). From an affective perspective, using a chatbot can enhance learners' motivation and engagement, enjoyment of learning, and willingness to communicate, while reducing their language anxiety (Ayedoun et al., 2019; Jeon, 2023; Lee & Jeon, 2024). A meta-analysis confirmed that using a chatbot increased overall language proficiency (Huang et al., 2021).

Prior studies have also pointed out the disadvantages of using a chatbot in L2 learning. Lee and Jeon (2024) found that while students' inclination to anthropomorphize the chatbot (i.e., regard the chatbot as a human partner) could further immerse them in learning, the students did not perceive the voice-based chatbot as an interaction partner due to the artificial nature of its communication, such as a mechanical voice and misrecognition. They viewed talking with the chatbot as beneficial to vocabulary learning, but they considered its interaction capabilities limited. While several studies have found interactions with voice-based chatbots to be more effective than those with text-based chatbots (Ayedoun et al., 2019; Lee & Jeon, 2024), others have criticized the higher extraneous cognitive load associated with interaction with voice-based chatbots due to the extra attention needed for auditory information processing (Fryer et al., 2020; Kim, 2016). Finally, technological limitations of chatbots, such as nonsensical outputs, unpredictable directions, a lack of emotions, and an inability to participate in long conversations, were listed as disadvantages of chatbots in the meta-analysis of Huang et al. (2021).

Despite the significant number of studies on chatbots in L2 learning, there is still a research gap. As emotion is associated with cognition and learning, studies have emphasized emotional, social, and motivational aspects of the role of chatbots in L2 learning (Lee & Jeon, 2024; Tsivitanidou & Ioannou, 2021). However, the affective domain in chatbot use has been under-researched (Huang et al., 2021). Moreover, the majority of previous studies have relied on self-reported surveys of students, and there is insufficient empirical evidence on students' outcomes, including vocabulary learning (Huang et al., 2021). In addition, pedagogical chatbots have focused mostly on drills and practice, and rarely on authentic communicative tasks in design, application, and research (Kim & Lee, 2023). Therefore, the present study examined students' actual outputs in interactions with a human partner (H-H) and with a chatbot (H-C) based on a communicative task and investigated their perceptions of the influence of the chatbot on vocabulary learning. This chapter addresses the following research questions:

1. Which method, human–human interaction or human–chatbot interaction, was more effective in students acquiring L2 vocabulary?
2. How did the students perceive the interaction with the chatbot compared with the interaction with a human partner? How did their affective and cognitive perceptions influence their L2 vocabulary learning and recall?

Method

Participants and procedures

The cohort of the current study was 36 Korean college students who enrolled in the Technology and Digital Contents course in 2022. The vocabulary pretest revealed a wide range of L2 vocabulary proficiency among the students; hence, rather than all students receiving the same vocabulary list, each student built their own target vocabulary list by selecting 20 unknown words from Nation's (2004) vocabulary list. Nation's list contains 10,000 words across 10 levels (1,000 words at each level), and most of the students selected words between levels 6 and 8. After they had selected the target words, they submitted their vocabulary list to the instructor and learned the meaning of the words using the dictionary.

The task was to converse first with a human partner and then with the chatbot, incorporating the 10 target words that they had selected into each dyad of the conversation (20 words in total) until they had used all the target words in the conversations. The instructor tested several chatbots and selected Replica, which performed the best at that time. The students tried the voice-based mode first; however, as many of them experienced trouble communicating through voice chat (e.g., the chatbot could not understand the students' pronunciations; it understood a simple imperative sentence but not a long prosaic sentence), the instructor decided to use the text-based mode. After completing both interactions, the students submitted a recording of the H-H interaction and screen captures of the H-C interaction. Four weeks after the task, they took a post-test (word recognition test) in which they were given their own vocabulary list and wrote down the meaning of each word. They also wrote a half-page reflection paper in which they explained which partner they preferred and why, and discussed the advantages and disadvantages of each conversation. Finally, they completed the post-test survey. The survey consisted of 20 questions about their perceptions of using the chatbot, their evaluation of the chatbot, the usefulness of the chatbot for learning English (with responses on a five-point Likert scale), and their preferred conversation partner.

Data analysis

This study employed a mixed methods approach. Quantitative data included the vocabulary post-test, the post-test survey, and the text of the interactions. The post-test scores on the vocabulary sets for the H-H and H-C interactions were compared using paired t-tests. The post-test survey was analyzed based on descriptive statistics. For the post-test survey, the reliability test was conducted and was found to be reliable (Cronbach's alpha = .710). The recordings of the H-H interaction were transcribed, and each student's lines were separated in each pair's conversation. The captures of the H-C interaction were converted to text files, and the chatbot's outputs and students' outputs were separated for comparison. Next, all outputs were analyzed in terms of word count, number of different words, percentage of difficult words, number of words per sentence, lexical density, and Gunning fog index (sentence complexity index). t-tests were employed to compare the results of text analysis.

The analysis of the students' reflection papers followed the qualitative analysis protocol. The researcher read the data carefully and identified emerging themes. Using the emerging themes as codes, the researcher then conducted axial coding. In the final step, the researcher categorized the codes into three groups based on the domain: affective, cognitive, or interactive. The affective domain included the students' anxiety, comfort, enjoyment, and nonverbal communication during the conversations. The cognitive domain included the students' evaluation of the chatbot and experience of learning English. The interactive domain included miscommunication, understanding, awkwardness, and feedback (for more detailed themes with indicators for each theme and category, refer to Table 6.5). Two trained coders analyzed the qualitative data for the reliability check, and the intercoder reliability was 89%.

Results

Quantitative data analysis

The current study analyzed the students' outputs in the H-H and H-C interactions, and descriptive statistics revealed the differences between them. Overall, the students produced a higher word count in their H-H interaction (mean = 570.12) than in the H-C interaction (mean = 476.51) in each pair. Noticeably, however, the range of the word count of each pair varied more widely in the H-H interaction. While it ranged from 77 to 996 in the H-C interaction, it ranged from 43 to 2208 in the H-H interaction. The students' output in the two dyads was also compared, and the findings revealed that the students' outputs in the H-C interaction

Table 6.1 Descriptive statistics of students' and chatbot's outputs

	H-H		H-C		H-C	
	Students' output		*Student's output*		*Chatbot's output*	
Aspect	Mean	SD	Mean	SD	Mean	SD
Word count	285.06	484.211	232.81	123.030	243.70	138.089
DW	103.34	131.795	128.07	52.208	131.26	60.234
HW	7.65	3.065	10.16	3.611	8.61	2.360
W/S	6.32	2.284	9.83	7.225	6.68	1.158
LD	43.32	13.852	49.46	3.464	51.14	8.529
GFI	5.59	1.855	8.00	3.292	6.11	1.010

DW = number of different words, HW = percentage of hard (difficult) words, W/S = number of words per sentence, LD = lexical density, GFI = Gunning fog index

Table 6.2 Paired t-test results of students' outputs in H-H and H-C interactions

	Mean	SD	t	Sig
WC	52.24	479.606	.566	.576
DW	-24.72	131.699	-.976	.338
HW	-2.51	4.504	-2.896	.008
W/S	-3.50	7.807	-2.334	.028
LD	-6.13	12.698	-2.511	.019
GFI	-2.41	3.580	-3.498	.002

exceeded those in the H-H interaction in all aspects (Table 6.1). In the comparison between the students' output and the chatbot's output, while the number of different words and lexical density were highest with the chatbot, the percentage of hard (difficult) words, number of words per sentence, and GFI were highest in the students' outputs in the H-C interaction. The students' outputs in the H-H interaction were lowest in all aspects.

Next, t-tests were conducted to examine whether the differences were statistically meaningful. A paired t-test between the students' outputs in the H-H and H-C interactions showed that except for word count and the number of different words, the differences were significant (Table 6.2). The results indicated that the students generated a more advanced level of language in the H-C interaction. An independent t-test to compare the students' outputs and the chatbot's outputs showed that the differences were significant only for the number of words per sentence and GFI

Table 6.3 Independent t-test results of outputs of the students and the chatbot

	Mean	SD	t	Sig
WC	10.88	144.441	.306	.340
DW	3.18	65.163	.208	.200
HW	-1.55	3.714	-1.872	.149
W/S	-3.15	7.68	-2.238	.032
LD	1.68	8.351	.950	.223
FGI	-1.88	3.312	-2.841	.034

(Table 6.3). The post-test results showed that the mean score of the H-H interaction (mean = 7.48) was higher than that of the H-C interaction (mean = 6.84); however, the t-test result showed that the difference was not statistically significant (t = 1.570, sig = .127).

Next, the survey results showed that the students had insufficient opportunities to speak in English previously, and their language anxiety was neutral. They had positive perceptions of the chatbot and regarded talking with the chatbot as enjoyable and helpful in learning English. On the question of their preference as a conversation partner, a slightly higher number of students answered that they preferred the human partner to the chatbot (human = 19, chatbot = 17), and the mean score for enjoyment was also higher for the H-H interaction. However, the students felt more comfortable with the chatbot. The students gave the intelligibility and communicability of the chatbot high scores and regarded the chatbot as a knowledgeable partner. The survey results are summarized in Table 6.4.

Reflection papers

The reflection papers demonstrated students' perceptions of the H-H and H-C interactions. Concerning the H-H interaction, the students showed appreciation and enjoyment of human interaction, such as emotional engagement, mutual understanding, and nonverbal extralinguistic communication. However, several students also experienced anxiety and conversational difficulties. In particular, they "felt nervous about [their] language mistakes and miscommunication." They also experienced difficulties understanding each other or explaining new vocabulary, and once communication difficulty or breakdown occurred, they said that "the interaction became awkward," or "it was hard to repair it." From the language learning perspective, the students remarked that they had good recall of the words in the post-test that they had used during the H-H interaction because they recalled the words along with the context, such

Table 6.4 Survey results

Category	Item	Mean	SD
Previous experience in English	I usually have a chance to speak English.	2.85	1.121
	It is hard to speak English.	3.18	1.236
	I have English speaking anxiety.	3.18	1.261
Intelligibility & communicability of the chatbot	The chatbot's English was accurate.	4.06	1.144
	The chatbot knew lots of vocabulary.	4.39	.747
	The conversation with the chatbot went well.	3.88	1.023
	The chatbot understood my English well.	3.97	.883
	I understood the chatbot's English well.	4.45	.711
	The chatbot's English sounded natural.	4.30	.810
Learning English with the chatbot	I will be able to remember the words or expressions that I learned/used during the conversation with the chatbot.	4.15	.972
	Talking with the chatbot can help me learn English.	4.27	.839
Interaction with the chatbot	I felt comfortable talking with the chatbot.	4.15	.972
	I felt more comfortable talking with the chatbot than with the human partner.	3.36	1.168
	Talking with the chatbot was enjoyable.	3.97	1.075
Interaction with the human partner	Talking with the human partner was enjoyable.	4.15	.870
	Talking with the human partner went well.	3.36	1.025
	Talking with the human partner was awkward.	3.09	1.128
	I felt comfortable talking with my partner.	3.76	.798
Learning English with the partner	I will be able to remember the words or expressions that I learned/used during the conversation with the human partner.	3.94	.899

as the atmosphere, the partner's nonverbal expressions, and the emotions that they felt at that time.

On the other hand, regarding the H-C interaction, the most frequently appearing themes were comfort, convenience of use, the accuracy of the chatbot's language, and opportunities to learn English. As in the survey, the reflection papers indicated that the students felt comfortable with the chatbot. During the H-C interaction, the students felt freer from worrying about "making mistakes," "incorrect grammar," and "not-very-good pronunciations." Some also mentioned that they did not have to be concerned about "hurting the partner's feeling," "cultural gaps," or "getting a judgmental look from the partner when [they] made mistakes." Moreover, several students perceived the H-C interaction as a smoother form of communication because the chatbot was able to handle all difficult vocabulary and diverse topics, which they found quite surprising. Due to the versatility and accuracy of the chatbot, the students considered talking with the chatbot helpful in learning English. Despite occasional occurrences of awkwardness, no total communication breakdown occurred in the H-C interaction because the "chatbot always filled up the silence with a new topic." However, they felt that the conversation was often "superficial" and could "not go deeper," and they felt "a lack of feedback in showing deeper understanding." They also pointed to abrupt responses and unpredictable directions of conversation as weaknesses. Despite a few shortcomings, the positive comments about the chatbot (N = 139) outnumbered the negative comments (N = 38). The students' responses are summarized in Table 6.5.

Table 6.5 Results of the reflection paper analysis

Dyad	Category	Theme	Freq.	Example
H-H	Affective	Enjoyment	11	We had a fun time talking.
		Emotional engagement	9	We could emotionally interact with each other.
		Nonverbal expressions	8	We could use nonverbal cues, such as tone, intonation, nuance, atmosphere, and context.
		Anxiety	5	I was anxious if I would make mistakes.
	Interactive	Feeling interactive	20	Being interactive and having feedback was more important than being efficient.
		Mutual/contextual understanding	13	We made jokes, and because of mutual background understanding, we had better communication.
		Conversational difficulties	10	I often talked awkwardly and stuttered.
		Smooth conversation	6	The conversation went smoothly.
	Cognitive	Language learning	12	Talking with my partner helped me remember the words because I remembered our laughs.
H-C	Affective	Feeling comfortable	24	I didn't have to worry about grammar.
		Being interesting	9	Talking with the chatbot was interesting and surprising.
		Feeling nonhuman	6	I didn't feel like I was talking to a real person.

Table 6.5 (Continued)

Dyad	Category	Theme	Freq.	Example
	Interactive	Lack of feedback	12	I was not sure if I was speaking correctly because of the lack of feedback.
		Better communication	10	The chatbot led the conversation better than my friends, and it was easier to understand.
		Abrupt flow	6	The chatbot abruptly changed the topic.
		Misunderstanding	6	The chatbot did not understand my intention.
		No shared understanding	5	We did not share contextual information.
	Cognitive/ Evaluative	Language learning	29	Speaking with the chatbot definitely helped me sustain my English skills.
		Convenience	19	I could talk with it any time and anywhere.
		Accuracy	16	I was very surprised at its accurate language.
		Awkward expressions	15	The conversation sometimes went astray.
		Better vocabulary	11	The chatbot knew difficult vocabulary.
		Versatility in topics	9	The chatbot knew lots of things, so we could talk about anything.

Italicized: negative comments

New understandings

This study compared the effectiveness of H-H and H-C interactions in students' L2 vocabulary learning and found that both types of interactions facilitated vocabulary learning. As prior studies have claimed that productive vocabulary knowledge tasks are more effective (González-Fernández & Schmitt, 2020, Teng & Xu, 2022), the positive learning outcomes of the current study were ascribed partly to the fact that the students were engaged in an intentional productive vocabulary learning task. According to Webb (2008), when learners learn vocabulary receptively, it is more likely that they will gain only receptive knowledge of the words, whereas when they learn it productively, they gain productive knowledge of the words, which leads to a deeper knowledge of vocabulary. The students in the current study performed a communicative task to incorporate the target vocabulary into their conversations, which encompassed need for, search for, and evaluation of the word (i.e., Involvement Load Theory, Laufer, & Hulstijn, 2001). In other words, both types of interactions had a high involvement load and demanded conscious attention to the words; as a result, they facilitated vocabulary learning. Furthermore, the present study showed that the chatbot could serve as an alternative pedagogical tool for L2 vocabulary learning, particularly in EFL situations. In this study, the H-C interaction was found to be as effective as the H-H interaction in vocabulary learning. Whatever their personal preferences between the two dyads, the students perceived the chatbot as an accurate and knowledgeable conversation partner and considered talking with the chatbot to be an efficient alternative language practice.

On the other hand, as human emotions strongly influence cognition and learning, particularly memory (Amran & Baker, 2020), the current study revealed that diverse aspects, including extralinguistic factors, intervened in the students' memory of L2 vocabulary. In the H-H interaction, as the students stored the words with the entire context of the conversation, such as atmosphere, context, gestures, facial expressions, and intonations, when they recalled a certain word, they tended to recall it along with the extra cues, including their feelings and their partners' nonverbal cues during the conversation. This helped them recall the vocabulary better. In the H-C interaction, although the chatbot lacked nonverbal cues, it had affective benefits. Most significantly, talking with the chatbot reduced anxiety and concerns about making mistakes, and increased comfort, which could lead to increases in the students' willingness to communicate and their achievement of language learning outcomes (Ayedoun et al., 2019; Lee & Jeon, 2024). While the students pointed out nonhuman-like interaction as a disadvantage of the H-C interaction, this dyad also contained extralinguistic factors, including their own feelings. The most notable feeling was surprise about the chatbot's language accuracy and capability to manage the conversation, which was related to the WOW, or novelty, effect (Zhang & Zou, 2022). For instance, the students were surprised by the chatbot understanding a trendy topic or political issues, or exhibiting human-like rapport. Moreover, several students tended to anthropomorphize the chatbot (e.g., "wondering whether I can build better rapport with the chatbot in the long term"). This inclination to anthropomorphize can increase students' engagement and enjoyment, thus facilitating L2 learning (Lee & Jeon, 2024). In addition, the word count range of the H-H interaction was far greater than that of the H-C interaction. The results indicated that while the H-H interaction relied greatly on the partner (i.e., language proficiency, shared interest, personality) to make the communication interesting or awkward, the chatbot was a more stable conversation partner.

Not only the strengths of the chatbot but also its weaknesses helped the students remember their H-C interaction by imprinting their feelings at the moment. For instance, in their reflection papers, the students remembered and pinpointed moments when they felt awkward (e.g., abrupt changes of topic, out-of-context remarks, misunderstanding). This indicated that both positive and negative feelings that the students experienced while talking with the chatbot were intertwined with their cognition and increased retention of a word and ultimately helped them trigger memory retrieval of that word. In short, not only in the H-H interaction but also in the H-C interaction, the students were able to create interconnectedness between the word and the context of use, which made their memory more robust. Moreover, from the cognitive perspective, the students viewed the chatbot as a competent conversational partner and valued the interaction with it. Their positive view of the chatbot enabled them to sustain the conversation with it. The text analysis of the interactions also revealed that the students produced more different words, difficult words, words per sentence, and higher lexical density and GFI during the H-C interaction. There are a few possible explanations for this result. First, as the students felt comfortable with the chatbot, they could take risks in using the target language without worrying about making mistakes. Second, as they considered the chatbot to be a "more knowledgeable partner than [their] peers," they used more advanced language with it. Finally, as Ayedoun et al. (2019) argued, although text-based interaction and voice-based interaction had the same involvement load, text-based interaction (H-C) seemed to have more benefits than voice-based interaction (H-H) in learning vocabulary because it included orthography and gave the students more time.

Implications

The results of this study suggest several pedagogical implications of using a chatbot for language learning. First, chatbots can be a useful pedagogical tool to assist L2 learning, particularly for those with limited L2 learning opportunities. However, when a chatbot is used in an L2 class, multiple factors should be considered, such as students' motivation, confidence, anxiety, and language proficiency, and language instructors should carefully design the task based on an understanding of these factors. They should also consider the technological affordance of the chatbot. For instance, students' engagement can increase more with an embodied voice-based chatbot with facial expressions and intonation (Lee & Jeon, 2024). Similarly, Ayedoun et al. (2019) claimed that during conversations with a chatbot, its capability for affective backchannels influences students' engagement more than its capability for communication strategies. As extralinguistic signals play an important role in social exchange, language instructors should select the chatbot mode (text, audio, or video) that best supports student learning.

Conclusion

This study investigated the effectiveness of a chatbot in L2 vocabulary learning and how students' perceptions affected learning outcomes. Whereas previous studies have focused on either students' perceptions or interaction outputs (Huang et al., 2021), the current study examined both perceptions and interactions, as well as the factors that affected L2 vocabulary learning. The results revealed that the H-C interaction was as effective as the H-H interaction in L2 vocabulary learning, and multiple cognitive and affective factors in the students' perceptions influenced the learning outcomes. While vocabulary learning often remains a decontextualized practice in many EFL classrooms (Lee, 2023), interaction with a chatbot can offer an authentic opportunity to use L2 vocabulary, which can, in turn, lead to better vocabulary learning and recall. The limitation of the study was that it was conducted over a short period with a small sample size. As the novel effect of the chatbot affects the learning outcomes, the effect of using the chatbot over a longer period should be examined. As technology advances, particularly with the recent advancement of ChatGPT, chatbots will be utilized more widely in L2 classrooms. This will offer a new arena for L2 learning, but at the same time, it may have unexpected downsides. Technology per se cannot guarantee successful learning; therefore, teachers will need to employ careful instructional design, implementation, and monitoring to benefit student learning.

Further reading

Huang, W., Hew, K., & Fryer, L. (2021). Chatbots for language learning – Are they really useful? A systematic review of chatbot-supported language learning. *Journal of Computer-Assisted Learning*, 38, 237–257.

This article presents the results of a systematic review on the effectiveness of chatbots in foreign language learning. It proposes design principles for meaningful integration of chatbots into language learning classrooms.

Lee, S., & Jeon, J. (2024). Visualizing a disembodied agent: Young EFL learners' perceptions of voice-controlled conversational agents as language partners. *Computer Assisted Language Learning*, 37(5–6), 1048–1073. doi.org/10.1080/09588221.2022.2067182

This article explores EFL students' perceptions of voice-controlled conversational agents using thematic analysis. The study found a strong tendency toward anthropomorphism, which indicates the agents' potential as conversational partners.

Teng, M., & Xu, J. (2022). Pushing vocabulary knowledge from receptive to productive mastery: Effects of task type and repetition frequency. *Language Teaching Research*, FirstView, 1–19. doi.org/10.1177/13621688221077
This study examined the effects of task type and repetition frequency on developing receptive vocabulary knowledge into productive mastery of vocabulary. The results of the study indicated that productive vocabulary tasks are more effective than receptive tasks. The study also showed that repetition helps promote students' vocabulary knowledge, but the effects declined after several retrievals.

References

Amran, M. S., & Bakar, A. Y. A. (2020). We feel, therefore we memorize: Understanding emotions in learning mathematics using neuroscience research perspectives. *Universal Journal of Educational Research*, 8(11B), 5943–5950. doi.org/10.13189/ujer.2020.082229

Ayedoun, E., Hayahshi, Y., & Seta, K. (2019). Adding communicative and affective strategies to an embodied conversation agent to enhance second language learners' willingness to communicate. *International Journal of Artificial Intelligence Education*, 29, 29–57.

Baixauli, E., (2017). Happiness: Role of dopamine and serotonin on mood and negative emotions. *Emergency Medicine*, 7, 1000350. doi.org/10.4172/2165-7548.1000350

Bao, G. (2019). Task type effects on English as a Foreign Language learners' acquisition of receptive and productive vocabulary knowledge. *System*, 53, 84–95. doi.org/10.1016/j.system.2015.07.006

Chen, C.-M., Liu, H., & Huang, H.-B. (2019). Effects of a mobile game-based English vocabulary learning app on learners' perceptions and learning performance: A case study of Taiwanese EFL learners. *ReCALL*, 31(2), 170–188. doi.org/10.1017/S0958344018000228

Chen, H-L., Widarso, G., & Sutrisno, H. (2020). A chatbot for learning Chinese: Learning achievement and technology acceptance. *Journal of Educational Computing Research*, 58, 1161–1189.

Fryer, L. K., Coniam, D., Carpenter, R., & Liapusneanu, D. (2020). Bots for language learning now: Current and future directions. *Language Learning & Technology*, 24(2), 8–22. http://hdl.handle.net/10125/44719

González-Fernández, B., & Schmitt, N. (2020). Word knowledge: Exploring the relationships and order of acquisition of vocabulary knowledge components. *Applied Linguistics*, 41, 481–505.

Huang, W., Hew, K., & Fryer, L. (2021). Chatbots for language learning – Are they really useful? A systematic review of chatbot-supported language learning. *Journal of Computer-Assisted Learning*, 38, 237–257.

Jeon, J. (2023). Chatbot-assisted dynamic assessment for L2 vocabulary learning and diagnosis. *Computer Assisted Language Learning*, FirstView, 36(7), 1338–1364. doi.org/10.1080/09588221.2021.1987272

Jeong, Y., & Choi, I-C. (2021). Exploring the efficacy of an AI chatbot-based automatic speech recognition based on a comparative error analysis. *Multimedia-Assisted Language Learning*, 24(4), 261–289.

Kim, H., & Lee, S. (2023). A study on task design of AI-based voice chatbot for elementary English speaking. *Multimedia-Assisted Language Learning*, 26(1), 31–58.

Kim, H., Yang, H., Shin, D., & Lee, J. (2022). Design principles and architecture of second language learning chatbot. *Language Learning & Technology*, 26(1), 1–18. http://hdl.handle.net/10125/73463

Kim, N.-Y. (2016). Effects of voice chat on EFL learners' speaking ability according to proficiency levels. *Multimedia-Assisted Language Learning*, 19(4), 63–88.

Kim, N-Y. (2018). Chatbots and Korean EFL students' English vocabulary learning. *Journal of Digital Convergence*, 16(2), 1–7.

Kim, S.-Y., & Kim, K.-S. (2022). Vocabulary transfer from reading to writing: A comparison of essay writing and synchronous CMC. *TESL-EJ*, 26(1), 1–21. doi.org/10.55593/ej.26101a8

Laufer, B., & Hulstijn, J. (2001). Incidental vocabulary acquisition in a second language: The construct of task-induced involvement. *Applied Linguistics*, 22(1), 1–26. doi.org/10.1093/applin/22.1.1

Lee, S.-M. (2023). Factors affecting incidental L2 vocabulary acquisition and retention in a game-enhanced learning environment. *ReCALL*, FirstView, 35(3), 274–289. doi.org/10.1017/S0958344022000209

Lee, S., & Jeon, J. (2024). Visualizing a disembodied agent: Young EFL learners' perceptions of voice-controlled conversational agents as language partners. *Computer Assisted Language Learning*, FirstView, doi.org/10.1080/09588221.2022.2067182

Lin, M. P.-C., & Chang, D. (2020). Enhancing post-secondary writers' writing skills with a chatbot. *Journal of Educational Technology & Society*, 23(1), 78–92.

Nation, I. S. P. (2004). A study of the most frequent word families in the British National Corpus. In P. Bogaards & B. Laufer (eds.), *Vocabulary in a second language: Selection, acquisition, and testing* (pp. 3–13). John Benjamins.

Sandi, C., & Haller, J. (2015). Stress and the social brain: Behavioural effects and neurobiological mechanisms. *Nature Reviews Neuroscience*, 16, 290–304.

Schmitt, N. (2008). Instructed second language vocabulary learning. *Language Teaching Research*, 12(3), 329–363. doi.org/10.1177/1362168808089921

Sundqvist, P., & Sylvén, L. K. (2016). *Extramural English in teaching and learning: From theory and research to practice*. Palgrave Macmillan.

Teng, F. (2020). Retention of new words learned incidentally from reading: Word exposure frequency, L1 marginal glosses, and their combination. *Language Teaching Research*, 24(6), 785–812. doi.org/10.1177/1362168819829026

Teng, M., & Xu, J. (2022). Pushing vocabulary knowledge from receptive to productive mastery: Effects of task type and repetition frequency. *Language Teaching Research*, FirstView, 1–19. doi.org/10.1177/13621688221077

Tsivitanidou, O., & Ioannou, A. (2021). Envisioned pedagogical uses of chatbots in higher education and perceived benefits and challenges. In P. Zaphiris & A. Ioannou (eds.), *Learning and collaboration technologies: Games and virtual environments for learning* (pp. 230–250). Springer. doi.org/10.1007/978-3-030-77943-6_15

Webb, S. (2008). Receptive and productive vocabulary sizes of L2 learners. *Studies in Second Language Acquisition, 30,* 79–95.

Xu, Y., Wang, D., Collins, P., Lee, H., & Warschauer, M. (2021). Same benefits, different communication patterns: Comparing children's reading with a conversational agent vs. a human partner. *Computers & Education, 161,* 4059. doi.org/10.1016/j.compedu.2020.104059

Zhang, F., & Zou, D. (2022). Types, purposes, and effectiveness of state-of-art technologies for second and foreign language learning. *Computer Assisted Language Learning, 35*(4), 696–742.

Zheng, D., Bischeoff, M., & Gilliland, B. (2015). Vocabulary learning in massively multiplayer online games: Context and action before words. *Educational Technology Research & Development, 63*(5), 771–790. doi.org/10.1007/s11423-015-9387-4

7 Training to use machine translation for vocabulary learning

Yijen Wang and Glenn Stockwell
Waseda University, Japan

Pre-reading questions

1. What is the role of MT tools in an EFL classroom?
2. How do EFL learners view MT tools for EFL learning?
3. How should we train learners to use MT tools for vocabulary learning?

Background

Machine translation (MT) applications, such as Google Translate, DeepL, Bing Microsoft Translator, and Amazon Translate, to name a few, have emerged as powerful tools for language learners and instructors alike, making use of the rapid advances in artificial intelligence (AI) technology that have taken place over the last few years. The proliferation of impressively accurate consumer-oriented free online MT tools—most notably Google Translate—has created both challenges and opportunities for language learners and the professional foreign language education community (Ducar & Schocket, 2018; Kol et al., 2018).

The literature indicates that MT can have a wide range of uses in the foreign language classroom, such as aiding in expanding students' vocabulary (Fredholm, 2019), improving accuracy and fluency (Fredholm, 2015; Kol et al., 2018), relieving learners' anxiety (Briggs, 2018), and for post-writing assistance (e.g., Tsai, 2019). However, its potential appears to be undervalued by foreign language instructors due to their concerns about inaccuracies (Lee, 2022) and the risk of students becoming overly reliant on MT tools (Moon, 2021; Zimotti et al., 2024). As such, resistance to permitting students to utilize MT technologies persists, and a significant disparity is frequently observed between learner and teacher perspectives on employing MT technology in language education and learning settings (Brown et al., 2022). Teachers are aware that students use MT tools, but they rarely endorse their use and may even choose to prohibit them

DOI: 10.4324/9781003367543-9

entirely, even though they use MT themselves (Nino Alonso, 2022). It is not uncommon for teachers to fail to provide clear guidelines on appropriate use of MT (Wang, 2024), and this may contribute to "inconsistent and inaccurate perceptions of (in)appropriate use of MT use" (Brown et al., 2022, p. 22). It is not inconceivable that this could cause learners to perceive MT negatively, feeling that its usage constitutes "breaking the rules" and could result in disciplinary measures if discovered. This adverse outlook on MT technologies may diminish their effectiveness as a resource, necessitating the education of learners on the realities and proper methods of employing MT in language learning. Furthermore, the best way to utilize MT tools to assist students with their writing remains uncertain (Lee, 2022).

Machine translation in vocabulary learning

It goes without saying that vocabulary acquisition is a fundamental aspect of language learning. In the past, students have depended on tools such as dictionaries, flashcards, and reading in context to enhance their collection of words. While these techniques remain essential, MT offers an extra opportunity to investigate and learn new vocabulary. MT systems deliver instant translations of words or expressions, reducing the time spent searching through dictionaries or other reference materials (Alm & Watanabe, 2022; Lo, 2023). This speed promotes a continuous flow of reading and writing, enhancing comprehension and fluency. MT can also supply numerous translations for a single word, each reflecting distinct contexts. This enables learners to grasp the subtle meanings of words and their appropriate usage in various scenarios. By understanding these contextual subtleties, learners can develop a more sophisticated command of vocabulary (Ducar & Schocket, 2018; Tsai, 2019). Additionally, MT provides learners with a vast range of translated words, offering exposure to diverse vocabulary across different languages. This exposure not only broadens their lexicon but also helps learners identify similarities and differences among languages, facilitating cross-linguistic connections. These potentials of MT tools empower learners to understand texts in languages they are not familiar with. Utilizing these tools enables students to decode the meanings of unknown words, thereby strengthening their comprehension and retention of the vocabulary.

The role of MT tools in EFL classrooms

While there has been a growing amount of research exploring the potential of MT in language education (e.g., Briggs, 2018; Chung & Ahn, 2021; Lee, 2022), much of this research has taken place in settings where students are encouraged to actively utilize MT tools, largely as a part of the research that is being conducted. Many, if not most, language teachers appear to maintain a pessimistic perspective on the use of MT tools in the classroom, perceiving them to be an all-too-convenient method that directly connects learners to their first language and results in a lack of mental involvement in the language learning process. As such, they regard students' usage as a sign of "laziness" or of cognitive disengagement (Nino Alonso, 2022; Van Praag & Sanchez, 2015).

As alluded to above, previous studies have found that teachers and learners have mixed and sometimes conflicting perceptions of using MT tools for second language learning. For example, students generally have positive attitudes toward the use of MT tools as the technologies help in post-editing their texts and generate translations to/from their target/first language, leading to gains in confidence in English writing (Chang et al., 2022; Tsai, 2022). On the other hand, teachers tend to acknowledge the usefulness of MT tools to some degree but remain skeptical about integration into classroom practices, with concerns about overreliance, accuracy of translations, and academic dishonesty issues (Ducar & Schocket, 2018; Moon, 2021; Tasmedir et al., 2023). Bridging the gap between these conflicting views to result in a pedagogy that capitalizes on the affordances of MT technologies has remained elusive, yet as these technologies become more sophisticated and accessible, it is a challenge that needs to be addressed. Thus, this study aims to investigate the changes in learner behavior resulting from an investigation of their current tactics and exploration of new MT approaches (cf. Lee, 2022). Additionally, the study aims to determine if learners' attitudes shift as a result of training, transitioning from viewing MT as a "prohibited" tool to recognizing it as a valuable component of their language learning arsenal.

A model of training in CALL

Although many teachers believe their students are familiar with digital technology, studies have shown that even students who are adept at using it for personal tasks, such as gaming and social networking, may not necessarily know how to apply it to language learning without sufficient training (Stockwell & Hubbard, 2013; Wang, 2020). Hubbard (2004) proposes a three-step instructional method to enhance the utilization of technology for language education: (1) *technical training*: during this initial phase, teachers instruct students on the various features of specific technology, without presuming that all students are already familiar with them; (2) *strategic training*: in this stage, learners receive guidance on strategies for specific language skills or domains, enabling them to select and employ the technology to support their learning objectives. The popular notion that the best way to learn is by teaching leads to the final step: (3) *pedagogical training*, where students are encouraged to share their technology-based learning strategies and instruct their peers on their application. It is important to note that these three steps should be implemented cyclically (Hubbard, 2013; Stockwell, 2022), and educators must provide students with sufficient opportunities to practice using the technology and exchange ideas about incorporating it for language learning purposes.

Research questions

In light of the growing use of MT technologies in foreign language education, it is crucial to understand their impact on vocabulary learning and English as a foreign language (EFL) learners' attitudes. By focusing on these two crucial aspects of academic writing, this study aims to unravel the complexities of MT usage in enhancing learners' linguistic abilities. In doing so, the study seeks to explore how MT technologies may contribute to the development of pedagogical practices and materials specific to vocabulary learning for EFL students. Ultimately, this research hopes to shed light on the ever-evolving relationship between emerging technologies and language education, paving the way for more effective and adaptive teaching strategies that embrace these advancements. The specific research questions posed for the current research are listed below:

1. How do learners perceive MT and AI tools used for English learning before and after training?
2. Do learners' vocabulary in writing practices change as a result of instruction and training by teachers in using MT and AI tools? If so, in what ways?
3. What are the affordances and limitations of using MT tools for academic writing?

Method

Participants

The convenience sampling method was adopted due to the availability of the participants. A total of 83 non-English major students were recruited from four intact EFL classes (three in-person and one online) at two universities in Japan. According to the course requirement, the students were at CEFR B1 level.

Machine translation tools used for this study

A pre-survey provided valuable insights into the prevailing practices of English writing among students at the two Japanese universities, revealing that Google Translate and DeepL were the preferred tools employed by students to aid their English writing endeavors. Consequently, recognizing the significance of these tools within the context of the study, they were selected as the primary focus for further investigation and analysis. The popularity of these tools can be attributed to their free accessibility to students.

Google Translate

Google Translate, known for its extensive language support and user-friendly interface, is widely utilized by language learners and educators for translating individual words, phrases, and entire texts. It allows users to translate not only text but also images, documents, and webpages. After 2016, Google Translate adopted neural MT technology, which no longer translates word-by-word as the old system did, but rather translates entire sentences at once.

DeepL

DeepL, like Google Translate, can translate text and files, but claims to have superior translation quality because of its advanced neural networks, although it does support fewer languages than Google Translate. It is equipped with functions such as the ability to adjust tone and a glossary, but a paid version is required for advanced functions and translations of unlimited words. With its contextually accurate and natural-sounding translations, it is not surprising that language learners often turn to DeepL to improve their vocabulary and language skills.

ChatGPT

ChatGPT, released by OpenAI in late 2022, is a large language model AI chatbot which can generate human-like text with responses to users' prompts. While it contains a massive knowledge base, it was trained on a database created before 2020, and this may cause a phenomenon called *hallucination*; that is, it provides factually incorrect or irrelevant responses due to limitations with its training data and architecture. Although it was not specifically designed for translation, users have started using ChatGPT as a translation and proofreading tool, aiding language learners in enhancing their conversational skills and understanding vocabulary usage in different contexts, thus prompting its inclusion in the investigation.

Research design and data elicitation

The study was conducted in three phases. Firstly, at the beginning of the study, an online pre-survey via Microsoft Forms was given out to investigate participants' EFL learning background and prior experience of using Google Translate, DeepL, and ChatGPT, as well as their attitudes toward using them for English learning. Secondly, three training sessions (see Table 7.1) based on Hubbard's (2004) training model were provided to help scaffold their knowledge. To ensure standardization of the training across different settings, the researchers collectively created the training guidelines and objectives. The researcher who conducted the initial class opened the classroom for observation to allow the subsequent instructor to replicate the training processes and content. However, recognizing that a one-size-fits-all approach may not be appropriate, both researchers retained the flexibility to adjust their interactions and instructional styles to better meet the learners' specific needs The details of each training session can be found in Table 7.1. By the end of each session, students had to practice the usages and take part in a discussion on the topics. During

Table 7.1 Training process

Training sessions	Training procedures
Session 1: Technical training	• Navigate through Google Translate, DeepL, and ChatGPT by presenting the basic functions • Practice the functions and sign up to an account for ChatGPT • Evaluate the functions of the three tools in groups
Session 2: Strategic training	• Introduce how to use the tools for vocabulary in writing • Ask students to evaluate the translation results across the three tools • In groups, discuss the practical uses of this to explore vocabulary while trying it out
Session 3: Pedagogical training	• Remind students of ethical issues and consequences of academic dishonesty through using the tools inappropriately • Practice the tools and try to develop individual strategies • In group, share the strategies for using the tools for EFL learning and discuss the advantages and disadvantages of the tools

the training sessions, the researchers observed how the students used the technologies during class by looking at the students' screens in the in-person classes or by asking them to share their screens in the online classes. The researchers took notes about the students' behaviors and the content of their debriefing discussions; students' notes recording their strategies used and discussion were also collected. Finally, an online post-survey was distributed to investigate the students' perceptions of using the tools for English vocabulary learning.

Quantitative data collected from the surveys were analyzed using Microsoft Excel to obtain descriptive and inferential statistics. For the qualitative data, including open-ended questions, the researchers' field notes and the students' notes were thematically coded using Microsoft Excel. Initially, one researcher read through the raw data to identify potential themes. The other researcher, who is an expert in the field, examined the themes. After discussing our observations, we agreed upon a preliminary set of codes. These were then applied to the entire dataset. We held regular meetings to resolve any discrepancies and refine the coding scheme as necessary. Following this, we aggregated similar codes into overarching themes. A list of strategies was created from the learner observations. Although we took steps to mitigate limitations by adopting inferential statistics and involving multiple coders in the qualitative analysis, future research might benefit from more sophisticated statistical techniques and additional validation methods.

Results

Student experience and perceptions before training

Figure 7.1 reveals the aspects of vocabulary use in English writing that the students were aware of. The results show that word choice holds the highest level of concern, accounting for 61% of the responses. Additionally, format is another important aspect, capturing the attention of 17% of the students, while spelling ranks third with 13% of the students indicating its significance. These findings emphasize the crucial role of word choice in effective English writing. With the majority of students recognizing its importance, they highlight the need for a diverse and accurate selection of words to convey ideas and express thoughts clearly. Furthermore, the significance attributed to format suggests that students are aware of the structural requirements and organizational principles that contribute to well-structured written work. Lastly, the attention given to spelling underscores the students' acknowledgment of its impact on overall written communication, as even minor spelling errors can diminish the quality and clarity of a piece of writing.

Training to use machine translation for vocabulary learning 139

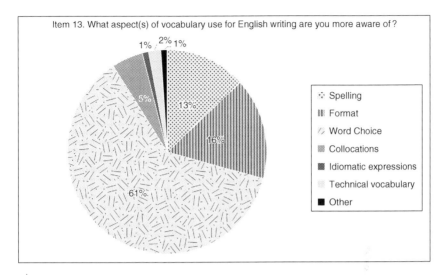

Figure 7.1 Students' awareness of vocabulary aspects for writing (N = 85)

Regarding the students' experience of using AI tools for English writing (item 14), the results indicate that 72 participants (85%) answered "Yes." On the other hand, 13 participants (15%) answered "No." This high percentage of participants who have used AI tools for English writing suggests a significant level of familiarity with and reliance on these tools among the EFL students. Conversely, the 15% of respondents who indicated that they have not used any AI tools for English writing could have various reasons for their choice. They may prefer more traditional methods, or they may not be aware of the existence or benefits of AI tools for English writing.

In order to understand which tools the students had used for English writing, the results from item 15 show the count of how many times each tool was mentioned: Google Translate: 44 times; DeepL: 26 times; Grammarly: 3 times; ChatGPT: 2 times; Weblio: 2 times; Papago: 1 time; NetEase Youdao Dictionary: 1 time. Table 7.2 categorizes how the students used the tools. Generally, the students used the tools to translate words and sentences from Japanese to English. It should be noted that some students mentioned using multiple tools, so the total count of mentions is higher than the total number of students who provided responses.

The results for the frequency of using the AI tools can be seen in Table 7.3. It indicates that Google Translate is the most frequently used AI tool among the respondents, with a significant proportion relying on it every time they

Table 7.2 Usage of AI tools for writing before training

Tool	Usage mentioned	Frequency counts (time)
Google Translate	Translating words and sentences from Japanese to English	25
	Checking grammar and correctness of English sentences	4
	Looking up word meanings	3
	Checking sentence order or spelling	1
	Checking vocabulary	1
	Checking grammar	1
DeepL	Translating Japanese sentences into English	5
	Understanding the meaning of words	4
	Confirming difficult expressions	3
	Translating English sentences into Japanese	1
	Checking grammar and correctness of English sentences	2
	Reading difficult materials with time constraints	1
	Checking the grammar	1
	Searching for new words	1
Grammarly	Checking and correcting English writing homework	3
ChatGPT	Asking for recommendations for English use	2
Weblio	Looking up words	2
Papago	Looking up words	1
NetEase Youdao Dictionary	Looking up words	1

Table 7.3 Frequency of students' MT tool usage

Total	Every time I write	Whenever needed	Often	Rarely	Never, but I'm interested	Never, and I'm not interested
Google Translate	35.6%	44.4%	40.4%	18.3%	6.4%	7.9%
DeepL	22.5%	31.4%	12.7%	11.4%	4.6%	7.1%
Grammarly	3.9%	3.1%	6.4%	14.4%	18.7%	24.3%
ChatGPT	17.3%	3.3%	7.3%	17.7%	49.3%	10.4%
Other	20.8%	18.3%	33.3%	38.3%	21.2%	50.4%

Table 7.4 Student perceptions of teachers' attitudes toward AI tools. Item 17. Did your teachers recommend or discourage AI tools for learning English?

Descriptions	Student responses (%)
Yes, we are allowed to use them in class.	12 (14%)
Yes, but not in class.	10 (12%)
Not sure.	35 (41%)
No, but not strictly banned.	20 (24%)
No, we are not allowed to use them.	8 (9%)
Other	0 (0%)

write (35.6%) or whenever needed (44.4%). DeepL is also widely used, although to a slightly lesser extent, with a notable percentage of respondents utilizing it regularly (22.5%) or whenever needed (31.4%). Grammarly is used less frequently overall, with only a small portion of respondents relying on it consistently (7%) or often (6.4%). ChatGPT sees moderate usage, primarily for generating or improving written content. This might be because the survey was conducted in April 2023 when ChatGPT was relatively new to the students, and they might not have been aware of the possibility of using it for English learning purposes. The "Other" category encompasses a range of AI tools, showing varying levels of usage frequency. Overall, the results highlight the prevalent use of AI tools for writing tasks, with Google Translate and DeepL being the most commonly used options.

The survey question in item 17 (Did your teachers recommend or discourage AI tools for learning English?) aimed to understand how the students perceived their teachers' attitudes towards the use of AI tools for English learning. The results indicated that most of the students (41%) were unsure about their teachers' stance on the matter. While some teachers may recommend or allow AI tool usage (26%), more teachers may discourage or restrict their use (33%). The diversity of perceived teachers' attitudes reported in the survey indicates the need for clear communication and guidance from teachers regarding the integration of AI tools into language learning.

The survey results from item 18, as show in Figure 7.2, indicate students' opinions on the ethical dimension of using AI tools for writing in English. Surprisingly, 44 (52%) students believed it is ethical, 13 students (15%) considered it unethical, and 28 (33%) stated they were unsure. These diverse viewpoints highlight the importance of fostering discussions and raising awareness about the ethical considerations associated with AI tool usage in language learning and writing tasks.

The survey results from item 19 (Figure 7.3) indicate that 52 students (61%) expressed their willingness to learn how to use AI tools more

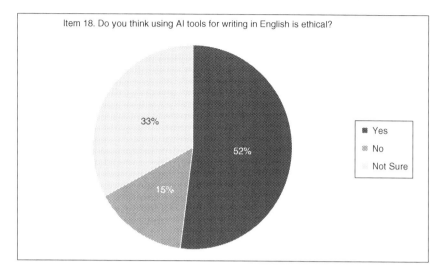

Figure 7.2 Perceptions of the ethicality of using AI tools for English writing

appropriately for English writing as they might recognize the potential benefits they offer. On the other hand, 13 students (15%) had no interest in acquiring such knowledge, while 20 (24%) were unsure. These findings underscore the need for comprehensive information and opportunities to explore the advantages of AI tools, allowing individuals to make informed decisions about integrating them into their English writing process.

In item 20, students were asked about their opinions of the potential benefits and drawbacks of using AI tools for writing in English, which revealed a range of interesting responses, although many of these were evident in the other questions asked and as such will not be dealt with in this chapter. From the responses to item 21 (Do you think AI tools can replace your English learning? Why or why not?), the results show that the majority of participants (68 out of 84) did not believe that AI tools can replace their English learning. They provided reasons such as the limitations of AI in language learning (36 times); preference for human interaction (15 times); the need for independent thinking and personal effort (16 times); skepticism about AI's current capabilities (8 times); and concerns about loss of individuality and identity (3 times). On the other hand, 13 participants expressed the belief that AI tools can replace their English learning. They mentioned the convenience and usefulness of AI tools (6 times), and they were optimistic about future advancements in AI (4 times). There was one participant who expressed uncertainty (not sure) about whether AI tools can replace their English learning. Additionally,

Training to use machine translation for vocabulary learning 143

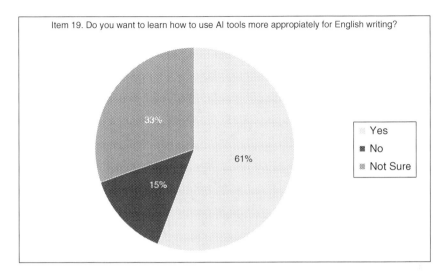

Figure 7.3 Desire to learn appropriate usage of AI tools for English writing

two students did not provide a clear "yes" or "no" answer but believed they can "learn English from the AI tools."

Overall, the majority of participants expressed skepticism towards the replacement of their English learning by AI tools, emphasizing the importance of human interaction, critical thinking, and personal effort in language learning.

Students' perceptions after training

Based on the data collected from the post-survey, the results indicate that 32 students (38%) believed they knew how to use the tools for English writing in a more ethical way after the training sessions (see Figure 7.4). This suggests that a proportion of the students gained more awareness of ethical issues, such as plagiarism, privacy, and data security, while using the tools. However, it is worth noting that 36 students (47%) responded with "Maybe," and ten students (15%) replied with "No." These uncertainties and lack of understanding imply that further guidance and additional support may be necessary, but they could be attributed to the time constraints as well.

From Figure 7.5, it can be seen that the vast majority of the students—76 of the 83 participants in total—viewed the training sessions on AI tools positively, including 20 who found them extremely helpful and 56 who found them helpful.

144　*Theory and Practice in Vocabulary Research in Digital Environments*

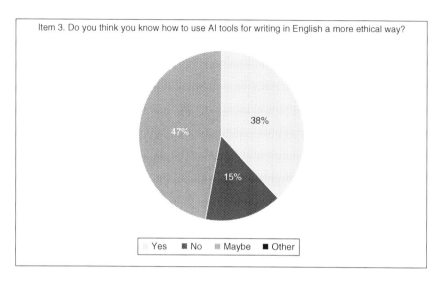

Figure 7.4 Perception of ethical usage of AI tools for English writing

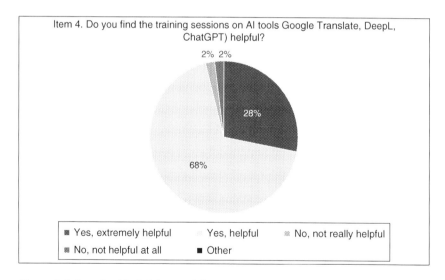

Figure 7.5 Perceived helpfulness of the training sessions

Regarding the reasons for choosing the level of helpfulness of the training sessions on AI tools, the responses are illustrated by the following brief extracts from answers to the open-ended questions:

"It is an opportunity to use AI tools that I've never used before."

"We can understand the differences between these three tools and consider how to use each tool properly before starting to write academic sentences."

"I didn't know much about DeepL and ChatGPT, so through these training sessions, I learned about them and the differences between these AI tools."

"I have used AI tools in the past, but I have discovered new ways to use them through this training."

"We use these AI tools every day, but we don't learn how to use them. In school, we study literacy, so we don't believe all the information from AI. However, it is just a way to prevent being deceived. We don't know how to use AI tools smartly and logically, so the training session was very helpful."

"I know the risks of using AI tools."

The data above indicate that the students generally acknowledged the training sessions were helpful, highlighting their appreciation for the opportunity to explore new tools, gain knowledge about their proper usage, discover new applications, and develop a better understanding of the risks and benefits associated with AI tools. Thus, when asking the students about the frequency of training on AI tools (item 6: How often do you think the training on AI tools should be given?), 61 students (82%) indicated that they believe the training on AI tools should be given occasionally, and 14 students (15%) regularly. This suggests that they perceive periodic training sessions as sufficient to maintain and enhance their knowledge and may value more updates and continuous learning opportunities to stay up-to-date with the utilization of AI tools.

In terms of the helpful features of AI tools for English writing (Figure 7.6), the majority of students valued the ability to find vocabulary meanings (56 responses) and understand sentence meanings (40 responses). Twelve participants appreciated the ability to find information to start writing, and 11 found assistance in understanding the tone of writing helpful. While two respondents mentioned other features, it was not clear what specific features they were referring to. Overall, the results highlight the importance of vocabulary assistance, sentence understanding, information

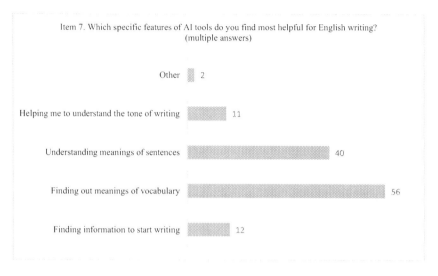

Figure 7.6 Perceived most helpful features of AI tools for English writing

retrieval, and tone interpretation as the most valued features of AI tools for English writing.

The affordances of using AI and MT tools to support academic writing

The affordances of the three target tools, according to the notes taken by the students and researchers during the training sessions, are presented in Table 7.5. In general, the students perceived Google Translate as easier to use, as it allows for the translation of a wider range of text types, and its availability for free may attract the students. However, Google Translate's results are viewed as less accurate and natural compared to DeepL. On the other hand, most of the students did not perceive ChatGPT as an appropriate translation tool, but rather as a tool that provides additional functions to translation. How the students used the tools for learning vocabulary will be presented in the following section.

The usage of the tools to support vocabulary learning

Generally, the students used Google Translate and DeepL to translate words and sentences from Japanese to English, as they stated that "We can learn several word expressions," and "If we use Google Translate and DeepL, we are more likely to get to know more expressions." DeepL was particularly valued for its ability to provide various synonyms, expanding

Table 7.5 The affordances of the AI and MT tools

Tool	Affordance	Example
Google Translate	User-friendly interface	It is easy for users to input text in various formats such as PDFs, images, and webpages. It eliminates the need for users to log in.
	Free to use	It is freely accessible to users, allowing them to utilize its translation services without any cost.
	Real-time translation	It translates the text of speech in real time, and can use the phone camera for instant translation.
	Quick response	It provides fast response times, allowing users to obtain translations promptly and efficiently.
DeepL	Higher-quality translations	The students regarded the translation results from DeepL as more accurate, and the use of language is considered more natural, although "they are not perfect."
	Context-aware translations	DeepL considers the context of the entire sentence rather than just individual words, resulting in more coherent translations.
ChatGPT	More functions	The students viewed ChatGPT as offering a range of additional functions beyond being a translation tool.
	Accessibility	ChatGPT provides information and answers more quickly compared to traditional search engines, making it a valuable resource for prompt inquiries. "It is available 24 hours."
	Search engine	ChatGPT is regarded as an alternative search engine. "ChatGPT can tell me something more quickly than I search." "It is like a Google that put all the searching results together."

students' vocabulary options and aiding in word choice. Many students also used the tools as a dictionary to look up word meanings, idioms, and slang, and search for synonyms and polysemous words as they "propose many kinds of words." The text-to-speech function enabled them to verify pronunciations and intonations, enhancing their language learning experience. ChatGPT served as a valuable tool for the students when seeking extra information about unfamiliar words. They utilized it to generate example sentences and explain difficult expressions. Additionally, ChatGPT was used to check spelling and create flashcards suitable for individual English proficiency levels.

From the observation during the training sessions, it was also found that the students compared the affordances and limitations of the tools and tailored their usage across the tools. For example, one student discovered that "Google Translate translates from the front of the sentences. Whereas DeepL translates the whole paragraph. So DeepL can translate sentences more naturally than Google Translate. But they cannot translate completely. For example, both systems cannot translate spoken words correctly." Other interesting observations from students included "Google Translate is for beginner learners, and ChatGPT can be useful for advanced learners," as "the example sentences ChatGPT created can be used as a language model for us to learn" and "We compare the translated texts and revise the unnatural languages [sic]." Some students used both Google Translate and DeepL to translate text from Japanese to English, and when there were differences in the words in the output, they asked ChatGPT to clarify differences between the words and to provide examples. In one example about the end of a winning streak for the Giants in the national baseball league, Google Translate produced "Giants' wins stopped" and DeepL produced "Giants' win snapped." The student then proceeded to ask ChatGPT about this by asking, "What's the difference between snap and stop?"

The limitations of using AI and MT tools to support academic writing

Although the students perceived the potential capabilities and functionalities of the tools, they also discovered their limitations by using the tools in practice. From the discussion notes taken by the students and the researchers during the training sessions, the main limitations can be thematically categorized (see Table 7.6). Overall, the students were aware of the accuracy of the translation results and the information source. ChatGPT was specifically mentioned as a tool that could create fictional evidence and provide inaccurate information, making it unsuitable for academic writing. Google Translate was noted to sometimes make mistakes, and there were instances of grammatical errors. DeepL was criticized for producing translations that were too formal and difficult to understand, indicating limitations in capturing appropriate tone and style. Moreover, the students also expressed uncertainty about the reliability of information obtained from the tools. They questioned the accuracy and validity of the information, highlighting concerns about outdated or potentially incorrect data. ChatGPT was viewed as a type of search engine but without clear verification of the information sources, making it questionable for business or academic use. Noticing the inaccuracy of the responses produced by the tools, one student stated that he preferred a proper dictionary: "it is better to use dictionaries to search for meanings of unknown words."

Training to use machine translation for vocabulary learning 149

Table 7.6 The limitations of the AI and MT tools (all responses are included as is)

Limitations	Extracts
Awareness of accuracy	"ChatGPT is a good tool, but it sometimes lies and creates fictional evidence, so it is not good for academic writing." "Google Translate sometimes makes mistakes." "There are still some grammatical errors in the tools." "The information might be wrong."
Suspicious information sources	Old information "ChatGPT is just a searching engine." "We don't know whether the information is true or not, and where it comes from." "ChatGPT can be used as a game to play with, but not for business or professional. The information is questionable." "(ChatGPT) The database closed in 2021, so the information is old, and it is often wrong."
Lack of accessibility and slow retrieval speed	"It is difficult to log in to ChatGPT." "It (ChatGPT) takes time to log in and wait for it to generate results."
Difficulties in capturing deeper meaning and misunderstanding	"ChatGPT doesn't understand the deep meaning of the words. It only provides the differences between the definitions." "ChatGPT doesn't understand the true meaning of our questions." "AI tools sometimes misunderstand expressions."
Inappropriate context use	"It (ChatGPT) is good for private use but not for public use." "In academic situations, DeepL is better." "Google Translate can be used in improper ways. For example, it is not good if it is used in exams or homework."
Reliance on the tools	"Google Translate is not always accurate, but if we always rely on it, we can't notice that." "Google Translate may replace our learning of language, as we can't make full use of what we've learned so far." "We shouldn't depend on these tools too much."

Some students experienced difficulties with logging in to ChatGPT and found it time-consuming to wait for the tool to generate results. This can hinder the efficiency and convenience of using the tool. The students also expressed that the AI tools lack the ability to understand the deep meanings of words and questions, leading to inaccurate or irrelevant results/responses. Regarding contextual use, students perceived ChatGPT as more suitable for private use rather than public or academic situations, and they noticed the improper use of the tools in exams or homework. The students acknowledged that overreliance on these tools might hinder language learning and prevent the full utilization of previously acquired knowledge.

Considering the potential limitations of the tools after the training sessions, the students became more aware of their role as language learners. Although the AI and MT tools may help by generating word meanings and texts, learners have to judge the results; as one student noted "Humans have to make final decisions." Most of the students did not agree that the tools will replace their learning process, but they will learn with the tools, as two of the students said:

> "The tools are indeed convenient, but we should not trust them totally. By judging if the results are appropriate or not, we can improve our English."

> "We still have to achieve a certain English level to evaluate the translation results."

These results highlight that the students do need training on how to learn with the aid of technology, as they noticed the affordances and limitations of the tools, and gradually developed their own strategies to support their language learning.

New understandings

Overall, the research results suggest that students can benefit from training in the use of AI tools for vocabulary learning for academic writing. The training can lead to a change in the students' attitude towards these tools, helping them recognize the value and potential benefits they offer, as one student noted that we can "see through the 'magic' of ChatGPT now." Additionally, through training, students can develop their own strategies for utilizing AI tools effectively in their writing process, enabling them to utilize the tools which meet their learning needs and learning styles (e.g., "We need to look for more productive ways to use it (ChatGPT)."). Moreover, the training helped the students become more aware of the affordances provided by AI tools, such as translation assistance, synonym suggestions, and additional language support. It is worth noting that the students also demonstrated an understanding of the limitations of these tools. This awareness highlights the importance of providing comprehensive training that not only emphasizes the benefits but also educates students about the limitations and encourages critical thinking in their use of AI tools for vocabulary learning.

Implications

It is important for students, teachers, and educators to recognize that AI tools can serve as valuable resources to aid in language teaching and learning processes. Teachers should be encouraged to embrace these tools as they can help facilitate personalized learning, provide instant feedback, and assist in individual learning strategies (see also Wang & Panahi, 2023).

It is worth noting that there might be a gap between teachers' and students' attitudes toward AI tools. Students may find the tools useful but have concerns that they will face consequences or be punished by their teachers for using AI tools in their academic work, as one student stated "We may be scolded by our teachers if we use these tools." This negative perception can discourage students from exploring and utilizing these tools, and thus they may miss the chance to develop creative and pedagogically appropriate learning strategies. To overcome this, training for both students and teachers is crucial, where students should be educated on the benefits and responsible use of AI tools, and teachers should receive training on how to effectively integrate AI tools into their teaching methods. This training can help them overcome any resistance or fear they may have about using AI tools, enabling them to fully leverage the potential of these technologies. Being open-minded and creating a safe space for exploration and communication, teachers can inspire students to utilize AI tools with greater awareness of the affordances and limitations of the technology. Finally, it is essential to emphasize that AI tools need not be threats to education and educators. They cannot replace teaching nor learning processes, but rather they act as a powerful supplement to enhance the language education experience.

Further reading

Jolley, J. R., & Maimone, L. (2022). Thirty years of machine translation in language teaching and learning: A review of the literature. *L2 Journal*, *14*(1), 22–44. https://doi.org/10.5070/L214151760
This review article provides historical and practical perspectives on MT in language education with a discussion on the potential benefits and limitations of usage. It also explores the use of MT as a tool in various aspects of the field, such as vocabulary learning, writing, and grammar.

Urlaub. P., & Dessein, E. (2022). Machine translation and foreign language education. *Frontiers in Artificial Intelligence*, *5*, 936111. https://doi.org/10.3389/frai.2022.936111
This article provides a very readable introduction to the fundamentals of MT and raises issues about perceptions and potential risks of using MT in language education. It also describes the potential way forward to making MT a more useful and integrated part of the language teaching and learning process.

References

Alm, A., & Watanabe, Y. (2022). Online machine translation for L2 writing across languages and proficiency levels. *Australian Journal of Applied Linguistics*, 5(3), 135–157. https://doi.org/10.29140/ajal.v5n3.53si3

Briggs, N. (2018). Neural machine translation tools in the language learning classroom: Students' use, perceptions, and analyses. *The JALT CALL Journal*, 14(1), 3–24. https://doi.org/10.29140/jaltcall.v14n1.221

Brown, A., Bennett. C., Bulman, G., Giannini, S., Habib, R., & Ticio Quesada, E. (2022). Machine translation: An enduring chasm between language students and teachers. *CALR Linguistics Journal*, 12, Article 3. https://web.aou.edu.lb/research/online-journals/PublishingImages/Pages/CALR---Issue-12/Article%203.pdf

Chang, P., Chen, P.-J., & Lai, L.-L. (2022). Recursive editing with Google Translate: The impact on writing and error correction. *Computer Assisted Language Learning*, 1–26. https://doi.org/10.1080/09588221.2022.2147192

Chung, E. S., & Ahn, S. (2021). The effect of using machine translation on linguistic features in L2 writing across proficiency levels and text genres. *Computer Assisted Language Learning*, 35(9), 2239–2264. https://doi.org/10.1080/09588221.2020.1871029

Ducar, C., & Schocket, D. H. (2018). Machine translation and the L2 classroom: Pedagogical solutions for making peace with Google Translate. *Foreign Language Annals*, 51, 779–795. https://doi.org/10.1111/flan.12366

Fredholm, K. (2015). El uso de traducción automática en la escritura en español como lengua extranjera: Efectos en fluidez, complejidad y corrección [Online translation use in Spanish as a foreign language essay writing : Effects on fluency, complexity and accuracy]. *Revista Nebrija de Lingüística Aplicada*, 9(18), 7–24. https://doi.org/10.26378/rnlael918248

Fredholm, K. (2019). Effects of Google Translate on lexical diversity: Vocabulary development among learners of Spanish as a foreign language. *Revista Nebrija de Lingüística Aplicada a la Enseñanza de Lenguas*, 13(26), 98–117.

Hubbard, P. (2004). Learner training for effective use of CALL. In S. Fotos & C. Browne (Eds.), *Perspectives on CALL for second language classrooms* (pp. 45–68). Mahwah, NJ: Lawrence Erlbaum.

Hubbard, P. (2013). Making a case for learner training in technology enhanced language learning environments. *CALICO Journal*, 30(2), 163–178. https://doi.org/10.11139/cj.30.2.163-178

Kol, S., Schcolnik, M., & Spector-Cohen, E. (2018). Google Translate in academic writing courses. *The EuroCALL Review*, 26(2), 50–57.

Lee, S.-M. (2020). The impact of using machine translation on EFL students' writing. *Computer Assisted Language Learning*, 33(3), 157–175. https://doi.org/10.1080/09588221.2018.1553186

Lee, S.-M. (2022). L2 learners' strategies for using machine translation as a personalized writing assisting tool. In J. Colpaert & G. Stockwell (Eds.), *Smart CALL: Personalization, contextualization, & socialization* (pp. 184–206). London: Castledown Publishers. www.castledown.com/reference/9781914291012-9/

Lo, S. (2023). Neural machine translation in EFL classrooms: Learners' vocabulary improvement, immediate vocabulary retention and delayed vocabulary retention. *Computer Assisted Language Learning*, 1–20. https://doi.org/10.1080/09588221.2023.2207603

Moon, D. (2021). Cyber learners' use and perceptions of online machine translation tools. *International Journal of Advanced Smart Convergence*, 10(4), 165–171.

Nino Alonso, A. (2022). Online translators in online language assessments. *CALL-EJ*, 23(3), 115–135.

Stockwell, G. (2022). *Mobile assisted language learning: Concepts, contexts and challenges.* Cambridge University Press. https://doi.org/10.1017/9781108652087

Stockwell, G., & Hubbard, P. (2013). Some emerging principles for mobile-assisted language learning. Monterey, CA: The International Research Foundation for English Language Education. www.tirfonline.org/english-in-the-workforce/mobile-assisted-language-learning

Stockwell, G., & Hubbard, P. (2014). Learner training in mobile language learning. In J. Colpaert, A. Aerts & M. Oberhofer (Eds.), *Proceedings of the 2014 CALL research conference* (pp. 320–322). Antwerp: University of Antwerp.

Tasmedir, S., Lopez, E., Satar, M., Riches, N. G. (2023). Teachers' perceptions of machine translation as a pedagogical tool. *The JALT CALL Journal*, 19(1), 92–112. https://doi.org/10.29140/jaltcall.v19n1.24

Tsai, S.-C. (2019). Using Google Translate in EFL drafts: A preliminary investigation. *Computer Assisted Language Learning*, 32(5–6), 510–526. https://doi.org/10.1080/09588221.2018.1527361

Tsai, S.-C. (2022). Chinese students' perceptions of using Google Translate as a translingual CALL tool in EFL writing. *Computer Assisted Language Learning*, 35(5–6), 1250–1272. https://doi.org/10.1080/09588221.2020.1799412

Van Praag, B., & Sanchez, H.S. (2015). Mobile technology in second language classrooms: Insights into its uses, pedagogical implications, and teacher beliefs. *Recall*, 27(3), 288–303. https://doi.org/10.1017/S0958344015000075

Wang, Y. (2020). Engagement in PC-based, smartphone-based, and paper-based materials: Learning vocabulary through Chinese Stories. *Technology in Language Teaching & Learning*, 2 (1), 3–21. https://doi.org/10.29140/tltl.v2n1.319

Wang, Y. (2024). Cognitive and sociocultural dynamics of self-regulated use of machine translation and generative AI tools in academic EFL writing. System, 126, 103505. https://doi.org/10.1016/j.system.2024.103505

Wang, Y., & Panahi, A. (2023). Technology and second language writing instruction. In H. Mohebbi & Y. Wang (Eds.), *Insights into teaching and learning writing: A practical guide for early-career teachers* (pp. 167–179). Castledown Publishers. https://castledown.online/reference/9781914291159-13/

Zimotti, G., Frances, C., & Whitaker, L. (2024). The future of language education: Teachers' perceptions about the surge of AI writing tools. *Technology in Language Teaching & Learning*, 6(2), 1–24. https://doi.org/10.29140/tltl.v6n1.1136

8 Korean EFL learners' vocabulary development through asynchronous CMC and synchronous CMC in content courses

Sung-Yeon Kim

Department of English Education, Hanyang University, Seoul, Korea

Pre-reading questions

1. What is your definition of lexical competence? What do you think is the role of lexical knowledge in language acquisition?
2. What do you think are the main differences in the characteristics of asynchronous CMC (ACMC) and synchronous CMC (SCMC)?
3. How can we use the different types of CMC in language teaching? For what purpose?
4. If you had to design a classroom task, which one would you prefer to use between ACMC and SCMC? Why?

Background

As computer-mediated communication (CMC) has proliferated with the acceleration of technological development, a myriad of studies have examined its impact on language learning (Lin, 2015). Many of these studies have attested to the pedagogical benefits of CMC, such as increasing learners' motivation, cultural understanding, social interaction, language proficiency, and pragmatic competence (Blake, 2000; De la Fuente, 2003; Eslami et al., 2015; Kitade, 2000; Lin, 2015; Pérez, 2003; Reynolds & Anderson, 2015; Roose & Newell, 2020). CMC is known to enhance L2 learners' motivation to learn a language by providing a more engaging and interactive learning experience (Roose & Newell, 2020; Stockwell, 2010). CMC also helps to reduce learner anxiety as learners feel comfortable interacting online (Mirzaei & Hayati, 2018). It can also facilitate cross-cultural communication, through which learners can acquire intercultural competence (Zeiss & Isabelli García, 2005). In addition, it can help learners improve their collaborative learning skills while working on computer-mediated language learning tasks (Kitade, 2000; Sotillo,

2000). Learners can share ideas, exchange feedback, and work together to solve problems.

Most of all, the interactive nature of CMC contributes to the development of L2 learners' communicative competence because CMC creates an environment where learners can use the language in the course of authentic interaction (Collentine, 2009; Sauro, 2011; Stockwell, 2010). Many studies have reported the positive effects of CMC on language learning. Abrams (2003) compared three groups (an ACMC group, an SCMC group, and a control group) in terms of fluency and linguistic complexity and found that the SCMC group improved in the quantity of language produced. Hirotani (2009) also examined an ACMC, an SCMC, and a control group in terms of their language output and lexical and syntactic measures. The study found positive correlations between the oral gain scores of the SCMC group and the number of speech units, and between the oral gain scores of the ACMC group and the syntactic complexity measures. However, the linguistic measures of oral proficiency did not differ significantly between the ACMC and SCMC groups. More recently, Shiroyama (2021) revived interest in the effects of CMC on linguistic development by analyzing the lexical diversity and syntactic complexity of learner output generated from decision-making tasks via ACMC and SCMC. The study found significant differences in measures of syntactic complexity between the two modes, with higher scores in the ACMC group, but the difference in lexical diversity was not significant.

In contrast, AbuSeileek and Qatawneh (2013) focused on discourse functions, such as question types and strategies, in their comparison of a SCMC group and an ACMC group. They found more positive effects in the ACMC group, which used more question types and strategies, and extended questions and answers. Likewise, Ajabshir (2019) investigated EFL learners' acquisition of the request speech act in ACMC, SCMC, and face-to-face communication (FFC) groups, but found no significant differences in their performance on a discourse completion task.

There have also been studies that have limited their scope to one of the modes, such as ACMC. For example, Stockwell (2005) analyzed learner output from ACMC, i.e., email exchanges involving L2 learners of English (n = 24), but found no significant improvement over time in terms of lexical and syntactic measures. In another study focusing on ACMC, Kitade (2006) examined negotiation routines and discourse strategies in jigsaw task-based email exchanges, and reported that more complex and formal signals were used in ACMC. More recently, Roose and Newell (2020) conducted an intertextual analysis of ESL students' online discussion of a news article. They found that the dialogic online space helped the students integrate their cultural repertoires as they negotiated the meaning of their peers' online postings. They suggested that online discussion allowed students to participate in writing as a social act, which developed their academic literacy.

Another line of CMC research has focused solely on the effects of SCMC. These studies delineate the facilitative effects of SCMC on fluency development (Blake & Zyzik, 2003; Sauro & Smith, 2010). Compared to FFC, SCMC can provide a non-threatening environment in which learners can take more risks and share their thoughts freely (Golonka et al., 2017; Kim, 2002; Kim & Kim, 2022; Rabab'ah, 2013; Reynolds & Anderson, 2015). Rabab'ah (2013) linked Arabic female participants' active participation in SCMC to the anonymous nature of the communication mode. SCMC is also known to facilitate the negotiation of meaning, leading to the acquisition of new vocabulary (Kim & Kim, 2022; Lai & Zhao, 2006; Salaberry, 2000). According to Coyle and Prieto (2017), SCMC creates a context in which students can notice gaps in their lexical knowledge in the course of interaction. It also helps learners focus on forms while they negotiate meaning with peers (Peterson, 2009). This process ultimately contributes to learner awareness raising and proficiency development in terms of linguistic complexity, diversity, and accuracy (Alwi et al., 2012; Lai & Zhao, 2006; Sauro & Smith, 2010; Smith, 2004).

While these studies indicate specific details about each mode, they do not show the relationship between the two modes. There are a few studies that have examined the two simultaneously (Abrams, 2003; Sotillo, 2000). The problem is that they were primarily interested in linguistic aspects other than the lexical properties of learner language, such as discourse functions and syntactic complexity (Sotillo, 2000). Abrams (2003) included lexical measures in his analysis, but only at the marginal level. In other words, lexical indices were either excluded from the analysis or not comprehensive enough to capture multidimensional components of lexical competence.

The current study attempts to fill this gap by employing a wide range of measures that represent lexical richness (Lu, 2012). The use of more comprehensive lexical measures is crucial for the accurate assessment of learners' lexical competence. Given that vocabulary is essential for processing language input and producing output not only in language classes but also in other disciplinary courses that require reading original texts in L2 (Lee, 2022; Ma, 2013; Mirzaei & Hayati, 2018), the use of more accurate indices is crucial. Therefore, this study aims to compare the effects of SCMC and ACMC on the lexical density, sophistication, and diversity of learners' language. The purpose is further specified in the following research questions:

1. Are there differences in written output between the two modes of CMC in terms of lexical density?

2. Do the texts from the two modes of communication differ in terms of lexical sophistication?
3. Are the texts from the two modes of CMC different in terms of lexical diversity?

Method

Research design

This study adopts a mixed-methods approach by combining a quantitative and a qualitative method. For the quantitative data analysis, the study used a within-subject design to compare the language output produced by Korean EFL learners in the ACMC and SCMC contexts. For the qualitative data analysis, the study analyzed the written texts produced in the ACMC and SCMC tasks.

Participants

The participants in the study were 40 Korean college students enrolled in two ESP writing courses (20 each) for pre-service teachers at a top university in Seoul, Korea. They were all seniors, and most of them (n = 37) were from the Department of English Education (EE), while the rest (n = 3) were from Educational Technology or German Language and Literature and were minoring in EE. In terms of gender, there were more female students (n = 27) than male students (n = 13). The students were quite advanced in English, having completed more than three years of an English-intensive curriculum at the university. Their writing proficiency was measured by an essay writing test scored by two native English teachers. The students' proficiency levels ranged from B2 to C1 according to the Common European Framework of Reference.

Instrument

For ACMC, the students used a discussion board on *Blackboard,* an online teaching and learning platform. The discussion board was used as an ACMC tool because the university adopted Blackboard as a learner management system (LMS) to support blended learning or distance learning during the pandemic. This allowed the students to participate in threaded discussions at convenient times. For SCMC, *KakaoTalk,* the Korean equivalent of *WeChat* or *WhatsApp,* was adopted as the medium of communication because it was one of the most widely used messenger apps in Korea and was familiar to the students.

For text analysis, the study used Lu's (2012) *Lexical Complexity Analyzer* (LCA) because the tool produces various indices of lexical richness, including measures of lexical density, lexical variation, and lexical sophistication (Uzun, 2019). The LCA produces 25 measures, such as LD, LS1, LS2, VS1, VS2, CVS1, NDW, NDWZ, TTR, CTTR, VV1, AdjV, and ModV, which can be classified into lexical density, lexical sophistication, and lexical diversity (see Lu, 2012 for more details on the indices). For example, LD was a measure of lexical density, and LS1, LS2, VS1, VS2, and CVS1 were measures of lexical sophistication. NDW, NDWZ, TTR, CTTR, NDW, and the other measures were indices of lexical variation.

Data collection

A total of 40 students enrolled in two different sections of the same course (20 in each) carried out a series of discussion tasks via both asynchronous and synchronous CMC. The study adopted a within-subject comparison, in that all the students completed the discussion tasks in both conditions: ACMC and SCMC. To control for the order effect, the participants in each class were divided into two groups and asked to perform the discussion tasks in counterbalanced order. The students performed both ACMC and SCMC tasks for two weeks, responding to the following prompts:

Time	Group 1	Group 2
Week 1	SCMC	ACMC
	Process vs. post-process	Process vs. post-process
Week 2	ACMC	SCMC
	Teaching methods	Teaching methods

- **Process vs. post-process**: Some scholars argue that a process approach is effective for L2 learners. Others claim that a post-process approach is useful as it helps learners acquire field- specific writing skills and writing strategies. Which approach do you support? Make sure to offer reasons for your argument. You should also react to your group members by expressing agreement or disagreement.
- **Teaching methods**: Approaches to writing instruction have been classified differently according to scholars. Among the three mentioned in Chapter 5, whose classification do you think is most comprehensive and valid? Explain how s/he has categorized writing instruction and discuss which one best accounts for secondary school English writing instruction in Korea. You should also react to your group members by expressing agreement or disagreement.

After completing each task, the students were asked to reflect on their CMC experience, and write reflection journals of more than 300 words in English.

Data analysis

The study analyzed learner-generated output with Lu's (2012) LCA. Because the scope of the study was confined to learners' productive vocabulary used in the different CMC tasks, the study focused on comparing learners' performance in different CMC tasks in terms of 25 lexical indices, such as lexical density (LD), lexical sophistication I (LS1), lexical sophistication II (LS2), number of different words (NDW), and type-token ratio (TTR). These measures were compared between the two sets of texts: bulletin board postings and real-time chat scripts. These measures are indicative of the lexical properties of the students' productive vocabulary in the two discussion tasks in terms of lexical density, lexical sophistication, and lexical diversity. To complement the results of the quantitative analysis, the students' texts were also analyzed qualitatively. For the qualitative analysis of the chat scripts, interactional discourse moves were coded based on Golonka et al.'s (2017) framework: offering assistance about language through meaning negotiation and peer- and self-correction, asking partners for help (e.g., clarifying, modelling, and helping with lexical and technical problems), and providing encouragement (eliciting, providing positive affect, and helping with task completion).

Results

The results section reports the findings from the analysis of the texts from the two modes of CMC. It was found that the students actively participated in CMC regardless of the mode, as evidenced by the multiple threads of discussion.

Productive vocabulary across the two modes of communication

Lexical density

Table 8.1 summarizes the descriptive statistics of LD, the lexical density measure, and the results of the paired-sample *t*-test. As seen in the table, the mean LD of ACMC was higher than that of SCMC, and the difference in mean scores was found to be statistically significant in the *t*-test. Given that lexical density refers to "the ratio of the number of lexical (as opposed to grammatical) words to the total number of words in a text" (Lu, 2012, p. 191), the statistically higher mean score of ACMC indicates that the students used more content words when discussing on the bulletin board than when discussing via *KakaoTalk*.

Table 8.1 Paired *t*-test of the lexical density measure between SCMC and ACMC

Measure	Group mean (SD) SCMC	ACMC	t-statistic t	p	Cohen's d d	CI
LD	0.54(0.04)	0.57(0.04)	-3.17	0.00	-0.52	-0.86 – -0.18

Notes. LD: lexical density, SD: standard deviation, Cohen's *d*: effect size, CI: confidence interval

The excerpts presented in Table 8.2 indicate the differences in the words the students used in the two modes. For comparable analysis, sample texts were taken from three students' postings, showing each student's statement of his or her position on the discussion topic.

Although four sample texts are not sufficient to generalize the lexical density of learner language, we can see differences in the first two or three sentences in the way the students used words to express their positions in each mode of communication. The students used a greater number of content words in presenting their opinions when they discussed on the bulletin board than when they communicated through SCMC.

Lexical sophistication

A higher level of lexical density of the learner language was found in ACMC; however, this difference did not result in the use of more sophisticated or advanced vocabulary on the bulletin board. As shown in Table 8.3, the learner language did not differ in terms of lexical sophistication according to the mode of communication.

Given that lexical sophistication represents "the proportion of relatively unusual or advanced words in the learner's text" (Read, 2000, p. 203), it is notable that the SCMC mean scores for lexical sophistication did not differ much from the ACMC scores. In fact, the differences in mean scores between the modes were not statistically significant for any of the five measures of lexical sophistication: LS1, LS2, VS1, VS2, and CVS1, as shown in Table 8.3. This means that the students' use of advanced words, that is, words beyond 2K according to Lu (2012), was about the same, regardless of the mode.

Lexical diversity

Despite the non-significant differences in lexical sophistication, the learner language displayed different patterns in terms of lexical variation. Table 8.4 summarizes the means (M) and standard deviations (SD) of the

Table 8.2 Examples of student postings across the two modes of communication

	ACMC	SCMC
Student A	"In my opinion, Ferris and Hedgcock's approach to L2 writing instruction is most comprehensive and valid, because they provided 7 specific writing instructions according to where we put focus of writing instruction on."	"if I had to choose between the two, I think that a post-process approach is more useful than a process approach to L2 learners"
Student B	"I think Raimes's classification best accounts for secondary school English writing instruction in Korea. Raimes focused on various factors for text production, such as content, syntax, grammar, mechanics, organization, word choice, purpose, audience, and the writer's process. And he described the teaching approach differs depending on which factor the teacher chooses in the instruction."	"I agree OO! It (post-process approach) could make students to learn so useful and frequent patterns and strategies by dealing with various genre or topic."
Student C	"I think post process approach is most beneficial and helpful for L2 learners. In current society, communication skill is emphasized more than ever. Demand for ESP is rising as well. According to the national curriculum (2015), English serves as lingua franca."	"I really liked F&H's approach, because it can be adapted to many different groups. I think having a theory that can actually connect to real life procedure is important." (two connected turns)

Table 8.3 Paired *t*-test of lexical sophistication measures between SCMC and ACMC

	Group mean (SD)		*t-statistic*		Cohen's d	
Measures	SCMC	ACMC	t	p	d	CI
LS1	0.28(0.07)	0.31(0.08)	-1.80	0.08	-0.30	-0.62 – 0.04
LS2	0.22(0.05)	0.22(0.05)	-0.05	0.96	-0.01	-0.33 – 0.31
VS1	0.09(0.05)	0.11(0.07)	-1.44	0.16	-0.24	-0.56 – 0.09
VS2	0.31(0.30)	0.33(0.35)	-0.19	0.85	-0.03	-0.35 – 0.29
CVS1	0.34(0.20)	0.35(0.21)	-0.14	0.89	-0.02	-0.35 – 0.30

Notes. LS1: lexical sophistication I, LS2: lexical sophistication II, VS1: verb sophistication I, VS2: verb sophistication II, CVS1: corrected VS1, SD: standard deviation, Cohen's *d*: effect size, CI: confidence interval

Table 8.4 Paired *t*-test of lexical variation measures between SCMC and ACMC

Measures	Group mean (SD) SCMC	Group mean (SD) ACMC	t-statistic t	t-statistic p	Cohen's d d	Cohen's d CI
NDW	106.46(31.09)	86.05(18.18)	3.56	0.00	0.59	0.23 – 0.93
NDW-50	39.46(2.70)	37.54(3.33)	3.53	0.00	0.58	0.23 – 0.93
NDW-ER50	39.94(1.60)	38.51(2.18)	3.29	0.00	0.54	0.19 – 0.88
NDW-ES50	39.62(2.00)	39.05(2.33)	1.21	0.24	0.20	-0.13 – 0.52
TTR	0.58(0.07)	0.58(0.07)	0.18	0.86	0.03	-0.29 – 0.35
MSTTR-50	0.79(0.04)	0.77(0.05)	2.36	0.02	0.39	0.05 – 0.72
CTTR	5.47(0.62)	4.96(0.54)	4.43	0.00	0.73	0.36 – 1.09
RTTR	7.73(0.87)	7.01(0.76)	4.45	0.00	0.73	0.36 – 1.09
LogTTR	0.90(0.02)	0.89(0.02)	1.27	0.21	0.21	-0.12 – 0.53
UBER	21.90(2.61)	20.43(3.77)	2.07	0.05	0.34	0.01 – 0.67
VV1	0.69(0.11)	0.72(0.13)	-1.08	0.29	-0.18	-0.50 – 0.15
SVV1	13.24(5.27)	10.57(3.88)	2.68	0.01	0.44	0.10 – 0.78
CVV1	2.52(0.50)	2.26(0.42)	2.69	0.01	0.44	0.10 – 0.78
LV	0.73(0.07)	0.70(0.08)	1.67	0.10	0.28	-0.06 – 0.60
VV2	0.19(0.05)	0.17(0.04)	1.87	0.07	0.31	-0.02 – 0.64
NV	0.71(0.09)	0.64(0.11)	3.10	0.00	0.51	0.16 – 0.85
AdjV	0.15(0.03)	0.14(0.04)	0.12	0.91	0.02	-0.30 – 0.34
AdvV	0.10(0.03)	0.08(0.03)	3.03	0.01	0.50	0.15 – 0.84
ModV	0.25(0.04)	0.23(0.04)	1.93	0.06	0.32	-0.02 – 0.65

Notes. NDW: number of different words (*T*), NDW-50: *T* in the first 50 words of the sample, NDW-ER50: Mean *T* of ten random 50-word samples, NDW-ES50: Mean *T* of ten random 50-word sequences, TTR: *T/N*, MSTTR-50: Mean segmental TTR, CTTR: corrected TTR, RTTR: Root TTR, LogTTR: Bilogarithmic TTR, Uber: Uber index, LV: lexical word variation; VV1: verb variation 1, SVV1: squared VV1, CVV1: corrected VV1, VV2: verb variation 2, NV: noun variation; AdjV: adjective variation, AdvV: Adverb variation, ModV: modifier variation (Lu, 2012, p. 195)

19 different measures of lexical diversity: NDW, NDW-50, NDW-ER50, NDW-ES50, TTR, MSTTR-50, CTTR, RTTR, LogTTR, UBER, VV1, SVV1, CVV1, LV, VV2, NV, AdjV, AdvV, and ModV.

Lexical diversity, also known as lexical variation, indicates the range of vocabulary used by learners (Lu, 2012) and includes various measures ranging from number of different words (NDW) to modifier variation (ModV). As shown in Table 8.4, the mean scores of the lexical variation measures were higher in SCMC than in ACMC for all of the measures except TTR and VV1. The differences in mean scores were found to be statistically significant for NDW, NDW-50, NDW-ER50, MSTTR-50, CTTR, RTTR, SVV1, CVV1, NV, and AdvV. These significant differences seem to indicate that the students used a more diverse range of words when chatting via SCMC than when discussing via ACMC. For example, the students used a greater number of new words, nouns, and adverbs when they chatted in real time than when they discussed via the bulletin board.

The following synchronous chat exchanges illustrate why the students used a greater number of new words in SCMC. The first excerpt shows how different lexical forms express a similar meaning, as in the examples of "incorporate," "apply," "accept," and "implement." It appears that as the students interacted with other participants in real time, they expanded their lexical repertoire by forming a chain of new words through association.

> Excerpt 1. Offering language-related assistance: Association of words in SCMC
>
> Student 1: However, post process approach is hard to be **accept**ed in the class. It's a problem.
> Student 2: I agree... although I know it is useful, I cannot really think of a way to **incorporate** it into class
> Student 3: yes, it goes back to the problem of the entrance examination system.
> Student 1: Also, English textbook cannot consider specific discourse, or student's needs
> Student 2: Exactly. Even if it can be **applied** into middle school classes, I do not think that parents nor the teachers would willingly **accept** the change
> Student 3: however it is still necessary to teach students the structure of certain texts
> Student 2: that is also true. However, unless the teachers can figure out a way to cleverly incorporate them into class, the struggles would always exist
> Student 4: To **implement** the system in an average Korean class, we have to make writing contextualized, which is the most difficult part.
> (*Discussion continues*)
> Student 2: All I'm saying is that not all of the Korean teachers are **fluent** enough to provide nor evaluate such writings
> Student 4: Interesting.. I was wondering the same thing. Are teachers really **capable**?
> (*Discussion continues*)

Student 2: Back to what I was saying... I think in order for changes to be made throughout, all of the teachers should be able to provide students with accurate examples and evaluate them accordingly.
Student 4: This leads to Y's opinion. Teachers should be **competent** enough.

This process of word association also allowed the students to retrieve words that referred to the same idea, as in the case of Student 2 and Student 4 who used "fluent," "capable," and "competent." In particular, Student 2 used additional new words while elaborating on the teachers' competence. Excerpt 2 shows how the chat participants influenced each other's use of synonyms. Specifically, Student 5 and Student 6 used words that were distinctive in form but similar in meaning, such as "cutting-edge," "latest," and "up-to-date." It seems that SCMC facilitated the association of various words, which then served as linguistic input for other learners and at the same time triggered output from other participants.

Excerpt 2. Offering language-related assistance: Use of synonyms in SCMC

Student 5: In that sense, J's opinion seems reasonable as Silva's EAP approach is a reflection of the most **cutting-edge** theory on EFL writing.

(*Discussion continues*)

Student 6: Maybe because their classification is the **latest,** many approaches consider the discourse community or the target reader.
Student 5: I also found my ideas in this sense. Ferris & Hedgcock's classification is by far the most **up-to-date** one.

In addition to using synonyms and words by association, the students often used modelling strategies. In other words, the students modelled their peers' words, even recycling them after several turns. As seen in Excerpt 3, Student 8 used the word "hierarchy" that Student 7 used in the previous turn.

Excerpt 3. Offering language-related assistance: Modelling of words in SCMC

Student 7: I think Ferris & Hedgcock's idea can provide the most ... encompassing view of writing teaching.
Student 8: wow good point

(Discussion continues)

Student 7: Because it deals with the hierarchy of writing that ranges from the most basic (e.g., writing for grammar practice) to the highest level (e.g., writing for social interaction writing for sociopolitical issues)!

(Discussion continues)

Student 8: I think the hierarchy makes it easier for the T and S to follow

(Discussion continues)

Student 9: Also, I thought he considered from sentence level to discourse level.

Student 7: That's true!

Student 8: oh, that's right, too.

Student 9: and also, he considered process of writing and academic purposes as well! So I thought he encompassed key factors?

There were times when the students modelled the words their peers had used much earlier in the course of interaction. For example, Student 9 transformed the word "encompassing" that Student 7 had used several turns earlier. In general, the students used a variety of vocabulary when communicating via SCMC. They used various communication strategies to negotiate meaning, such as expanding topics, asking questions for clarification, eliciting output from their peers, and managing communication, as seen in Excerpt 4 and Excerpt 5.

Excerpt 4. Using partners as a resource: Expanding topic and asking for clarification

Student 12: Still, it is difficult, but I think with combining with other subjects, it could be more helpful and more valuable to implement.

Student 13: Now, the educational trend is changing to 융합교육?

Student 14: **What's that, S13?**

Student 13: It incorporate two or three different subjects… to develop creative thinking

Student 13: If we incorporate other subjective with writing, it can be a post approach

Student 14: yeah. I agree with S. And honestly, I think both of approaches can be usefully used supplementing each other.

For example, in Excerpt 4, Student 13 began to talk about the changing trend in education and introduced the concept of convergence education. This idea prompted a question from Student 14, and helped to broaden the scope of the discussion. A few words like "incorporate," and "supplement" were used to clarify the concept. Similarly, in Excerpt 5, Student 18 asked if CBI writing was identical to theme-based writing. In responding to this question, the participants used a diverse range of words to clarify the concept, such as "subcategory," "collaborating," "theme," "Halloween," "necessarily," "academic," and "subject."

Excerpt 5. Providing encouragement: Eliciting output and managing conversation

> Student 15: I think what TH is saying is similar to theme-based learning, and I also think that is a good method. But I still have doubts whether it can be applied well in real middle and high school settings, since I have not experienced it. **Has any of you guys experienced or witnessed theme-based learning before?**
>
> Student 16: Hmm I think JI's opinion is somehow possible way because people who has intrinsic motivation can try writing journals themselves in their daily life.
>
> Student 17: I haven't either. In fact I have never received proper writing classes in school, so I do have doubts about how any writing classes can be done in school.
>
> Student 17: I'm just 'supposing' that there may be separate writing classes in the future. 😄
>
> Student 18: Sorry to interrupt, but **is CBI writing exactly same with theme-based writing?**
>
> Student 15: yes I think we all are, since there are not many writing classes held in Korean English classrooms.
>
> Student 17: I think theme-based learning is a subcategory under CBI.
>
> Student 17: Very similar.
>
> Student 18: thanks
>
> Student 15: I believe theme-based learning is collaborating with other subjects such as science and music to learn the same theme just in different subjects
>
> Student 17: I only remember that theme-based learning can also be about basketball, Halloween, not necessarily academic subjects

Student 15: I think we can agree upon using process approach teaching method but applying post-process approach to provide the context to the writing? Can this summarize our discussion?

Student 17: Ok 👍

In addition to asking questions for clarification, the participants used communication strategies such as encouraging output production and managing conversation. For example, Student 15 asked a question to elicit other members' thoughts about theme-based learning, but toward the end of the discussion, she asked a conversation management question, "Can this summarize our discussion?" to bring the discussion to a close.

As seen in the excerpts above, SCMC was particularly effective in developing lexical diversity. The students used a variety of words while negotiating meaning in SCMC contexts. They provided language input, and at the same time produced output, modelling what their peers used as they exchanged ideas during online interaction. This may be because online communication allows learners to "rely on a buffer zone (the editing window) that gives them the opportunity to reflect on the best type of language form to express their ideas" (Salaberry, 2000, p. 9).

New understandings

The findings of this study indicate the differential effects of CMC on vocabulary learning. The study noted the positive effects of ACMC in improving lexical density. Given that cognitive processing demands vary according to the mode of CMC, ACMC may have allowed learners more processing time (Kern, 1995; Sotillo, 2000). In general, learners are expected to have more time to process input and produce output in ACMC, whereas the rapid pace of synchronous or real-time CMC makes it difficult for them to edit language, often resulting in a lack of accuracy and coherence (Kern, 1995). Because students had more time to process input and plan their output in ACMC than in SCMC, they may have been able to generate more content words when posting their opinions on the online bulletin board.

However, the students did not differ in terms of lexical sophistication due to the mode of CMC. In other words, the modes of CMC did not have a significant influence on the learners' use of advanced vocabulary. This finding may be attributable to the fact that cyber language in CMC is close to quasi-spoken communication with features of spoken English (Kim & Kim, 2022). Thus, the words used in online communication may have shifted from formal and academic language to more casual and colloquial forms. The participants in the study may have used the first (K1) or the second (K2) thousand most frequent words rather than advanced, academic vocabulary, regardless of the type of CMC.

Despite the non-significant differences in lexical sophistication, the students did display differences in terms of lexical diversity. SCMC was found to be more effective in increasing lexical diversity than ACMC, as the students used a more diverse range of words in the real-time chat rather than on the asynchronous bulletin board. Kim and Kim (2022) associated the lexical diversity in SCMC with the interactive nature of chatting, reporting that the participants were able to expand their lexical repertoire while engaged in a synchronous chat. Kim and Kim (2022) also attributed the increase in lexical diversity to the unique features of SCMC that facilitate language-related episodes (LREs) or interactional moves (Coyle & Prieto, 2017; Golonka, et al., 2017; Reynold et al., 2015). SCMC provides an optimal context for interlanguage lexical development because it allows for constant negotiation of lexical meaning and supports the interactive exchange of modified output (Blake, 2000; Jackson, 2011). SCMC also facilitates a focus on form through LREs (Peterson, 2009). More specifically, the ongoing and fluid nature of SCMC makes it easier for learners to notice target language forms in the course of interaction and recycle them in their output production (Lai & Zhao, 2006; Teng, 2015). In particular, the inherent features of text-based CMC discourse make SCMC "a pedagogically sound environment for increasing metalinguistic awareness in the L2" (Salaberry, 2000, p. 9).

The present study also noted such interactive exchanges, confirming the LREs from Golonka et al.'s (2017) framework. The participants in the study provided language-related assistance in the form of meaning negotiation and peer modelling, used their partners as resources, or provided encouragement to keep the conversation going. In particular, when the students noticed a gap between their interlanguage and their L2, they actively negotiated meaning to fill the gap. This synchronous co-construction of meaning seems to have made the L2 input more comprehensible, and allowed the learners to use various words, which may have led to lexical diversity (Blake, 2000; Blake & Zyzik, 2003; Ma, 2013; Rezaee & Ahmadzadeh, 2012; Salaberry, 2000).

Implications

The results of the study have several pedagogical implications. First, CMC tools are useful for language acquisition, especially for lexical development. Therefore, classroom teachers should try to incorporate CMC tasks into their lessons. For example, they could ask their students to read texts and discuss the readings via CMC in order to develop productive vocabulary.

Especially considering that CMC can provide a non-threatening environment, the use of CMC would be effective in engaging learners with high levels of foreign language anxiety. CMC can be used as a stand-alone activity or in combination with face-to-face sessions, depending on the needs of the learners. Second, because the effects of CMC vary by mode, the types of tools should be chosen judiciously according to the objectives of the CMC activities. For example, real-time CMC tools, such as synchronous text chat, can be used when the focus of instruction is on promoting lexical diversity, whereas ACMC tools, such as bulletin boards, can be used to develop lexical density. Third, teachers can introduce some useful communication strategies that can facilitate their students' meaning negotiation in CMC contexts (Kim & Kim, 2022). The use of meaning negotiation strategies would make CMC more interactive and contribute to L2 learners' vocabulary acquisition.

Conclusion

The present study investigated if and to what extent different modes of CMC would influence L2 learners' lexical development. This study is unique and distinctive, in that it compared EFL learners' productive vocabulary in different modes of CMC and explored the pedagogical value of CMC tasks for mediating discussion in content courses. The study focused on the differential effects of ACMC and SCMC on a variety of lexical measures, and it found facilitative effects of CMC on vocabulary learning. This was not surprising, as CMC is known to engage learners in initiating, negotiating, constructing, and reconstructing meaning (Coyle & Prieto, 2017). Of particular note was that the effects varied depending on the mode of CMC. This finding is pedagogically beneficial for teachers in that they can consider the relationship between the modes of CMC and lexical density, sophistication, and diversity when designing classroom tasks. Despite the significance of the study, it has some limitations. As it was a cross-sectional study, it was not possible to examine the long-term effects of CMC on vocabulary acquisition. In addition, the instruments used in the study may have influenced its results. Therefore, it would be interesting to replicate the study with other CMC tools or with different participant groups for a comparative analysis, as in Kim et al. (2024). In conclusion, the pedagogical potential of CMC is indeed promising. However, it is evident that both task design and the choice of CMC tools play crucial roles in determining learning outcomes in classroom contexts. Teachers should, therefore, carefully consider instructional goals, learning styles, and learner proficiency when designing tasks with CMC tools. The success of technology-enhanced learning depends not only on the selection of appropriate tools but also on the effective use of these tools.

Further reading

Golonka, E., Tare, M., & Bonilla, C. (2017). Peer interaction in text chat: Qualitative analysis of chat transcripts. *Language Learning & Technology*, *21*(2), 157–178.

This study examines the interactions of 25 intermediate-level adult learners of Russian during text chat activities, analyzing their chat transcripts. The findings indicate frequent instances of language-related assistance, modelling, and encouragement among peers, suggesting that real-time interactive tasks foster behaviors beneficial for language learning.

Kim, S.-Y., & Kim, K.-S. (2022). Vocabulary transfer from reading to writing: A comparison of essay writing and synchronous CMC. *TESL-EJ*, *26*(1), 1–21.

This study explores vocabulary transfer from a reading text to essay writing and synchronous text chat produced by 100 Korean college students, revealing that chat scripts incorporated more diverse vocabulary than essays, though without a significant difference in lexical diversity. The findings suggest that synchronous chat is as effective as essay writing for promoting vocabulary transfer, highlighting the value of reading as a source for language input and output production.

Kim, S.-Y., Shin, D., & Kim, K.-S. (2024). Association of lexical and collocation knowledge: A comparative analysis of native speakers and nonnative learners of English. *Vigo International Journal of Applied Linguistics*, *21*, 67–96.

This study compares the use of single words and collocations between EFL learners and native speakers. While advanced EFL learners are on a par with native speakers concerning the diversity of single words, all EFL learners, regardless of proficiency, were significantly behind in collocational knowledge. It underscores the importance of integrating a wider range of collocations into the curriculum, instruction, and assessment to bridge the gap in language proficiency.

References

Abrams, Z. I. (2003). The effect of synchronous and asynchronous CMC on oral performance in German. *The Modern Language Journal*, *87*(2), 157–167.

AbuSeileek, A. F., & Qatawneh, K. (2013). Effects of synchronous and asynchronous computer-mediated communication (CMC) on oral conversations on English language learners' discourse functions. *Computers & Education*, *62*, 181–190.

Ajabshir, Z. F. (2019). The effect of synchronous and asynchronous computer-mediated communication (CMC) on EFL learners' pragmatic competence. *Computers in Human Behavior*, *92*, 169–177.

Alwi, N., Adams, R., & Newton, J. (2012). Writing to learn via text chat: Task implementation and focus on form. *Journal of Second Language Writing*, *21*(1), 23–39.

Blake, R. (2000). Computer mediated communication: A window on L2 Spanish interlanguage. *Language Learning & Technology*, *4*(1), 120–136.

Blake, R., & Zyzik, E. (2003). Who's helping whom? Learner/Heritage-speakers' networked discussions in Spanish. *Applied Linguistics*, *24*(4), 519–544.

Collentine, K. (2009). Learner use of holistic language units in multimodal, task-based synchronous computer-mediated communication. *Language Learning & Technology, 13*(2), 68–87.

Coyle, Y., & Prieto, M. (2017). Children's interaction and lexical acquisition in text-based online chat. *Language Learning & Technology, 21*(2), 179–199.

De la Fuente, M. J. (2003). Is SLA interactionist theory relevant to CALL? A study on the effects of computer-mediated interaction in L2 vocabulary acquisition. *Computer Assisted Language Learning, 16*(1), 47–81.

Eslami, Z. R., Mirzaei, A., & Dini, S. (2015). The role of asynchronous computer-mediated communication in the instruction and development of EFL learners' pragmatic competence. *System, 48*, 99–111.

Golonka, E., Tare, M., & Bonilla, C. (2017). Peer interaction in text chat: Qualitative analysis of chat transcripts. *Language Learning & Technology, 21*(2), 157–178.

Hirotani, M. (2009). Synchronous versus asynchronous CMC and transfer to Japanese oral performance. *CALICO Journal, 26*(2), 413–438.

Jackson, D. (2011). Convergent and divergent computer-mediated communication tasks in an English for academic purposes course. *TESL-EJ, 15*(3), 1–18.

Kern, R. G. (1995). Restructuring classroom interaction with networked computers: Effects on quantity and characteristics of language production. *The Modern Language Journal, 79*, 457–476.

Kim, S.-Y. (2002). Korean college students' reflections of English language learning via CMC and FFC. *Multimedia-Assisted Language Learning, 5*(2), 9–28.

Kim, S.-Y., & Kim, K.-S. (2022). Vocabulary transfer from reading to writing: A comparison of essay writing and synchronous CMC. *TESL-EJ, 26*(1), 1–21.

Kim, S.-Y., Shin, D., & Kim, K.-S. (2024). Association of lexical and collocation knowledge: A comparative analysis of native speakers and nonnative learners of English. *Vigo International Journal of Applied Linguistics, 21*, 67–96.

Kitade, K. (2000). L2 learners' discourse and SLA theories in CMC: Collaborative interaction in internet chat. *Computer Assisted Language Learning, 13*(2), 143–166.

Kitade, K. (2006). The negotiation model in asynchronous computer-mediated communication (CMC): Negotiation in task-based email exchanges. *CALICO Journal, 23*(2), 319–348.

Lai, C., & Zhao, Y. (2006). Noticing and text-based chat. *Language Learning & Technology, 10*(3), 102–120.

Lee, S.-M. (2022). Factors affecting incidental L2 vocabulary acquisition and retention in a game-enhanced learning environment. *ReCALL, 35*(3), 274–289. doi.org/10.1017/S0958344022000209

Lin, H. (2015). A meta-synthesis of empirical research on the effectiveness of computer-mediated communication (CMC) in SLA. *Language Learning & Technology, 19*(2), 85–117.

Lu, X. (2012). The relationship of lexical richness to the quality of ESL learners' oral narratives. *The Modern Language Journal, 96*(2), 190–208.

Ma, Q. (2013). Computer assisted vocabulary learning: Framework and tracking user data. In P. Hubbard, M. Schulze, & B. Smith (Eds.), *Learner-computer interaction in language education* (pp. 230–243). San Marcos, Texas: Computer Assisted Language Instruction Consortium.

Mirzaei, S., & Hayati, A. F. (2018). Effects of the computer mediated communication interaction on vocabulary improvement. *TELKOMNIKA, 16*(5), 2217–2225.

Pérez, L. C. (2003). Foreign language productivity in synchronous versus asynchronous computer-mediated communication. *CALICO Journal, 21*(1), 89–104.

Peterson, M. (2009). Learner interaction in synchronous CMC: A sociocultural perspective. *Computer Assisted Language Learning, 22*(4), 303–321.

Rabab'ah, G. (2013). Discourse functions and vocabulary use in English language learners' synchronous computer-mediated communication. *Turkish Online Journal of Distance Education, 14*(2), 99–118.

Read, J. (2000). *Assessing vocabulary.* Oxford: Oxford University Press.

Reynolds, B., & Anderson, T. (2015). Extra-dimensional in-class communications: Action research exploring text chat support of face-to-face writing. *Computers and Composition, 35,* 52–64.

Rezaee, A., & Ahmadzadeh, S. (2012). Integrating computer mediated with face-to-face communication and EFL learners' vocabulary improvement. *Journal of Language Teaching and Research, 3*(3), 346–352.

Roose, T. M., & Newell, G. E. (2020). Exploring online discussions through an academic literacies approach. *ELT Journal, 74*(3), 258–267.

Salaberry, R. (2000). L2 morphosyntactic development in text-based computer-mediated communication. *Computer Assisted Language Learning, 13,* 5–27.

Sauro, S. (2011). SCMC for SLA: A research synthesis. *CALICO Journal, 28*(2), 369–391.

Sauro, S., & Smith, B. (2010). Investigating L2 performance in text chat. *Applied Linguistics, 31*(4), 554–577.

Shiroyama, T. (2021). Task-based language learning and teaching using synchronous and asynchronous CMC. *English Usage and Style, 38,* 35–55.

Smith, B. (2004). Computer-mediated negotiated interaction and lexical acquisition. *Studies in Second Language Acquisition, 26*(3), 365–398.

Sotillo, S. M. (2000). Discourse functions and syntactic complexity in synchronous and asynchronous communication. *Language Learning & Technology, 4*(1), 82–119.

Stockwell, G. (2005). Syntactical and lexical development in NNS-NNS asynchronous CMC. *The JALT CALL Journal, 1*(3), 33–49.

Stockwell, G. (2010). Effects of multimodality in computer-mediated communication tasks. In M. Thomas & H. Reinders (Eds.), *Task-based language learning and teaching with technology* (pp. 83–104). New York: Continuum.

Teng, X. (2015). *Languaging in cyberspace: A case study of the effects of peer-peer collaborative dialogue on the acquisition of English idioms in task-based synchronous computer-mediated communication.* Unpublished doctoral dissertation, Iowa State University, Iowa.

Uzun, K. (2019). Lexical indicators of L2 writing performance. *The Literacy Trek*, 5(1), 23–36.

Zeiss, E., & Isabelli García, C. L. (2005). The role of asynchronous computer mediated communication on enhancing cultural awareness. *Computer Assisted Language Learning*, 18(3), 151–169.

9 The anatomy of word lists in New Word Level Checker
Description and comparison

Atsushi Mizumoto
Kansai University, Japan

Pre-reading questions

1. Why was there a need to develop a new vocabulary profiling tool optimized for Japanese EFL learners?
2. What are the key differences between flemma and lemma counting methods for word lists? How do these impact the vocabulary profiles generated?
3. Beyond just profiling vocabulary difficulty, how can a tool like New Word Level Checker aid in data-driven learning? What specific features allow for deeper analysis of lexical patterns and usage?

Introduction

Vocabulary profiling involves analyzing texts to determine vocabulary frequency and coverage against pre-defined word lists. This process is crucial for researchers, material developers, teachers, and learners to evaluate texts based on the percentage of words at each frequency or difficulty level, pinpointing challenging or unfamiliar words (Nation, 2016). Advantages include selecting texts aligned with learners' proficiency levels, such as graded readers, creating teaching materials, assessing vocabulary development over time (e.g., Pigada & Schmitt, 2006), and facilitating autonomous vocabulary learning. Overall, vocabulary profiling plays a pivotal role in enhancing instruction and assessment for the acquisition of high-frequency vocabulary. This chapter presents the New Word Level Checker (NWLC) as an exemplar of vocabulary profiling programs.

NWLC (https://nwlc.pythonanywhere.com/) is a web application for vocabulary profiling. Using the core concept of its predecessor, Word Level Checker, developed by Someya (2006), NWLC analyzes English texts submitted by users and produces a coverage profile based on the built-in, user-selected word lists.

DOI: 10.4324/9781003367543-11

The anatomy of word lists in New Word Level Checker 175

The rationale for the development of NWLC was twofold: (1) vocabulary lists developed overseas are not designed specifically for Japanese English as a foreign language (EFL) learners, and (2) vocabulary lists tailored for Japanese EFL learners are not included in other online vocabulary profiling applications such as VocabProfiler (www.lextutor.ca/vp/comp/). Thus, NWLC is an online application specifically created to provide vocabulary profiling that has been optimized for Japanese EFL learning contexts.

Figures 9.1–9.3 illustrate the core functionalities of NWLC. Upon initial access to the system, users are presented with a text area and a dropdown menu that enumerates all available word lists, as depicted in Figure 9.1. When clicking on the '1. Check' button, a range of key metrics appears: the specific word level within the selected list, the categories of words at that level, the aggregate word frequency, and the proportion of words at that level relative to the entire list. These metrics are shown in the form of both individual and cumulative percentages. In addition, the coverage rate for each word level is graphically illustrated in a section labeled 'Word Level Distribution & Cumulative Percentage'. When creating a new word list,

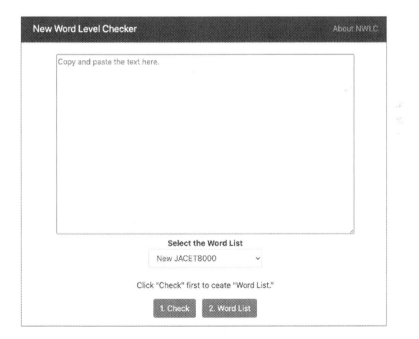

Figure 9.1 Initial user interface of NWLC with text area and word list dropdown menu

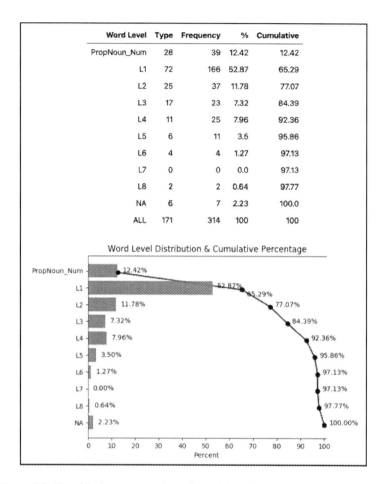

Figure 9.2 Graphical representation of word level coverage rates in NWLC

users are navigated to the interface shown in Figure 9.3. This interface provides several functionalities, enabling users to: (1) search for specific terms within the list, (2) sort columns of data, and (3) download the entire list in CSV format. As a result, the downloaded data allows users to tailor the vocabulary list to meet their unique requirements.

Word lists in NWLC

NWLC incorporates several word lists that have been developed specifically for Japanese EFL learners. The selection of appropriate word lists

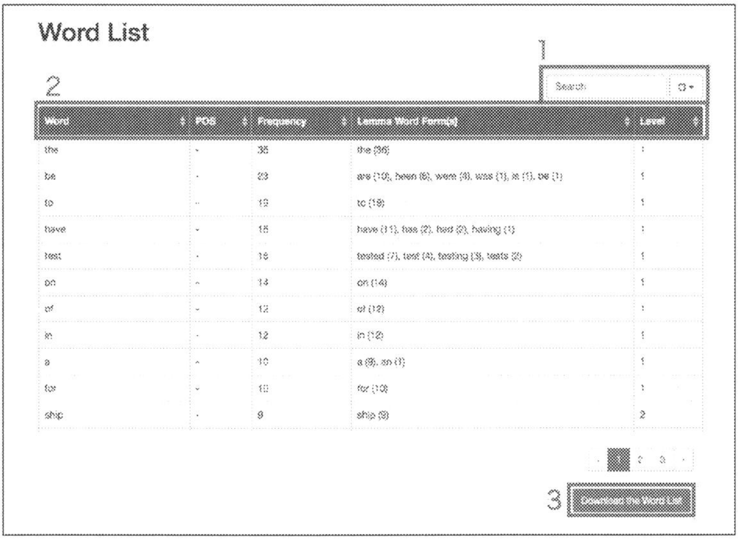

Figure 9.3 Interface for user-created word lists with search and sort functionalities

is critical, as it determines the accuracy and usefulness of the vocabulary profiling output. In the following section, I will introduce the word lists included in NWLC, detailing their key characteristics and intended purposes. The word lists adopted in NWLC are: New JACET8000, SVL12000, New General Service List, CEFR-J Wordlist, and SEWK-J. Each list offers unique benefits tailored to Japanese EFL learning contexts, which I will elucidate below. While NWLC is optimized for Japanese learners, the word list comparisons and insights presented here have broader implications for vocabulary research and EFL learning globally.

New JACET8000

The New JACET List of Basic Words (New JACET8000) (JACET, 2016) is the updated version of JACET8000 (JACET, 2003), compiled by the Japan Association of College English Teachers (JACET). Based on the British National Corpus (BNC) and the Corpus of Contemporary American English (COCA), New JACET8000 serves as an educational word list for Japanese learners of English, especially university students. The list has 8,000 words, and for each 1,000 words, the level (i.e., from 1 to 8) is provided by the NWLC profiler. The New JACET8000 is available from Dr. Shin Ishikawa's website (http://language.sakura.ne.jp/s/voc.html).

SVL12000

SVL12000 (Standard Vocabulary List 12000) was developed and published in 2001 by ALC Press, Inc. It is based on the BNC. Like New JACET8000, the word list is intended to be used for educational purposes, and many ALC-published materials use this list. As the name suggests, the list has 12,000 words and can be divided into 12 levels for each 1000-word band.

New General Service List

The New General Service List (NGSL) was conceived as a modern update of the General Service List (West, 1953). It was created from the Cambridge English Corpus (CEC), and it covers about 92% of general texts of English with a list of approximately 2,800 high-frequency words (Browne et al., 2013). Browne and his colleagues subsequently produced a secondary series of word lists for learners who have mastered the first 2,800 words in NGSL. These include the New Academic Word List (NAWL), the TOEIC Service List (TSL), and the Business Service List (BSL), which have the following number of headwords in each list:

1. NGSL (general): 2,801 words (Ver. 1.01)
2. NAWL (academic): 963 words (Ver. 1.0)
3. TSL (TOEIC): 1,259 words (Ver. 1.1)
4. BSL (business): 1,754 words (Ver. 1.01)

The secondary word lists (i.e., NAWL, TSL, and BSL) exclude all words in NGSL, but some words appear in more than one secondary list. For example, the word 'impact' is in all three lists (NAWL, TSL, and BSL). Also, while the word 'quit' is in both TSL and BSL, the word 'syndicate' only appears in BSL. For this reason, NWLC considers the overlapping of words in the three lists and produces the output using the criteria shown below. In total, NWLC has 5,621 words for word profiling.

1. Level 1: NGSL = 2,801 words
2. Level 2: NAWL & TOEIC & BSL = 183 words
3. Level 3: NAWL & TOEIC, NAWL & BSL, or TOEIC & BSL = 790 words
4. Level 4: Only in NAWL, TOEIC, or BSL = 1,847 words

CEFR-J Wordlist

CEFR-J Wordlist was based on an English textbook corpus consisting of textbooks for primary and secondary schools in China, Korea, and Taiwan (Tono, 2019). The word levels were classified according to the Common

Table 9.1 CEFR-J level, number of headwords and school levels in Japan

CEFR-J level	Number of headwords	School level in Japan
A1	1,164	Elementary
A2	1,411	Junior high
B1	2,446	Senior high
B2	2,778	University
Total	7,799	

European Framework of Reference for Languages (CEFR) levels, and they were aligned with the English Vocabulary Profile (www.englishprofile.org/wordlists). All headwords, as a result, have part of speech information and their corresponding CEFR(-J) levels, as shown in Table 9.1. NWLC uses CEFR-J Wordlist Version 1.5.

SEWK-J

The Scale of English Word Knowledge–Japanese (SEWK-J) was developed to estimate the difficulty that the vocabulary in a text presents to Japanese learners of English. Thus, the SEWK-J list estimates the likelihood that a word is known to Japanese university students. The probability of knowledge of a word is based on a multiple regression performed by Pinchbeck et al. (2022) using vocabulary test data of the 149-item New Vocabulary Levels Test (McLean & Kramer, 2016) administered to Japanese University EFL students as the criterion (dependent) variable. The regression formula includes the following predictive variables to provide estimates for about 75,000 flemma headwords:

1. English L2 vocabulary yes/no test data—accuracy
2. English L2 vocabulary yes/no test data—reaction time
3. English-Japanese loan words—identity
4. English-Japanese loan words—frequency in Japanese
5. Age of acquisition
6. Age of exposure
7. Word frequency in a large general corpus of English

Word counting units and rules

Proper nouns and numerals

In NWLC, proper nouns and numerals (numbers) are first identified using an open-source part of speech tagger, *spaCy* (https://spacy.io/), and are then treated as possibly *known* words because they can be assumed to be understood by learners. The possessive *'s* (e.g., Todd's dog) is also put into the *known* category in word profiler output. For the remaining words in the text, the following lemmatization (tokenization) rules are applied.

Lemmatization

A variety of word counting methods have been used in previous studies (for a review, see McLean, 2018). In some word counting methods, 'happy', 'happily', 'happiness', and 'unhappy' can be counted as one word family, with the headword 'happy' (e.g., Nation, 2012). Four out of the five word lists in NWLC adopt flemma counting (i.e., a base form as a headword and its inflected forms are counted as one word). For example, for the headword 'study', the following word forms are included and counted as one word: study, studies, studied, and studying. The flemma—a portmanteau of 'family' and 'lemma'—was first introduced by Pinchbeck (2014, 2017) to distinguish between word lists that include part of speech information and those that do not and is a recommended word counting method in the field of applied linguistics and in EFL teaching contexts (McLean, 2018; Pinchbeck et al., 2022). Flemma counting combines inflections of lemma groups but does not distinguish the part of speech (POS). That is, with flemma counting, the verb 'study' and the noun 'study' are both counted under the same headword 'study'.

A distinction between the terms *flemma* and *lemma* is not always made. For example, a type of resource used by the AntConc software that is termed a 'lemma list' has no requirement for POS tag information. In fact, the resource labeled as 'lemma list', as used in the NWLC (see below) is all based on *flemma*-grouped word lists.

In contrast to the family and flemma grouping methods, lemma counting can detect the POS differences. The CEFR-J Wordlist adopts lemma counting because the original CEFR word lists are also lemmatized. Thus, in the CEFR word lists, the *verb* 'study' is classified as A1 and the *noun* 'study' is A2.

When a user selects the New JACET8000 or the SVL12000, NWLC uses the flemma list *AntBNC Lemma List* (www.laurenceanthony.net/software/antconc/), which is based on all words in the BNC corpus with a frequency greater than two, for flemmatization. Modifications were manually made to match the headwords of New JACET8000 and SVL12000. For example, the words 'interesting' and 'interested' are listed as two headwords in both New JACET8000 and SVL12000, so they were excluded from the flemma entry 'interest' in these lists (i.e., interest = interest, interests). In addition, words with British spellings in New JACET8000 and SVL12000 are

The anatomy of word lists in New Word Level Checker 181

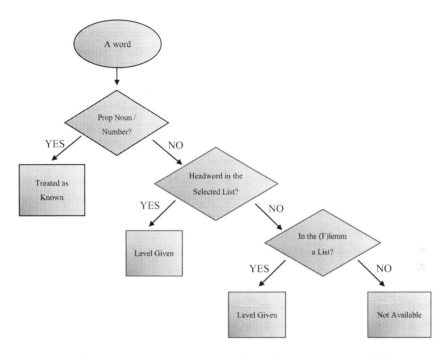

Figure 9.4 Flowchart representing the algorithm of lemmatization in NWLC
Note: For CEFR-J, spaCy is used to lemmatize the word.

included in the revised flemma list (e.g., advertise = advertise, advertises, advertised, advertising, advertize, advertizes, advertized, advertizing).

For the NGSL, flemmatization is simple because all NGSL lists are provided as flemma groupings. NWLC uses the flemma lists available at the NGSL website. For the CEFR-J Wordlist, NWLC utilizes spaCy to assign a POS and its lemma form. For SEWK-J, NWLC refers to a flemma list developed by Pinchbeck (manuscript in preparation).

Figure 9.4 shows a flowchart representing the algorithm of (f)lemmatization in NWLC. As can be seen, the application does its best to provide, by referring to the selected word list, the vocabulary profile of the text uploaded by the users.

Capitalized letters

As the headwords in New JACET8000, SVL12000, and CEFR-J Wordlists include capital letters (Table 9.2), they are treated as they are (e.g., 'I' not 'i'). However, when the NGSL or the SEWK-J is used, NWLC treats all

182 *Theory and Practice in Vocabulary Research in Digital Environments*

Table 9.2 List of words with capitalized letters

New JACET8000 (20 words)
April, August, December, English, February, Friday, I, January, Japanese, July, June, Monday, November, October, Saturday, September, Sunday, Thursday, Tuesday, Wednesday

SVL12000 (44 words)
April, August, Bible, Buddhism, Buddhist, Catholic, Christ, Christian, Christianity, Christmas, December, Easter, Fahrenheit, February, Friday, God, I, Islam, January, July, June, March, May, Messrs., Miss, Monday, Mr., Mrs., Ms., Muslim, November, OK, October, Protestant, Renaissance, Satan, Saturday, September, Shinto, Sunday, Thanksgiving, Thursday, Tuesday, Wednesday

CEFR-J (72 words)
A.M., AM, Apr, April, Atlantic, Aug, August, CD player, CD, CD-ROM, CV, Christian, DJ, DNA, DVD, Dec, December, Dr, Dr., E-mail, Englishman, Feb, February, Friday, HIV, I, ID card, ID, IT, Internet, Jan, January, July, June, MP3 player, Mar, March, May, Mediterranean, Miss, Monday, Mr, Mr., Mrs, Mrs., Ms, Ms., Nov, November, OK, OK, Oct, October, Olympia, Olympiad, Olympic, Olympics, PC, P.M., PM, Saturday, Sept, September, Shakespearean, Soviet, Sunday, T-shirt, TV, Thursday, Tuesday, Wednesday, X-ray

words as lowercase because all headwords in these lists are lowercase. In other words, the New JACET8000, SVL12000, and CEFR-J profilers are case-sensitive, whereas those using the NGSL and SEWK-J are case-insensitive.

Contracted forms

NWLC detects contracted forms by using spaCy and reverts them to their uncontracted forms (e.g., 'I'm' => 'I am'). Note that, as contracted forms such as 's' as in 'he's' (he has, he is) and 'd' as in 'we'd' (we had or we would) are not distinguished by the spaCy tagger, NWLC regards 's' and 'd' as they are. We consider this lack of precision acceptable because the headwords 'be', 'is', 'have', 'has', 'would', etc. are all among the most frequent words. For users who need to accurately distinguish between these contracted forms, the results may need to be checked carefully.

The SVL12000, NGSL, and CEFR-J contain words with apostrophes (Table 9.3). If those words are in the input text, NWLC treats them as they are.

Table 9.3 List of words with apostrophes

SVL12000 (1 word)
o'clock

NGWL (2 words)
o'clock, ma'am

CEFR-J (6 words)
driver's license, 'm, o'clock, 're, 's, 'd

Table 9.4 List of words with periods

SVL12000 (4 words)
Mr., Mrs., Ms., Messrs.

CEFR-J (8 words)
a.m., A.M., Dr., Mr., Mrs., Ms., p.m., P.M.

Abbreviations with periods

The SVL12000 and CEFR-J include abbreviations that use periods. If those word lists are selected and the input text has those words, shown in Table 9.4, NWLC treats them as they are.

Hyphenated words

Hyphenated words are first divided into two words (e.g., 'Osaka-based' is treated as two words, 'Osaka' and 'based') in all word lists except for the cases where the selected list has hyphenated words as headwords (Table 9.5).

Compounds/multi-word units

If a headword in the selected word list consists of more than one word (e.g., 'bank account' and 'mobile phone' in CEFR-J), it is counted as one word (unit), and NWLC returns the word profiling accordingly. NGSL and its three secondary lists (NAWL, TSL, and BSL) have only one compound, 'ice cream', while CEFR-J has 145 compounds (Table 9.6).

Comparison of word lists

Table 9.7 summarizes the word counting units and rules, as described in the previous section, for the word lists adopted in NWLC.

184   *Theory and Practice in Vocabulary Research in Digital Environments*

Table 9.5 List of hyphenated words

NGWL *(3 words)*
e-book (in TSL), e-book (in BSL), by-law

CEFR-J *(62 words)*
bad-tempered, brand-new, brother-in-law, CD-ROM, check-in, check-in counter, check-in desk, daughter-in-law, duty-free, easy-going, e-mail, E-mail, face-to-face, father-in-law, film-maker, first-floor, full-time, good-looking, grown-up, half-price, hand-held, hard-working, heart-warming, high-tech, hip-hop, hi-tech, last-minute, left-hand, long-distance, long-term, make-up, middle-aged, mother-in-law, next-door, non-smoking, old-fashioned, out-of-date, part-time, right-hand, second-hand, self-confidence, self-confident, self-service, semi-final, short-term, sister-in-law, so-called, son-in-law, take-off, tee-shirt, T-shirt, up-to-date, washing-up, well-balanced, well-built, well-dressed, well-known, well-organised, well-organized, well-paid, worn-out, X-ray

Table 9.6 List of compounds

NGWL *(1 word)*
ice cream

CEFR-J *(145 words)*
according to, air conditioning, air force, alarm clock, all right, bank account, because of, board game, bus station, bus stop, capital letter, car park, carbon dioxide, carbon footprint, carbon monoxide, CD player, central heating, chat show, check-in counter, check-in desk, chest of drawers, chewing gum, classical music, climate change, common sense, credit card, de facto, debit card, definite article, department store, digital camera, dining room, disc jockey, disk jockey, driver's license, driving licence, each other, environmentally friendly, exchange rate, exclamation mark, extreme sports, face to face, fast food, fed up, fire brigade, fire station, first floor, first lady, first language, first name, first person, frying pan, full stop, global warming, good afternoon, good morning, good night, grocery store, ground floor, hard drive, have to, health care, heart attack, high school, hip hop, human rights, ice cream, ice hockey, ice skating, ID card, identity card, indefinite article, instead of, inverted commas, junk food, last minute, last name, living room, main course, martial art, message board, mineral water, mixing bowl, mobile phone, modal verb, MP3 player, native speaker, navy blue, net surfer, next door, next to, no one, olive oil, on to, ought to, out of, owing to, pen friend, per cent, petrol station, phrasal verb, pocket money, point of view, polar bear, police officer, police station, post office, primary school, prime minister, public transport, question mark, real estate, remote control, rush hour, science fiction, second person, secondary school, shop assistant, sitting room, soap opera, social networking, soft drink, sports center, sports centre, steering wheel, stock market, swimming costume, swimming pool, table tennis, text message, third person, tour guide, traffic jam, traffic light, travel agent, upside down, used to, vice president, video clip, video game, virtual reality, washing machine, weather forecast, web page, worn out

Table 9.7 Summary of word counting units and rules

	NewJ8	*SVL*	*NGSL*	*CEFR-J*	*SEWK-J*
Total words	8,000	12,000	5,621	7,799	74,810
Lemma or flemma	Flemma	Flemma	Flemma	Lemma	Flemma
(F)lemma list	No	No	Yes	No	Yes
Capitalized	20	44	0	72	0
Case	Sensitive	Sensitive	Insensitive	Sensitive	Insensitive
Apostrophe	0	1	2	6	0
Abbreviation with period	0	4	0	8	0
Hyphen	0	0	3	62	0
Compound	0	0	1	145	0

Given the variability in rules and word definitions across the word lists in NWLC, direct comparisons are complex. To address this, I evaluated the coverage rates of each list, aiming to offer users a guideline for selecting the most suitable word list for specific educational needs.

While the focus of this description is on the word lists within NWLC in the Japanese EFL context, its implications are broader. The primary objective is to elucidate the characteristics and efficacy of these lists, extending the aforementioned guideline. Although the evaluation described below is based on a high-stakes test in Japan, the methodology and insights are applicable to other educational contexts and EFL/ESL settings. Thus, this description not only clarifies the challenges and opportunities within the Japanese context but also offers valuable insights for a broader audience.

An example of text was analyzed with NWLC using all five word lists. The text was composed of (a) the Center Test in 2020 and (b) the Kyotsu Test from 2021 to 2023, and both the reading and listening sections including the script for the listening section were used. The test materials were sourced from the National Center for University Entrance Examinations (www.dnc.ac.jp/) and are available for download in PDF format. These PDF files were then subjected to optical character recognition (OCR) to extract textual data, which served as the analytical corpus for this study. After deleting question numbers, symbols, and Japanese, the Center and Kyotsu Tests comprised 53,001 words. The Kyotsu Test (Kyotsu means 'common' in English), which was called the Center Test until 2020 with a different test format, is a standardized exam for students who intend to enter a national, public, or private university in Japan. Over 470,000 test-takers sat for the Kyotsu Test in 2023. As the Center and Kyotsu test items reflect the Course of Study (national curriculum guidelines) in Japan, the

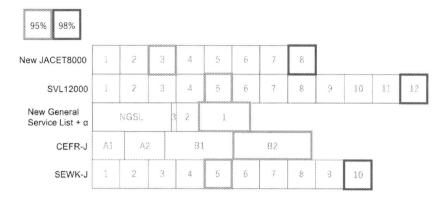

Figure 9.5 Coverage rates of five word lists in NWLC

Note: For New General Service List + α (three other lists), 3 indicates NAWL & TOEIC & BSL (183 words), 2 indicates NAWL & TOEIC, NAWL & BSL, or TOEIC & BSL (790 words), and 1 indicates that the word appears only in NAWL, TOEIC, or BSL (1,847 words). In this analysis, SEWK-J has only 10 levels, each with 1,000 words, for comparison with other lists.

test items from 2020 to 2023 used in this comparison can serve as a yardstick for evaluating the coverage rate, with each word list, of the standard English text that high school graduates in Japan are likely to encounter.

Figure 9.5 shows the results of the coverage rate of five word lists in NWLC. The level or category marked by the thick grey boxes indicates 95% coverage of the text by each word list. As is clear from the results, all five lists reach the 95% coverage threshold, which indicates that the vocabulary included in these word lists is within the range of practical use for this important, high-stakes test in Japan.

The thick black boxes in the figure indicate 98% coverage of the text by each word list. This result demonstrates that reaching the 98% coverage threshold, which is posited by vocabulary research literature (Schmitt et al., 2011), requires several thousands more words in New JACET8000, SVL12000, and SEWK-J. In the case of the NGSL plus the three secondary lists (NAWL, TOEIC, and BSL) and the CEFR-J, it was not possible to reach the 98% coverage threshold for the Center and Kyotsu Tests. This is not surprising given the fact that the number of words included in NGSL plus the three secondary lists is 5,621, and 7,815 for CEFR-J. It should be noted that when it comes to the coverage rate of text, CEFR-J has a disadvantage because it adopts the lemma counting unit, and the same word may have a different POS, which is not the case with the other four lists in NWLC; this means that many more lemmas are required to cover the same amount of text compared to flemmas.

From the results of the comparisons of word lists used in NWLC, it can be claimed that all word lists could be used to examine the coverage rate of text because all the lists proved to have sufficient coverage of English texts, up to 95%. Although only the results of analyzing one type of English text were reported in this article, the same tendency can also be observed with other texts.

If the purpose of using the list is to learn the first 3,000 words in the flemma form, NGSL may be a good choice. NGSL was reported to cover 92% of most general English texts (Browne et al., 2013). In this sense, the learning efficiency is much higher for learners. As CEFR-J distinguishes POS of the words, it could be used for assessing learners' productive vocabulary use in writing or speaking, which in turn implies that CEFR-J could be used to measure the depth of vocabulary knowledge.

Among New JACET8000, SVL12000, and SEWK-J, New JACET8000 had better coverage than the other two in the current comparisons. As New JACET8000 is an updated word list integrating other word lists derived from large corpora, the coverage performance seems to be better than other word lists. If the user needs to learn more than 8,000 words, which is what the New JACET8000 covers, the SVL12000 or SEWK-J could be utilized. In particular, the SEWK-J list contains 74,810 headwords, and thus it is possible to inspect how many words learners need to know to reach the 98% coverage threshold, which cannot be accomplished with the other word lists in NWLC.

Although the degree of coverage of texts can be used as a measure of how efficiently a word list represents a target register, word lists can also be used for other purposes. Notably, SEWK-J was not designed to increase coverage performance; rather, it was intended to map Japanese university students' vocabulary knowledge on the word list. In this sense, it is unique in that the rank order of the headwords in SEWK-J represents the likelihood that a word in the list is known to the learners in the target population (i.e., Japanese university students). Thus, while frequency-based lists are of great value in directing learners towards the most frequent—and so valued—words in a list, when matching learners with texts, we should consider basing tests and lexical profilers on what learners *do* know (i.e., by using word lists based on learners' actual vocabulary knowledge such as SEWK-J), rather than frequency-based lists, which indicate what learners *should* know (Schmitt et al., 2021). By matching learners with texts, vocabulary profiling will allow teachers and material developers to estimate how difficult candidate texts might actually be for learners at a given level of proficiency.

In terms of the assessment of vocabulary knowledge, word profilers and vocabulary tests should be based on the same word list scale to match the vocabulary level of a text with learners' lexical knowledge. To this end, the Vocableveltest.org website (https://vocableveltest.org/) can be utilized because it facilitates the creation and administration of meaning-recall vocabulary level tests, which better measure the type of vocabulary knowledge that can be employed when reading than meaning-recognition (multiple-choice or matching) tests (McLean et al., 2020; Stewart et al., 2021), on several of the same word lists that are used in NWLC (e.g., SEWK-J, NGSL, NAWL, TSL, and New JACET 8000).

NWLC as a data-driven learning tool

In the previous section, I demonstrated that NWLC is most commonly employed to check the level of vocabulary from built-in lists and assess how comprehensively these lists cover a given target text. This is often conducted by researchers or material developers. Similarly, NWLC allows learners to insert texts they are studying to identify specific words for further learning. Teachers can also use NWLC to analyze texts and select level-appropriate vocabulary for instructional purposes. For instance, the analysis of the Center and Kyotsu Tests revealed content words unique to the test—such as 'food', 'friend', 'dog', 'lunch', and 'money'—appear frequently. This utilization highlights NWLC's potential as a valuable data-driven learning (DDL) tool.

DDL is an inductive approach to foreign language learning that treats language as data and students as researchers undertaking guided discovery tasks (Johns, 1990). Underpinning this pedagogical approach is the data-information-knowledge paradigm, which is informed by a pattern-based approach to grammar and vocabulary, and a lexico-grammatical approach to language in general. The basic task in DDL is to identify patterns at all levels of language. As O'Keeffe (2021) notes, DDL is grounded in constructivist learning theory, which emphasizes learner-centered active knowledge construction through hypothesis testing and inductive corpus exploration. The independent discovery process aligns with constructivism's focus on inference, open-ended exploration, and learner autonomy. Furthermore, sociocultural theory highlights the role of scaffolding and mediation in DDL. Peer collaboration and teacher guidance can provide vital support as students analyze corpus data, balancing the constructivist emphasis on unguided discovery. From these findings, students can understand how certain lexico-grammatical items are typically used, informing their own usage in speaking and writing. DDL connects to key SLA notions like attention, noticing, input enhancement, and involvement load hypothesis (O'Keeffe, 2021). DDL concordances may increase input salience, aiding acquisition.

A wealth of primary studies and meta-analyses (e.g., Boulton & Cobb, 2017; Lee et al., 2019) have confirmed that DDL is effective for

Figure 9.6 Demonstration of contextual word analysis using NWLC's KWIC feature

the acquisition of lexico-grammatical items. Moreover, DDL is instrumental in fostering independent language learners, as it teaches them how to frame language questions and utilize resources to obtain and interpret data, thereby contributing to learner autonomy (Boulton, 2009).

Beyond merely identifying individual words, NWLC offers a more nuanced analysis of their contextual usage. Specifically, the tool allows for the exploration of formulaic sequences, which are recurrent combinations of words, such as collocations. Similar to dedicated corpus concordancing software like AntConc (Anthony, 2023), NWLC's 'Key Word in Context' (KWIC) feature displays concordance lines (see Figure 9.6). This feature provides both learners and teachers with deeper insights into lexical items, not limited to simple measures like frequency or difficulty level. For instance, in the previously analyzed Center and Kyotsu Tests,

NWLC's KWIC feature showed that the term 'experience' functions both as a verb and a noun. Detailed inspection of the concordance lines reveals that 'experience' appears 16 times as a verb and 19 times as a noun and is also used as a countable noun.

Building on the pedagogical implications of NWLC, specific guidelines can be developed for educators to harness its full potential. For instance, teachers can use the KWIC feature to create lesson plans that focus on the contextual usage of frequently occurring words like 'experience'. A classroom activity could involve students examining the concordance lines for 'experience' and categorizing its usage as a noun or a verb. This would not only deepen their understanding of the word but also improve their grammatical skills. Furthermore, teachers can use NWLC to tailor vocabulary lists that align with the curriculum and learning objectives. These lists can then be integrated into teaching materials such as quizzes or flashcards. By doing this, teachers can provide a more targeted and interactive vocabulary learning experience, thereby bridging the gap between technology and pedagogy.

In the broader 21st-century language learning landscape, mastering DDL tools like NWLC is essential. When combined with other resources like generative AI platforms such as ChatGPT, these tools offer a comprehensive approach to language instruction (see Mizumoto, 2023, for a research and practice framework). Therefore, NWLC has a significant role to play in the realm of resource utilization for language learning and teaching, setting the stage for future research and advancements in this area.

Conclusion

In this chapter, I have introduced NWLC, an online vocabulary profiling tool optimized for Japanese EFL learners. This tool was developed with the aim of offering a comprehensive and customizable vocabulary analysis, integrating various word lists like New JACET8000, SVL12000, NGSL, CEFR-J Wordlist, and SEWK-J, among others. I have discussed the different counting units and rules adopted in NWLC, such as flemma and lemma counting methods, and how these influence the vocabulary profile generated.

Furthermore, I have delved into the comparative study of the coverage rates of different word lists using standardized tests in Japan as a benchmark. These analyses revealed that all lists are effective up to a 95% coverage rate for these high-stakes tests. This has significant implications for material developers and educators in selecting the most appropriate word list for their specific needs.

Lastly, I have explored the potential of NWLC as a tool for DDL. With features like KWIC concordance lines, NWLC offers nuanced analysis of lexico-grammatical patterns, making it a powerful resource not just for researchers, but also for teachers and learners. It complements other language resources, thus setting the stage for future research and advancements in vocabulary profiling and EFL learning and teaching.

New vocabulary lists for general purposes (e.g., Cobb & Laufer, 2021) and discipline-specific lists based on corpora (e.g., Miller, 2022) continue to be developed to this day. Their usefulness is beyond doubt; however, they are primarily intended for researchers and material developers, not for learners and teachers. This gap is where tools like NWLC, which enables the effective use of vocabulary lists, bridge theory and practice. The more specific the demography and needs of the learners, the more specialized lists are developed. Concurrently, profiling tools are also developed to convey their benefits to learners and teachers, empowering them in the process. With advancements in specific applications, the accessibility of vocabulary lists and profiling tools is likely to improve (e.g., Finlayson et al., 2023), allowing learners and teachers to independently customize these resources, thus enhancing the efficiency of learning and teaching vocabulary. I hope that this chapter has elucidated the latent potential of NWLC in this regard.

Further reading

1. Finlayson, N., Marsden, E., & Anthony, L. (2023). Introducing Multilingprofiler: An adaptable tool for analysing the vocabulary in French, German, and Spanish texts. *System*, *118*, 103122. https://doi.org/10.1016/j.system.2023.103122

This paper introduces a tool called MultilingProfiler for analyzing vocabulary in French, German, and Spanish texts. It allows customization of word counting units and can handle the complex language systems. It also profiles texts against various word lists and provides detailed statistics. The paper presents two case studies demonstrating the tool's use in creating leveled texts for different learner groups.

2. Nation, I. S. P. (2016). *Making and using word lists for language learning and testing*. John Benjamins. https://doi.org/10.1075/z.208

This book is a practical guide for vocabulary researchers and curriculum designers on creating useful word lists for language teaching and testing. It focuses on key considerations like corpus design, counting units, and definitions of 'words' when developing frequency-based lists. The author draws on existing research to provide guidelines on these factors, aiming to aid the development of word lists that effectively inform vocabulary instruction, materials, and assessment.

3. Pinchbeck, G. G., Brown, D., Mclean, S., & Kramer, B. (2022). Validating word lists that represent learner knowledge in EFL contexts: The impact of

the definition of word and the choice of source corpora. *System*, *106*, 102771. https://doi.org/10.1016/j.system.2022.102771

This paper investigates how word lists created from corpus data can best represent the vocabulary knowledge of EFL learners. It compares different definitions of words (word type, lemma, flemma, and word family) and different types of corpora to see which ones correlate most with learner word knowledge. It finds that flemma-based word lists are more predictive of learner knowledge than word-family-based lists across 18 corpora.

Acknowledgments

This research was made possible by a Grant-in-aid for Scientific Research (21H00553) from the Japan Society for the Promotion of Science.

References

Anthony, L. (2023). AntConc (Version 4.2.3) [Computer Software]. www.laurenceanthony.net/software

Boulton, A. (2009). Testing the limits of data-driven learning: Language proficiency and training. *ReCALL*, *1*(21), 81–87. https://doi.org/10.1007/s13398-014-0173-7.2

Boulton, A., & Cobb, T. (2017). Corpus use in language learning: A meta-analysis. *Language Learning*, *67*(2), 348–393. https://doi.org/10.1111/lang.12224

Browne, C., Culligan, B., & Phillips, J. (2013). *New general service list project*. www.newgeneralservicelist.com/

Cobb, T., & Laufer, B. (2021). The nuclear word family list: A list of the most frequent family members, including base and affixed words. *Language Learning*, *71*(3), 834–871. https://doi.org/10.1111/lang.12452

Finlayson, N., Marsden, E., & Anthony, L. (2023). Introducing Multilingprofiler: An adaptable tool for analysing the vocabulary in French, German, and Spanish texts. *System*, *118*, 103122. https://doi.org/10.1016/j.system.2023.103122

Japan Association of College English Teachers (JACET). (2003). *JACET8000*.

Japan Association of College English Teachers (JACET). (2016). *The new JACET list of 8000 basic words*. Kirihara Shoten.

Johns, T. (1990). From printout to handout: Grammar and vocabulary teaching in the context of data-driven learning. *CALL Austria*, *10*, 14–34.

Lee, H., Warschauer, M., & Lee, J. H. (2019). The effects of corpus use on second language vocabulary learning: A multilevel meta-analysis. *Applied Linguistics*, *40*(5), 721–753. https://doi.org/10.1093/applin/amy012

McLean, S. (2018). Evidence for the adoption of the flemma as an appropriate word counting unit. *Applied Linguistics*, *39*(6), 823–845. https://doi.org/10.1093/applin/amw050

McLean, S., & Kramer, B. (2016). The development of a Japanese bilingual version of the New Vocabulary Levels Test. *Vocabulary Education and Research Bulletin (VERB)*, *5*(1), 2–5.

McLean, S., Stewart, J., & Batty, A. O. (2020). Predicting L2 reading proficiency with modalities of vocabulary knowledge: A bootstrapping approach. *Language Testing*, *37*(3), 389–411. https://doi.org/10.1177/0265532219898380

Miller, D. (2022). Replication as a means of assessing corpus representativeness and the generalizability of specialized word lists. *Applied Corpus Linguistics*, *2*(3), 100027. https://doi.org/10.1016/j.acorp.2022.100027

Mizumoto, A. (2023). Data-driven learning meets generative AI: Introducing the framework of metacognitive resource use. *Applied Corpus Linguistics*, *3*(3), 100074. https://doi.org/10.1016/j.acorp.2023.100074

Nation, I. S. P. (2016). *Making and using word lists for language learning and testing*. John Benjamins. https://doi.org/10.1075/z.208

Nation, P. (2012). *The BNC/COCA word family lists*. Victoria University of Wellington, New Zealand. www.wgtn.ac.nz/__data/assets/pdf_file/0004/1689349/Information-on-the-BNC_COCA-word-family-lists-20180705.pdf

O'Keeffe, A. (2021). Data-driven learning: A call for a broader research gaze. *Language Teaching*, *54*, 259–272. https://doi.org/10.1017/S0261444820000245

Pigada, M., & Schmitt, N. (2006). Vocabulary acquisition from extensive reading: A case study. *Reading in a Foreign Language*, *18*(1), 1–28. https://nflrc.hawaii.edu/rfl/item/114

Pinchbeck, G. G. (2014, March). *Lexical frequency profiling of a large sample of Canadian high school diploma exam expository writing: L1 and L2 academic English* [Roundtable presentation]. American Association for Applied Linguistics Annual Conference 2014, Portland, Oregon. https://app.box.com/s/2772oofxkg6jyzmd3l7j

Pinchbeck, G. G. (2017). *Vocabulary use in academic-track high-school English literature diploma exam essay writing and its relationship to academic achievement* [Doctoral dissertation, University of Calgary]. https://prism.ucalgary.ca/handle/11023/3676

Pinchbeck, G. G., Brown, D., Mclean, S., & Kramer, B. (2022). Validating word lists that represent learner knowledge in EFL contexts: The impact of the definition of word and the choice of source corpora. *System*, *106*, 102771. https://doi.org/10.1016/j.system.2022.102771

Schmitt, N., Dunn, K., O'Sullivan, B., Anthony, L., & Kremmel, B. (2021). Introducing knowledge-based vocabulary lists (KVL). *TESOL Journal*, *12*(4), e622. https://doi.org/10.1002/tesj.622

Schmitt, N., Jiang, X., & Grabe, W. (2011). The percentage of words known in a text and reading comprehension. *The Modern Language Journal*, *95*(1), 26–43. https://doi.org/10.1111/j.1540-4781.2011.01146.x

Someya, Y. (2006). *Word level checker* [Web app]. https://mizumot.com/wlc/

Stewart, J., Stoeckel, T., McLean, S., Nation, P., & Pinchbeck, G. G. (2021). What the research shows about written receptive vocabulary testing: A reply to Webb. *Studies in Second Language Acquisition*, *43*(2), 462–471. https://doi.org/10.1017/S0272263121000437

Tono, Y. (2019). *CEFR-J Wordlist version 1.5*. www.cefr-j.org/download.html#cefrj_wordlist

West, M. (1953). *A general service list of English words*. Longman.

10 Mobile-assisted vocabulary learning in an EAP context

Jeong-Bae Son and Sang-Soon Park
University of Southern Queensland, Australia

Pre-reading questions

1. How can EAP students improve their academic vocabulary knowledge?
2. How can mobile devices be used for academic vocabulary learning?
3. How can online vocabulary learning activities be designed for EAP students?

Background

Points of departure

It is essential for English for academic purposes (EAP) students to increase their academic vocabulary knowledge, which is a key component of academic success (Gardner & Davies, 2014; Nagy & Townsend, 2012; Nation, 2001). With an increasing need for the use of technology in EAP teaching, it is also important for EAP teachers to integrate technology into their EAP courses (Arnó-Macià, 2012). Lawrence et al. (2020) point out the need for the effective use of technology in EAP programs. Taking into consideration the questions of how to improve EAP students' academic vocabulary knowledge and how to offer the students opportunities to learn academic English words in digital environments, the study reported in this chapter explores EAP students' experiences in informal mobile-assisted academic vocabulary learning (i.e., academic vocabulary learning with mobile devices outside formal classrooms). The study involved designing online vocabulary learning activities using online tools such as *Quizlet* (https://quizlet.com/), which is a mobile and web-based study application offering flashcards, games, and quiz activities, and *Kahoot!* (https://kahoot.com/), which is a game-based learning tool with a classroom response system. Both tools were freely available and easy to access in the context of the study. The activities were then used and evaluated by two groups of EAP students who could access them with their mobile devices in and out of the classroom.

DOI: 10.4324/9781003367543-12

Academic vocabulary learning

Academic vocabulary is a key element of academic communication. Coxhead and Nation (2001) divide English vocabulary into four groups: high frequency words; academic vocabulary; technical vocabulary; and low frequency words. While emphasizing the importance of specialized English vocabulary, they state that academic vocabulary is "common to a wide range of academic texts, and generally not so common in non-academic texts" (p. 254). Paquot (2010) defines academic vocabulary as "a set of options to refer to those activities that characterize academic work, organize scientific discourse and build the rhetoric of academic texts" (p. 28). She asserts that "EAP courses need to ensure that sufficient attention is given to vocabulary development" (p. 26).

Previous studies such as Park and Son (2011) and Son and Park (2014) reported that non-English speaking background (NESB) university students strongly felt that they should expand their knowledge of academic vocabulary. In this respect, it should be valuable to provide NESB students with quality resources (e.g., a context-specific vocabulary list, a discipline-specific vocabulary list) which help them improve their vocabulary knowledge. Although there is some disagreement about the need for a single core vocabulary list and the effects of teaching general academic vocabulary items in different disciplines (e.g., Hyland & Tse, 2007), the value of academic vocabulary knowledge is generally accepted, and the development of academic vocabulary lists for direct teaching is commonly encouraged in EAP programs (e.g., Coxhead, 2000; Gardner & Davies, 2014; Paquot, 2010). While pointing out that disciplines clearly differ in vocabulary use, Durrant (2016) also supports the idea that frequency-based vocabulary lists can be a reference point that informs "pedagogical decisions" (p. 51). Lists of academic words can be devised to achieve specific learning goals and can be "a very valuable part of a learner's vocabulary" (Coxhead & Nation, 2001, p. 267). Related to this point, there have been a number of specialized academic word lists (e.g., Li & Qian, 2010; Martinez et al., 2009; O'Flynn, 2019; Vongpumivitch et al., 2009; Wang et al., 2008).

In the present study, Son's (2019) academic English word list (AEWL) was used in creating online vocabulary learning activities in a specific EAP context. The list was originally developed as an academic vocabulary resource for NESB students in EAP programs and compiled from an analysis of Coxhead's (2000) academic word list (AWL: 570 words), Paquot's (2010) academic keyword list (AKL: 930 words), Gardner and Davies's (2014) academic vocabulary list (AVL: 3014 lemmas), and academic words from various EAP materials and doctoral theses. It contains 450 words that are divided into three difficulty levels (from easiest to most difficult): Level 1 (320 words), Level 2 (82 words), and Level 3 (48 words). These difficulty levels are based on a survey of the 450 words with a group of EAP students, and the difficulty level of each word is not fixed and is subject to change.

Mobile-assisted vocabulary learning

Mobile-assisted language learning (MALL) offers opportunities to learn anytime and anywhere (Burston, 2014; Son, 2016). The potential of MALL has been discussed in a range of contexts (Burston, 2013), and the view that mobile technology can be useful for vocabulary learning has been supported by previous research (e.g., Chen et al., 2019; Daly, 2022; Ko, 2019; Lin & Lin, 2019). Kim et al. (2013), for example, examined 53 MA TESOL students' perceptions of the use of mobile devices for learning and the students' mobile language learning experiences in 12-week class projects. They divided the participants into two user groups based on the types of mobile devices the participants owned (i.e., smartphone and tablet user group; and mobile computer user group). Their findings indicate that those who owned smartphones or tablets were more likely to be receptive to innovation and eager to use mobile devices for their learning, while many of them tended to switch to a more comfortable means (e.g., laptops) of completing their tasks when they had issues with practicality and difficulty in using small mobile devices. They suggested that teachers should use mobile learning activities that are practical and meaningful to individual language learners.

In a different context, Tran (2016) investigated 21 Vietnamese English as a foreign language (EFL) learners' engagement in mobile-based vocabulary and grammar learning activities using *Quizlet*. She provided the learners with technical training in class and strategic and pedagogical training through in-class activities and *Facebook* (https://www.facebook.com/). She collected data from a learning journal, a *Facebook* page, a pre-questionnaire, a post-questionnaire, and a focus group discussion over a five-week period. She found that the learners' participation in *Quizlet* and *Facebook* was not high, but there was some possibility of using social networking such as *Facebook* as a support for learner training. Dizon (2016), on the other hand, examined the effects of using *Quizlet* on nine Japanese university students' academic vocabulary development. His EFL students studied Coxhead's (2000) AWL with *Quizlet* for ten weeks. He found that the students were able to demonstrate significant improvement in their post-test scores and showed positive attitudes toward the use of *Quizlet* for vocabulary learning. Bueno-Alastuey and Nemeth (2022) and Li and Hafner (2022) also reported similar positive attitudes associated with increased engagement with mobile-assisted vocabulary learning.

Through a four-week experimental study, Chen et al. (2019) investigated the effects of a mobile English vocabulary learning app on 20 EFL learners' perceptions and learning performance. Their experimental group used the app with gamified functions such as gamified assessment and ranking of learning peers while their control group used the app without gamified functions. They found that, in vocabulary acquisition and retention, the experimental group's performance was significantly higher than the control group's performance. They also found that those learners in the experimental group rated the app as more effective and more satisfactory than those learners in the control group. Based on these findings, they argued that mobile game-based learning is helpful in promoting learners' motivation for vocabulary learning, leading to improved learning outcomes.

As shown in the studies reviewed above, there has been increasing attention on mobile-assisted vocabulary learning. However, little attention has been given to the implementation of informal mobile-assisted vocabulary learning in EAP contexts. The present study addresses this gap. Mobile-assisted vocabulary learning activities can be more attractive to learners than merely memorizing lists. They can be presented in a variety of formats (e.g., text, audio, video, animation). In response to the importance of activity design (Son, 2018), the instructional design of mobile-assisted vocabulary learning activities needs to be widely discussed and examined in MALL in order to take advantage of mobile pedagogies and technologies.

Method

Design and aims

The study used a mixed methods research design together with a quasi-experimental one-group pre-test-post-test design. It consisted of two sub-studies: Sub-Study 1 (eight weeks) and Sub-Study 2 (eight weeks). Each sub-study was conducted with a different group of students in a different term. The study aimed to investigate EAP students' experiences in informal mobile-assisted vocabulary learning and find out the students' attitudes toward mobile-assisted vocabulary learning and how they used mobile learning activities outside the classroom. To achieve these aims, the following research questions were addressed:

1. What are EAP students' attitudes toward mobile-assisted vocabulary learning?
2. How do the students use a specific range of mobile-assisted vocabulary learning activities to improve their academic vocabulary knowledge?

3. What effects do the activities have on the students' academic vocabulary development?

Participants

Participants in the study were two groups of EAP students who enrolled respectively in an elective course offered by an EAP program at an Australian university in a ten-week term. The course normally had 7–10 students in each term. The entry requirements for the EAP program were IELTS 5.5 or equivalent. A total of 17 students (ten students in Sub-Study 1 and seven different students in Sub-Study 2) agreed to participate in the study by completing a consent form prior to the study, in accordance with the ethics guidelines of the university. They all possessed their own mobile devices such as smartphones and laptops at the time of the study. Table 10.1 shows demographic information on the participants.

Instruments

In each sub-study, data were collected from a pre-questionnaire, a pre-test, discussion forums in a learning management system (Moodle), a post-questionnaire, a post-test, and focus group discussions. The pre-questionnaire (consisting of six short answer questions and one 5-point Likert scale question containing ten statements to respond to) was

Table 10.1 Participant profiles

	Sub-Study 1 (n = 10)	Sub-Study 2 (n = 7)
Gender	8 males 2 females	6 males 1 female
Age	Ranging from 21 to 31 (Mean: 26 years old)	Ranging from 21 to 31 (Mean: 28 years old)
Native language	2 Chinese 2 Gujarati 2 Nepali 1 Arabic 1 Hindi 1 Kurdish 1 Punjabi	2 Chinese 2 Gujarati 2 Nepali 1 Russian
Length of smartphone ownership	Less than 1 year: 1 (10%) 1–5 years: 8 (80%) Over 5 years: 1 (10%)	Less than 1 year: 2 (29%) 1–5 years: 4 (57%) Over 5 years: 1 (14%)

Note. N = 17

employed to document the participants' background, while the post-questionnaire (consisting of four short answer questions, two 5-point Likert scale questions each containing ten statements to respond to, and five open-ended questions) was employed to document the participants' experiences with mobile-assisted vocabulary learning. The pre-test and the post-test consisted of 20 vocabulary questions each. Among the 20 words given in the pre-test, ten words were practiced together with 38 other words through the online learning activities in each sub-study. The post-test consisted of the same 20 vocabulary questions as the pre-test – this means that a half of the post-test (ten questions) could be considered a proficiency test (measuring general vocabulary knowledge) whereas the half of the post-test (another ten questions) could be considered an achievement test (measuring knowledge learned through the online learning activities). The sequence of questions in the post-test was different from the sequence used for the pre-test. For the online discussion forums on Moodle, the participants were given five guiding questions for weekly posts (e.g., asking when and how they used the activities). For the focus group discussions, on the other hand, the participants (3–5 participants in a group) were given seven guiding questions they could discuss (e.g., asking which activities they liked and disliked) and asked to come out with group answers at the end of the discussions.

Procedures

The participants in each sub-study were asked to complete the pre-questionnaire in the first week of the study and then the pre-test in the second week of the study. After the pre-test, the participants were given 30-minute learner training that was offered to help them understand what digital technologies, digital devices, and MALL are, and guide them on how to use the mobile learning tools and activities. Once they had been introduced to the mobile learning activities using *Quizlet* and *Kahoot!*, they were encouraged to explore the activities themselves (for information on types of *Quizlet* activities, see https://quizlet.com/en-gb/features/study-modes; and for information on how *Kahoot!* works, see https://kahoot.com/schools/how-it-works/). From the third week to the sixth week (four weeks), all participants were invited to use the activities with their mobile devices and participate in the discussion forums on Moodle. Each week the participants were given 12 new academic English words through both the *Quizlet* and *Kahoot!* activities. In the seventh week, the participants completed the post-questionnaire and the post-test, which were followed by the focus group discussions (20 minutes each) in the eighth week. All groups in the focus group discussions, which were audio recorded, submitted a written summary of their group responses to the guiding questions at the end of the discussions. Two researchers independently coded qualitative data into common themes and then finalized the themes through an agreement.

Results

Questionnaires

There was a difference in the way the groups in Sub-Study 1 and Sub-Study 2 viewed their self-perceived competence in digital literacy. All participants in Sub-Study 1 had initially indicated that their abilities to use digital technologies were good or very good, but 30% of the participants changed their ratings of their self-perceived digital literacy level to acceptable at the end of the study. On the other hand, the participants in Sub-Study 2 had indicated that their digital literacy level was varied: poor (14%), acceptable (29%), good (14%), and very good (43%). At the end of the study, however, they rated their digital literacy as good (71%) or very good (29%).

Table 10.2 shows the average ratings of the participants' attitudes toward the use of digital technologies and tools. In the pre-questionnaire and post-questionnaire, overall, the two different groups from the two sub-studies indicated that they had more positive attitudes at the end of the study. There were also some exceptions. After they experienced mobile-assisted vocabulary learning, for example, the Sub-Study 1 participants indicated that they felt somehow less comfortable using digital devices, while the Sub-Study 2 participants indicated that they were a little less aware of various types of digital devices. Another thing to note is that the Sub-Study 2 participants expressed the view that they were much more willing to learn more about digital technologies than before.

Regarding their mobile learning experiences, both groups in the two sub-studies generally indicated that their experiences were positive by choosing "Agree" or "Strongly agree" on the scale (see Table 10.3). It is noted that the Sub-Study 1 participants' positive responses to the question of whether they gained confidence in their ability to use mobile devices for learning purposes was slightly weaker than other items. Another thing to note is that both groups indicated that *Quizlet* was a bit more useful than *Kahoot!* for their learning.

Through their responses to the open questions in the post-questionnaires, the participants in both sub-studies made meaningful comments. In response to the question of whether the mobile activities were helpful for their academic vocabulary learning, all students said "Yes". The following are some example responses:

Table 10.2 Average ratings of attitudes toward digital technologies and tools

	Sub-Study 1 (n = 10)		Sub-Study 2 (n = 7)	
	Pre-questionnaire	Post-questionnaire	Pre-questionnaire	Post-questionnaire
I enjoy using digital devices.	4.6	4.5	4.3	4.4
I feel comfortable using digital devices.	4.4	3.9	4.1	4.3
I am aware of various types of digital devices.	4.2	4.0	4.4	4.1
I am willing to learn more about digital technologies.	4.4	4.3	4.1	4.9
I feel threatened when others talk about digital technologies.	2.1	2.4	2.3	2.4
I feel that I am behind my fellow students in using digital technologies.	2.8	2.9	2.9	2.3
I think that it is important for me to improve my digital fluency.	3.6	3.9	4.3	4.9
I think that my language learning can be enhanced by using digital tools and resources.	4.0	4.2	4.3	4.3
I think that my academic vocabulary learning can be enhanced by using digital tools and resources.	4.0	4.1	4.1	4.6
I think that training in technology-enhanced language learning should be included in language education programs.	4.1	4.2	4.3	4.4

Note. 1 Strongly disagree; 2 Disagree; 3 Uncertain; 4 Agree; 5 Strongly agree

Table 10.3 Average ratings of mobile-assisted vocabulary learning experiences

	Sub-Study 1 (n = 10) Post-questionnaire	Sub-Study 2 (n = 7) Post-questionnaire
I enjoyed the online vocabulary learning activities.	4.1	4.4
I found the mobile activities helpful for my vocabulary learning.	4.0	4.7
I was comfortable using mobile devices during the online vocabulary learning activities.	4.3	4.7
The online vocabulary learning activities were valuable for learning academic English words.	4.6	4.7
The experiences in mobile-assisted language learning made this course more interesting.	4.2	4.1
I gained confidence in my ability to use mobile devices for learning purposes.	3.7	4.3
I am now comfortable using mobile devices for language learning.	4.1	4.7
I think that *Quizlet* is a useful learning tool.	4.5	4.6
I think that *Kahoot!* is a useful learning tool.	4.2	3.9
I would like to use online learning tools myself outside class time.	4.1	4.9

Note. 1 Strongly disagree; 2 Disagree; 3 Uncertain; 4 Agree; 5 Strongly agree

> *Yes, the mobile activities were helpful for my academic vocabulary learning because they gave me knowledge of how they are used, when and where.* (Participant S1-1)
>
> *Yes, they were helpful because they allowed me to learn a lot of academic words in an interesting way.* (Participant S1-6)
>
> *Yes, by using them, I can study words at any time.* (Participant S2-4)
>
> *Yes, the mobile activities were helpful for academic vocabulary learning because they helped me remember terms and words that are beneficial for my study.* (Participant S2-7)

In terms of the selection of online tools, most participants indicated that, as noted earlier in the results of the post-questionnaires, they tended to prefer *Quizlet* although they all found both *Quizlet* and *Kahoot!* were helpful to them:

> *While both Quizlet and Kahoot are very helpful for learning new vocabulary, I think that Quizlet is more helpful for me.* (Participant S2-1)

Both Quizlet and Kahoot are beneficial, but I feel that Quizlet is particularly very useful because I can learn word meanings and do practices, which help me correct my spellings and evaluate myself how much I remembered. (Participant S2-7)

When the participants were asked about the strengths of MALL, they mentioned easy access and convenience of use as two main strengths:

Mobile devices are convenient to use anytime and anywhere. (Participant S1-1)
It is easy to use anywhere and anytime. (Participant S1-5)
Easy to use and convenient because I can use it anytime, anywhere. (Participant S2-4)
They are easy to use; they are effective and efficient as well; we do not have to engage in it for long time; repeating nature of the activities was helpful. (Participant S2-6)

When they were asked about the weaknesses of MALL, on the other hand, most participants indicated that there were no particular weaknesses, while a few participants pointed out difficulty in concentrating (three participants) or small screen size (two participants). For example:

Difficult to concentrate on small screen for long time; mind gets diverted to other social media apps than learning applications. (Participant S1-2)
Maybe when I use the phone to assist in learning, it is hard to concentrate because I always want to play others such as games or communicating with other people. (Participant S1-9)
For me, I prefer using my laptop because the screen size on our mobiles is still small. (Participant S1-6)

Other comments include the following:

At the moment, I am using Quizlet and Kahoot as online learning platforms and I have found some improvement in my vocabulary, so I recommend them to other students. (Participant S1-2)
I really like to use mobile devices to study. I will use them in my leisure time in a day. Maybe 5–10 minutes each day. Repeating words is a good way to help me remember those words. (Participant S1-9)
These applications are very useful because they helped us learn more words, but more examples would be more beneficial. (Participant S2-7)

Table 10.4 Results of the pre-test and the post-test

		Pre-test (out of 20)	Post-test (out of 20)
Sub-Study 1 (n = 10)	Score range	4–14	6–17
	Mean	8.9 (44.5%)	12.2 (61%)
Sub-Study 2 (n = 7)	Score range	6–14	8–20
	Mean	10.3 (51.5%)	13.6 (68%)

Tests

As mentioned earlier, 20 vocabulary questions were set in the pre-test and another 20 in the post-test. Table 10.4 shows the participants' scores from the pre-test and the post-test. The Sub-Study 1 participants' mean scores were 8.9 in the pre-test and 12.2 in the post-test, while the Sub-Study 2 participants' mean scores were 10.3 in the pre-test and 13.6 in the post-test. A paired t-test showed that, in Sub-Study 1, there was a significant difference in the scores for the pre-test (M = 8.9, SD = 3.35) and the post-test (M = 12.2, SD = 3.23): $t(9) = 3.25$, $p = 0.01$. Similarly, in Sub-Study 2, there was also a significant difference in the scores for the pre-test (M = 10.3, SD = 2.60) and the post-test (M = 13.6, SD = 4.20): $t(6) = 3.16$, $p = 0.02$.

Discussion forums

All participants posted their responses to the five guiding questions in the discussion forums on Moodle every Friday or Saturday for the specified four weeks. Their overall responses to the first question of when and which devices they used for the mobile activities indicate that nine students (53%) used smartphones, four students (23.5%) used laptops, and another four students (23.5%) used both smartphones and laptops at various times, including morning, afternoon, evening, night, and/or weekends. The length of time they engaged with the mobile activities was from five minutes per day or 30 minutes per week on 2–3 days to 20 minutes per day or 120 minutes per week on 4–5 days. The participants' posts in the discussion forums also indicate that they all felt that the mobile activities were useful for their vocabulary learning and they could enjoy them. A Sub-Study 2 participant's weekly posts below show how he/she felt about the mobile learning throughout the four weeks:

> *I really like Kahoot and Quizlet. I think that they can help me remember word meanings.* (Participant S1-8's first week discussion forum post)

I feel that the use of the apps is more convincing than online links. I think that it is useful to learn new vocabulary. (Participant S1-8's second week discussion forum post)

I enjoy using them very much. I feel them very useful. As those words are academic words, I can use them in my academic papers. (Participant S1-8's third week discussion forum post)

I like using these two apps to learn academic vocabulary, and I find that I remember those words for a long term. (Participant S1-8's fourth week discussion forum post)

Similar to the results of the post-questionnaires, most participants from both sub-studies indicated in their discussion forum posts that they liked both apps, although the number of participants who preferred *Quizlet* was a little higher than the number of participants who preferred *Kahoot!*. The following comments from three participants briefly summarize how they regarded the apps:

With Quizlet we learn new words, and Kahoot allows us to review those words. (Participant S1-9's second week discussion forum post)

Both applications are beneficial to all the students, and I hope in future other useful activities are added for our study. (Participant S1-7's third week discussion forum post)

I liked Kahoot before because it was interesting. However, I now find Quizlet more helpful because it allows me to study by using flashcards to remember words at any time. (Participant S2-6's third week discussion forum post)

Focus group discussions

For the focus group discussions, the Sub-Study 1 participants (n = 10) were divided into two groups of five participants, while the Sub-Study 2 participants (n = 7) were divided into one group of three participants and one of four. The four groups' overall responses to the seven guiding questions were similar to the results of the post-questionnaires and the discussion forums reported earlier. In response to the question about their views on the vocabulary learning activities, for example, the groups summarized their responses as follows:

Easy to visualize (remember); learn pronunciation; fun. (Group S1-A)
New learning approach. (Group S1-B)
We think that online vocabulary activities are convenient, beneficial. They also improve our vocabulary knowledge. (Group S2-A)

Online vocabulary learning activities are very useful to improve our vocabulary, which we can use in our current courses as well as for future. (Group S2-B)

The groups also made the following comments:

It is a different learning method, which gives people other styles of learning. We feel that it is suitable for us. (Group S1-A)
It is a good idea for blended learning practice. (Group S1-B)
It would be better if there would be some examples of the words in sentences. (Group S2-A)
At first, it was quite difficult for us to engage in it. However, as time passes by, we got used to it and started enjoying it. (Group S2-B)

These responses confirm that all groups found the mobile activities useful for their vocabulary learning and wanted to have more online learning activities.

New understandings

The study involved designing academic vocabulary learning activities, implementing learner training, and using mobile devices for self-directed learning. Findings indicate that it was a worthwhile effort. Mobile-assisted vocabulary learning was a new experience to the EAP students who participated in the study. They generally found it helpful and enjoyable, and showed considerable interest in the use of digital tools and resources for further learning. They valued anywhere anytime learning using mobile devices and appreciated vocabulary learning with the mobile activities. This finding is similar to the results of Chen et al. (2019) who reported that online vocabulary learning enhanced their students' motivation.

As seen from the post-questionnaires, the discussion forums, and the focus group discussions, the participants' overall reactions to their mobile-assisted vocabulary learning experience were positive, while the participants in Sub-Study 2 showed more positive attitudes toward and more comfort with MALL than the participants in Sub-Study 1. With regard to the weaknesses of mobile learning, three participants mentioned difficulty in concentrating, and two participants mentioned small screen size, which was an issue raised in Kim et al. (2013). It was also found that some of the participants became more realistic in assessing their digital literacy and realized the need to improve their digital competence and have more digital language learning opportunities. This finding can be considered to be positive and encourages the development and implementation of more MALL activities in and out of the language classroom.

In relation to learner engagement, the participants used smartphones only, laptops only, or both smartphones and laptops to engage with the online learning activities for 5–20 minutes in each attempt on a regular basis. While they liked both *Quizlet* and *Kahoot!*, there was some preference for *Quizlet*, which allowed them to learn new academic English words first before moving to challenge mode in *Kahoot!*. This finding supports Dizon's (2016) study on the positive use of *Quizlet* for vocabulary learning. Through weekly posts in the discussion forums and contributions to the focus group discussions, the participants were guided and encouraged to reflect and express themselves on their mobile learning experiences. As a result, they could become self-reflective learners who thought about what they learned and how they developed critical thinking skills. This was demonstrated by their regular posts in the discussion forums and active contributions to the focus group discussions.

In terms of the participants' vocabulary development, there were significant differences between the pre-test scores and the post-test scores in both Sub-Study 1 and Sub-Study 2. However, any suggestion that the improvement in the participants' vocabulary knowledge came about solely because of the MALL activities needs to be treated with caution. The time the participants spent in their EAP program and the learning they gained from their EAP courses could also be factors contributing to their vocabulary development. Nevertheless, it can be stated that there were positive overall outcomes in the participants' learning achievements, and the mobile-assisted vocabulary learning activities were helpful in increasing the participants' knowledge of the selected academic English words.

Implications

As a way to help EAP students improve their academic vocabulary knowledge, mobile-assisted academic vocabulary learning using online tools was designed, implemented, and evaluated in the study. After it was introduced to the students in the classroom, the students were guided to use the tools and activities informally outside the classroom whenever they wanted. The study found that the students showed positive attitudes toward MALL, and the mobile activities they used regularly during the specific period of time were helpful for their academic vocabulary learning. This suggests that informal mobile-assisted vocabulary learning as part of EAP programs can be regarded positively, and online learning resources and activities containing context-specific academic vocabulary can be useful for EAP students. Therefore, EAP teachers are encouraged to develop their digital competence and explore the possibility of using mobile devices and the provision of learner training and mobile activities for their students.

Limitations of the study include the small number of the participants recruited from only one EAP program at one university and the lack of random assignment, which is a weakness of quasi-experimental designs (Head & Harsin, 2017). Also, the duration of the study was short; the number of items in the vocabulary tests was small; and the study focused on only two online tools. Therefore, the results of the study cannot be generalized, and it would be beneficial to avoid these limitations in future studies. The study, however, offers some insights into the implementation of mobile-assisted vocabulary learning in an EAP context. The findings of the study contribute to our understanding and knowledge of the use of informal mobile-assisted academic vocabulary learning. Further research is recommended to find out whether other types of online tools and mobile activities are useful for academic vocabulary learning and how they can be used effectively in various contexts.

Further reading

Daly, N. P. (2022). Investigating learner autonomy and vocabulary learning efficiency with MALL. *Language Learning & Technology*, 26(1), 1–30. https://doi.org/10125/73469
This article presents the results of a study that evaluated the effectiveness of individual vocabulary learning strategies: only flashcard app; paper-based notes and word lists; and both notes and the flashcard app.

Li, Y., & Hafner, C. A. (2022). Mobile-assisted vocabulary learning: Investigating receptive and productive vocabulary knowledge of Chinese EFL learners. *ReCALL*, 34(1), 66–80. https://doi.org/10.1017/S0958344021000161
This article presents the results of a study that investigated English vocabulary learning in a mobile learning group and a paper-based learning group. The mobile application group showed greater gains than the physical word card group.

Wang, A. I., & Tahir, R. (2020). The effect of using Kahoot! for learning – A literature review. *Computers & Education*, 149, 103818. https://doi.org/10.1016/j.compedu.2020.103818
This article presents a literature review on the effects of using *Kahoot!* for learning, with a specific focus on learning performance, classroom dynamics, and students' and teachers' attitudes and perceptions.

References

Arnó-Macià, E. (2012). The role of technology in teaching languages for specific purposes courses. *The Modern Language Journal*, 96(Supplement 1), 89–104. https://doi.org/10.1111/j.1540-4781.2012.01299.x

Bueno-Alastuey, M. C., & Nemeth, K. (2022). Quizlet and podcasts: Effects on vocabulary acquisition. *Computer Assisted Language Learning*, 35(7), 1407–1436. https://doi.org/10.1080/09588221.2020.1802601

Burston, J. (2013). Mobile-assisted language learning: A selected annotated bibliography of implementation studies 1994–2012. *Language Learning & Technology*, 17(3), 157–225. https://doi.org/10125/44344

Burston, J. (2014). MALL: The pedagogical challenges. *Computer Assisted Language Learning*, 24(4), 344–357. https://doi.org/10.1080/09588 221.2014.914539

Chen, C.-M., Liu, H., & Huang, H.-B. (2019). Effects of a mobile game-based English vocabulary learning app on learners' perceptions and learning performance: A case study of Taiwanese EFL learners. *ReCALL*, 31(2), 170–188. https://doi.org/10.1017/s0958344018000228

Coxhead, A. (2000). A new academic word list. *TESOL Quarterly*, 34(2), 213–38. https://doi.org/10.2307/3587951

Coxhead, A., & Nation, P. (2001). The specialised vocabulary of English for academic purposes. In J. Flowerdew & M. Peacock (Eds.), *Research perspectives on English for academic purposes* (pp. 252–267). Cambridge University Press.

Daly, N. P. (2022). Investigating learner autonomy and vocabulary learning efficiency with MALL. *Language Learning & Technology*, 26(1), 1–30. https://doi.org/10125/73469

Dizon, G. (2016). Quizlet in the EFL classroom: Enhancing academic vocabulary acquisition of Japanese University students. *Teaching English with Technology*, 16(2), 40–56. https://tewtjournal.org/download/4-quizlet-in-the-efl-classroom-enhancing-academic-vocabulary-acquisition-of-japanese-university-students-by-gilbert-dizon/

Durrant, P. (2016). To what extent is the Academic Vocabulary List relevant to university student writing? *English for Specific Purposes*, 43, 49–61. https://doi.org/10.1016/j.esp.2016.01.004

Gardner, D., & Davies, M. (2014). A new academic vocabulary list. *Applied Linguistics*, 35(3), 305–327. https://doi.org/10.1093/applin/amt015

Head, K. J., & Harsin, A. M. (2017). Quasi-experimental design. In M. Allen (Ed.), *The SAGE encyclopedia of communication research methods* (pp. 1384–1387). SAGE Publications.

Hyland, K., & Tse, P. (2007). Is there an "academic vocabulary"? *TESOL Quarterly*, 41(2), 235–253. https://doi.org/10.1002/j.1545-7249.2007.tb00058.x

Kim, D., Rueckert, D., Kim, D.-J., & Seo, D. (2013). Students' perceptions and experiences of mobile learning. *Language Learning & Technology*, 17(3), 52–73. https://doi.org/10125/44339

Ko, M.-H. (2019). Students' reactions to using smartphones and social Media for Vocabulary Feedback. *Computer Assisted Language Learning*, 32(8), 920–944. https://doi.org/10.1080/09588221.2018.1541360

Lawrence, G., Ahmed, F., Cole, C., & Johnston, K. P. (2020). Not more technology but more effective technology: Examining the state of technology integration in EAP programmes. *RELC Journal*, 51(1), 101–116. https://doi.org/10.1177/0033688220907199

Li, Y., & Hafner, C. A. (2022). Mobile-assisted vocabulary learning: Investigating receptive and productive vocabulary knowledge of Chinese EFL learners. *ReCALL*, 34(1), 66–80. https://doi.org/10.1017/S0958344021000161

Li, Y., & Qian, D. (2010). Profiling the academic word list (AWL) in a financial corpus. *System*, *38*(3), 402–411. https://doi.org/10.1016/j.system.2010.06.015

Lin, J. J., & Lin, H. (2019). Mobile-assisted ESL/EFL vocabulary learning: A systematic review and meta-analysis. *Computer Assisted Language Learning*, *32*(8), 878–919. https://doi.org/10.1080/09588221.2018.1541359

Martinez, I. A., Beck, S. C., & Panza, C. B. (2009). Academic vocabulary in agriculture research articles: A corpus-based study. *English for Specific Purposes*, *28*(3), 183–198. https://doi.org/10.1016/j.esp.2009.04.003

Nagy, W., & Townsend, D. (2012). Words as tools: Learning academic vocabulary as language acquisition. *Reading Research Quarterly*, *47*(1), 91–108. https://doi.org/10.1002/RRQ.011

Nation, I. S. P. (2001). *Learning vocabulary in another language*. Cambridge University Press.

O'Flynn, J. (2019). An economics academic word list (EAWL): Using online resources to develop a subject-specific word list and associated teaching-learning materials. *Journal of Academic Language & Learning*, *13*(1), A28–A87. https://journal.aall.org.au/index.php/jall/article/view/592

Paquot, M. (2010). *Academic vocabulary in learner writing: From extraction to analysis*. Continuum International.

Park, S.-S., & Son, J.-B. (2011). Language difficulties and cultural challenges of international students in an Australian university preparation program. In A. Dashwood & J.-B. Son (Eds.), *Language, culture and social connectedness* (pp. 35–55). Cambridge Scholars Publishing.

Son, J.-B. (2016). Selecting and evaluating mobile apps for language learning. In A. Palalas & M. Ally (Eds.), *The international handbook of mobile-assisted language learning* (pp. 161–179). China Central Radio & TV University Press. https://drjbson.com/papers/MALL_Ch6_JS_2016.pdf

Son, J.-B. (2018). *Teacher development in technology-enhanced language teaching*. Palgrave Macmillan.

Son, J.-B. (2019). *Academic English word list*. https://drjbson.com/projects/aewl/

Son, J.-B., & Park, S.-S. (2014). Academic experiences of international PhD students in Australian higher education: From an EAP program to a PhD program. *International Journal of Pedagogies and Learning*, *9*(1), 26–37. https://doi.org/10.1080/18334105.2014.11082017

Tran, P. (2016). Training learners to use Quizlet vocabulary activities on mobile phones in Vietnam with Facebook. *The JALT CALL Journal*, *12*(1), 43–56. https://doi.org/10.29140/jaltcall.v12n1.201

Vongpumivitch, V., Huang, J.-Y., & Chang, Y.-C. (2009). Frequency analysis of the words in the academic word list (AWL) and non-AWL content words in applied linguistics research papers. *English for Specific Purposes*, *28*(1), 33–41. https://doi.org/10.1016/j.esp.2008.08.003

Wang, J., Liang, S. L., & Ge, G. C. (2008). Establishment of a medical academic word list. *English for Specific Purposes*, *27*(4), 442–458. https://doi.org/10.1016/j.esp.2008.05.003

11 Vocabulary learning with Netflix

Exploring intraformal learning practices through the lens of Complex Dynamic Systems Theory

Antonie Alm and Yuki Watanabe
University of Otaga, New Zealand

Pre-reading questions

1. How can digital platforms such as Netflix be purposefully integrated into formal contexts to enrich vocabulary learning?
2. What insights does Complex Dynamic Systems Theory offer regarding the development of vocabulary learning practices through technology?
3. How do individual differences influence learner interaction with lexical affordances in digital environments?

Background

Vocabulary knowledge is essential for language learning, comprehension, and use (Nation & Webb, 2011). Learners require extensive vocabulary knowledge to understand spoken and written texts, articulate ideas, and communicate effectively in the target language (Schmitt, 2019). Several theoretical models have contributed to our understanding of vocabulary development. The noticing hypothesis posits that conscious attention to lexical items is required to convert input into intake for learning (Schmidt, 1990). The involvement load hypothesis states that word retention depends on the depth of cognitive engagement (Laufer & Hulstijn, 2001). Increasingly, usage-based perspectives recognise vocabulary learning as a dynamic process that occurs over time through multiple contextual encounters (Ellis, 2017). Words are not isolated units, but are acquired and used in phrases, patterns, and meaningful contexts. Usage-based models emphasise the central role of formulaic language, collocations, and multiword units in language learning and use (Conklin & Schmitt, 2012). Knowledge of a word evolves gradually from recognition of basic form-meaning connection to understanding of grammatical functions, collocational properties, and appropriate usage across diverse contexts (Henriksen, 1999). Learner factors such as motivation, proficiency level,

DOI: 10.4324/9781003367543-13

cognitive abilities, and learning strategies impact vocabulary development (Folse, 2004; Hu & Nassaji, 2016).

Both incidental and intentional learning contribute to lexical growth (Karami & Bowles, 2019). Incidental vocabulary uptake occurs as a by-product of meaning-focused communication without deliberate memorisation (Webb, 2020). Studies show the importance of out-of-class incidental exposure, as increased input predicts vocabulary gains (Peters, 2018). Digital technology assists incidental learning by providing varied multimodal L2 input via resources like TV, websites, and apps (Arndt & Woore, 2018; Godwin-Jones, 2018). However, the potential depends on learner engagement and cognitive processing (Feng & Webb, 2020). In contrast, intentional vocabulary learning utilises strategies to consciously acquire lexical information (Webb, 2020). Multimedia glosses combining textual definitions with visual and audio input promote intentional learning (Mohsen & Balakumar, 2011). Moreover, greater attention and elaboration appear vital for retention (Teng, 2020).

Studies have examined vocabulary gains through viewing captioned and subtitled videos, which provide multimodal input by combining visual, textual, and auditory information (Montero Perez et al., 2014; Rodgers, 2013). Subtitles provide written translation of the spoken language, while captions transcribe the speech verbatim. Research shows both formats can support learning, with greater gains for less proficient learners. Captions help learners parse the speech stream and notice new words, while subtitles convey meaning and promote noticing. Individual differences in factors like working memory, vocabulary knowledge, and aptitude influence outcomes (Pellicer-Sanchez, 2016; Peters & Webb, 2018). Bilingual subtitles present simultaneous L1 and L2 lines on screen. Some studies have shown the benefits of these captions, suggesting they integrate the advantages of captions and L1 subtitles by enabling L1 translation and L2 comprehension (Lunin & Minaeva, 2015). However, studies in multimedia learning have cautioned that redundant information may hinder processing (Sweller, 2005). Empirical studies report conflicting results on the benefits of bilingual subtitles over other formats (Wang, 2019). Methodological factors may explain inconsistencies (Liao et al., 2020).

The digital media platform Netflix offers a range of features that can support language learners' vocabulary development (Fievez et al., 2023; Godwin-Jones, 2018 Vanderplank, 2016). The platform's extensive selection of international content including TV series, movies, and shows is complemented by flexible language options such as multiple audio tracks and subtitles. The ability to pause, rewind, and replay lexical sequences provides learners with the opportunity for repeated exposure to vocabulary in context. Furthermore, TV series provide repeated exposure to vocabulary, expressions, and structures (Godwin-Jones, 2018), aligning with usage-based theories of language learning, which emphasise the role of patterned language use (Ellis, 2017). Furthermore, watching L2 content can also provide insight into cultural aspects and authentic language as it is used in everyday situations, enhancing the development of pragmatic competence (Godwin-Jones, 2018).

The browser extension Language Learning with Netflix (or Language Reactor, www.languagereactor.com) offers additional language learning support on top of the Netflix features, including dual-language subtitles, a pop-up dictionary, and word-saving features. The extension features enable learners to exercise enhanced control over their intentional language learning experience and have been shown to positively influence vocabulary development and listening comprehension (Dizon & Thanyawatpokin, 2021; Fievez et al., 2023). The effectiveness of such multimodal input for language learning has been demonstrated in experimental studies (Gass et al., 2019; Rodgers & Webb, 2017), as well as in contexts where language learners engage informally in watching TV series and making their own content and subtitling choices (Peters & Muñoz, 2020). Therefore, the combination of Netflix and the Language Learning with Netflix (LLN) extension offers a valuable resource for language learners seeking to develop their vocabulary through multimodal input.

Despite growing insights into vocabulary learning through audiovisual input, limited research has examined how individual learner factors and the learning affordances of digital media dynamically shape vocabulary development. The availability of authentic L2 content through digital media provides opportunities for vocabulary development outside classroom settings. This aligns with the concept of intraformal learning, which involves intentionally integrating informal digital resources into formal educational contexts to enrich language instruction (Alm, 2019). For vocabulary development, intraformal approaches allow for a contextual balance between discovery and explicit study. Learners can drive their own vocabulary expansion by selecting motivating materials, while having pedagogical support. However, research on how learners construct intraformal vocabulary learning experiences through digital engagement is limited.

This study applies Complex Dynamic Systems Theory (CDST) as a framework to analyse the adaptive nature of vocabulary learning (Larsen-Freeman, 1997). CDST recognises learning as an emergent process shaped by the dynamic interplay between individual learner factors, contexts, and self-organisation. This perspective aligns with intraformal learning environments by examining the heterogeneity of learners and their evolving approaches to vocabulary building through digital resource engagement. The study aims to address the limited understanding of how learners develop and engage in intraformal vocabulary learning practices by analysing how tertiary Spanish language learners integrate the use of Netflix and the browser extension LLN into their vocabulary learning. The research questions are as follows:

1. How do university students learning Spanish construct vocabulary learning practices when integrating self-directed viewing of Netflix series into their formal educational context?
2. What individual learner factors shape their self-organisation of vocabulary learning processes as they engage with Netflix series and the browser extension LLN?
3. How do contextual constraints and affordances interact to influence the trajectory of vocabulary learning for university students learning Spanish using Netflix to enrich classroom language instruction?

Method

Research design and context

This exploratory qualitative case study was conducted at a university in New Zealand. The participants were adult Spanish learners (18–37) enrolled in an advanced (B2 level) university Spanish course. The study aimed to gain an in-depth understanding of how these learners constructed vocabulary learning practices by integrating the digital platform Netflix into their formal language study. As part of the course, 28 students participated in a seven-week project using Netflix to supplement their vocabulary learning: students were required to watch at least two episodes of their chosen series per week and write a weekly 350-word blog entry in Spanish about their viewing experience. In addition, students were encouraged to read and comment on each other's blog entries (see Table 11.1 for the timeline of activities and blog topics). The COVID-19 pandemic led to the closure of the university and a move to online learning during the project, but students were able to continue the Netflix viewing and blogging activities remotely. This project provided the context for the study.

Complex Dynamic Systems Theory

CDST provides a comprehensive framework for understanding language learning as an interconnected, evolving process shaped by multiple factors interacting in complex ways (De Bot et al., 2007; Larsen-Freeman, 1997). Grounded in concepts from systems theory and complexity science, CDST recognises that language development is dynamic, adaptive, interconnected, and self-organising (Toffoli, 2020). This perspective offers a valuable lens

Table 11.1 Timeline of activities

Week	In class	Blog topics	Out-of-class viewing
1	Introduction of Netflix task	Reflection on Netflix experiences for language learning	Selection of Netflix series
2	Discussion of the Netflix series	Description of Netflix series, including characters, plot, and selection process	Viewing activity starts
3	Introduction of LLN	Reflection on LLN's impact on comprehension	Viewing of series using LLN
4	COVID lockdown, classes halted	Reflection on viewing routines	Viewing continues
5		Reflection on vocabulary learning	Focus on vocabulary while viewing the series
6		Sharing of updates on Netflix series and discussion of shifts in perceptions and reflections	Viewing continues
7		Evaluation of the Netflix project, identifying successes, shortcomings, and areas for improvement	Viewing continues and concludes with the last episodes of the series

for examining the fluid, nonlinear nature of vocabulary learning and its emergence from the complex interplay of diverse variables (Hiver & Al-Hoorie, 2019).

Some key principles of CDST relevant to this study include the following:

- *Dynamism*: CDST views learning as nonlinear and dynamic, continually changing over time. Vocabulary learning is recognised as an adaptive process influenced by diverse variables like learner traits, input types, and social contexts.
- *Initial conditions*: This refers to the unique set of circumstances learners begin with, including their prior experiences, proficiency, motivations, and learning preferences. These conditions shape their potential learning trajectories and interactions with new learning environments.
- *Attractor and repeller states*: Attractors are patterns or behaviours learners gravitate towards, such as a TV show that engages them. Repellers are states learners have difficulty maintaining, like strategies that hamper enjoyment. The interplay between attractor and repeller states evolves as learners progress.
- *Self-organisation*: Learners self-organise by spontaneously adapting strategies and behaviours to shape their learning without explicit external direction. For example, learners may develop personalised

routines for vocabulary learning by creatively utilising available tools and resources.
- *Interconnectedness*: CDST highlights relationships between components of the learning system. Vocabulary learning is impacted by connections between learner traits, contextual factors, and self-organisation processes.

For this study, CDST provides a useful framework to conceptualise vocabulary learning with Netflix as a complex dynamic process shaped by individual differences and emergent learner-environment interactions. Key CDST concepts guide analysis of how learners utilise the platform to construct personalised learning experiences.

Participants

Three learners were purposefully selected based on their Netflix engagement as listed below. To protect the anonymity of the participants, pseudonyms are used to report the findings. Ethical approval was obtained for this study, and informed consent was received from the participants prior to commencement of the study.

- Mario (19 years) – highly motivated, avid Netflix user
- Emma (19 years) – cautious of technology overuse
- Tom (27 years) – independent learner who preferred YouTube over Netflix

Data collection

This study adopted a qualitative case study approach for an in-depth investigation of participants' experiences and engagement with Netflix for vocabulary learning. The case study method is widely used in language learning research (Duff, 2014) and is particularly suitable for examining second language learning within the CDST framework, as it allows for in-depth examination of individuals (Toffoli, 2020).
Data were collected from two sources:

- *Reflective blogs*: Students wrote seven weekly Spanish blog entries describing their Netflix viewing experiences. Prompts elicited reflections (see Table 11.1). The blogs captured participants' experiences and reflections in the target language.
- *Focus group interviews*: Semi-structured online focus group interviews were conducted via Zoom in English to explore the blog themes.

Questions focused on the viewing experience, the use of tools such as the LLN browser extension, and the impact on vocabulary learning. The interviews were audio-recorded and transcribed.

Case study data consisted of the three participants' blog entries over the seven weeks of the study. The blogs were translated into English by a research assistant to facilitate analysis. The following abbreviations are used throughout: M = Mario, E = Emma, T = Tom, B = Blog, 1–7 numbered blog entry (e.g., MB1 = Mario's first blog entry). The English translations of the blogs are used to present the results.

Data analysis

The translated blog texts and interview transcripts were analysed using an inductive thematic approach (Braun & Clarke, 2006). The qualitative data analysis software Nvivo was used to organise and support the coding process. Both authors participated in the coding process. Initial open coding was carried out independently by each researcher reviewing the data corpus and identifying relevant features and patterns related to vocabulary learning experiences. Following this independent open coding, the researchers discussed their initial codes and reached a consensus on an initial coding scheme. This set of codes was then applied to the data corpus again. The codes were iteratively refined into categories and emerging themes based on the examination of connections and relationships between codes. The themes were developed using key concepts from CDST as a conceptual framework for understanding the dynamic patterns and trajectories of vocabulary learning.

Limitations

Potential limitations of this study should be acknowledged. The use of self-reported data from learner blogs and interviews relies on participants' perceptions and accuracy of recall. The case study approach also has inherent biases in the purposeful selection of participants to illustrate diverse experiences. To address these limitations, strategies were used to enhance credibility and transparency. Data sources were triangulated to obtain both ongoing reflections (blogs) and retrospective insights (interviews). While the findings may not be generalisable, this in-depth case study provides valuable insights into the complex, dynamic process of developing vocabulary learning practices using digital platforms. Readers can evaluate the relevance of findings to their contexts.

Results

This case study examines the L2 viewing experiences of three Spanish learners, illuminating their individualised ways of engaging with vocabulary learning. It shows how the learners adopted different approaches shaped by their unique initial motivations, preferences, and social contexts.

Mario

Initial conditions

Mario is a highly motivated Spanish student, convinced that he will be "speaking Spanish fluently one day" (MB3). His goal is to serve as an ambassador for New Zealand in Spain. He learned Spanish in his high school years; however, he reported experiences with an uninspiring teacher (MB3), and expressed dissatisfaction with language apps, notably referring to "that green owl" (MB3). An enthusiastic user of Netflix, Mario recognises the platform's potential for language learning, particularly for "expanding vocabulary" (MB2). His choice of the series *Elite*, a popular Spanish high school drama, is determined by his familiarity with Castilian Spanish (MB2) and his interest in Spanish culture and society (MB3).

Mario's initial conditions, characterised by high motivation, a clearly defined future self-image, and a preference for creative, immersive language learning, provide the starting point for his learning trajectory. These conditions shape how he perceives and interacts with the affordances offered by Netflix.

The dynamic stage

As Mario initiates his journey with the series *Elite*, begins using the LLN extension, and starts sharing his viewing experiences in his blog, key affordances come into play, significantly influencing his language learning experience and the way he engages with vocabulary.

His fascination with *Elite* rapidly draws him into a strong positive attractor state. He describes *Elite* as a "very, very addictive thriller. Seriously, I never want to stop watching!" (MB2). This enthusiasm is reinforced by his classmates, who comment on his blog. Maria teasingly asks him not to give away any spoilers (MB2), and Anna agrees, eagerly awaiting season three of the show (MB2). These social interactions validate his enjoyment and contribute to the stability of the attractor state.

Mario finds a valuable affordance in the dual subtitle feature of the LLN extension, describing it as "a lifesaver", as it helps him follow everyday interactions among Spanish speakers (MB3). The LLN extension affords him an immersive viewing experience. In his words, "When I discovered LLN, I wanted to jump over the moon. There's nothing better than watching Elite with English and Spanish subtitles in my cosy bed with my warm blanket, hot chocolate with marshmallows in one hand and delicious buttery popcorn in the other" (MB4). This learning experience stands in stark contrast to Mario's perception of textbook-based language classes, which he describes as "not remotely effective. You'll end up becoming a walking textbook. Lifeless, tasteless" (MB3).

Finally, Mario embraces the affordance of writing blogs to share his vocabulary learning experiences with his peers. He enjoys the informality and interaction that come with blogging, as expressed by his statement, "I hope you enjoy reading this. It gives me an excuse to be informal in an environment that would expect sterile pieces of modern literature. Just kidding!" (MB4). This suggests that writing for an audience in an informal, conversational style encourages him to use his language skills in an authentic context.

Self-organisation for vocabulary learning

Mario's language learning trajectory exemplifies the concept of self-organisation, a process characterised by his engagement with the affordances provided by the series, the LLN extension, his physical environment, and his blogging activity. This self-organisation is evident in his ability to adapt his learning strategies, make effective use of available resources, and actively shape his learning in response to the experiences he encounters and the feedback he receives.

His use of the dual subtitle feature of LLN is instrumental in his vocabulary learning process. Instead of looking up unfamiliar terms, Mario takes a context-driven approach, deriving meaning from the captions and subtitles, and his inference skills. The dual subtitles enable him to immerse himself in the narrative universe of the series. He writes passionately, "That's what I love. The rich and incredible use of language – very powerful" (MB5), indicating the integral role of LLN in facilitating his access to conversational Spanish.

Additionally, Mario embraces text conversations shown in *Elite*, documenting the texting shortcuts (Table 11.2) and urging his peers to use them (MB5).

Mario's learning journey is demonstrated in the way he utilises his blog as a space for individual reflection and as a platform to apply and experiment with the vocabulary from *Elite*. In his original words, "Pensé que los jóvenes en Nueva Zelanda juraban mucho. ¡Incorrecto! España gana la corona. Por ejemplo; joder, (hijo de) puta, culo, follar, los cojones, mierda, coño y la lista continúa. ¡Guauu! Nunca pensé que escribiría estas

Table 11.2 Texting shortcuts recorded in Mario's blog

Que = k o q
Genial = gnl
Ahora = aora
Quiero = kiero
Clase = kls
Aquí = aki
Gracias = grax
Ok = okas
También = tb
Por favor = x fa
Porque = xq
Bien = bn
Espero = spro*
Te quiero mucho = tqm
Estoy = toy*
Esta = ta*
*si una palabra comienza con es, se omiten.

palabrotas en papel. ¡Jajajajaja!" [This is not an exaggeration, but there's a lot of swearing. I thought young people in New Zealand swear a lot. Wrong! Spain wins the crown. For example; fuck, (son of) a bitch, ass, fuck, bollocks, shit, cunt, and the list goes on. Wow! I never thought I'd write these swear words on paper. Hahahaha!] (MB5). His appreciation for the vernacular is met with positive reinforcement from his peers, such as Maria, who affirms, "The curses, yes, make it more authentic, and so we learn something" (MB5). In this sense, the blog serves as an effective affordance, a safe space that enables Mario to engage with the colloquial language he encounters in *Elite*.

Mario's learning system demonstrates his dynamic and adaptable approach to vocabulary learning. He creatively utilises diverse learning affordances, challenges traditional methods, and fosters an interactive language learning community through his blog. This exemplifies self-organisation, highlighting the interplay between individual agency, resource utilisation, and the influence of others in shaping his evolving language system.

Emma

Initial conditions

Emma is not a frequent Netflix user. While she acknowledges the appeal of its "large selection of shows and movies" (EB1), she is cautious about getting too caught up in TV series, explaining, "I don't have self-control and would watch each chapter consecutively, without pause to do my homework" (EB1). She expresses her preference for non-technological activities, stating, "I'd rather ... bake, chat with my friends, or call my family or go to the beach" (EB1). However, she enjoys Netflix as a social activity, "when all of the people in my flat come together to watch a movie, relax and have a tea". While Emma has previously started watching a Spanish series, *Cable Girls*, she admits that she "didn't finish it" (EB1). Despite this, she shows enthusiasm for the idea of watching a Netflix series for her Spanish study, expressing, "I'm excited to do this assignment because I can watch Netflix and relax while I study, so lucky" (EB1).

The dynamic stage

Encouraged by her boyfriend, Emma chooses to watch the crime drama *La Casa de Papel*, a genre shift from her usual preference for romance or comedy series. This choice, coupled with her initial uncertainty, sets the stage for a dynamic process in her engagement and learning trajectory. As she finds her attention heightened by the suspenseful elements of the series, a perceptual shift occurs that triggers an attractor state. Emma observes, "I realised that I was more attentive when there was suspense and crime ... it will help me with the language because you learn more when you are attentive" (EB2). At this stage, the attractor state serves a dual function: stabilising her viewing patterns and enriching her language learning process, exemplifying the dynamic interplay of engagement and attention in language learning.

However, her engagement with the series is not without tension. Her initial conditions, characterised by a wariness of binge-watching due to her perceived lack of self-control, resurface when she expresses concerns about potential overconsumption, suggesting a possible negative attractor state. This is further complicated by her desire to watch the series with her roommates, which requires the use of English subtitles, an aspect she views as a potential obstacle to her language learning goal, expressing that "it didn't help me learn Spanish" (EB3) as her focus was diverted to reading rather than listening. Once she settles into her viewing practice with her boyfriend, however, she finds herself increasingly invested in the show, making it easier to allocate viewing time (EB3).

Self-organisation for vocabulary learning

By week four, Emma's language learning system has self-organised into a routine with set times for watching and writing (EB4). She has found a balance between studying and relaxing, positioning Netflix as an effective tool for language learning. Her boyfriend continues to play an important role in her language learning system, serving as a consistent interlocutor, facilitating her exploration of unfamiliar words and phrases, and allowing her to put her vocabulary to practical use in everyday conversation. She uses the dictionary feature on LLN to look up unfamiliar words and discuss idioms with him, "When I find a new word, I go back to the part with the word and click to find the definition. Sometimes I'll explain the phrase to my boyfriend if it's an idiom" (EB5).

She also keeps vocabulary lists on her blog. Emma acknowledges the importance of written lists and emphasises her reliance on visual memory: "For me, to remember or learn something, I need to see it written ...That's why Netflix subtitles help me so much" (EB6). Unlike Mario, she exercises discretion over her list entries, revealing, "A lot of times the word is rude, so I don't put it in a list" (EB5). Explaining her approach further, she says, "After looking up the definition, I say a phrase using the word as an example of how to use it. The next day, I try to remember the word and use it in my normal day" (EB5).

Emma's blog becomes a forum for social interaction, where she recommends series to her classmates and solicits feedback on her study techniques. This feedback not only validates and fine-tunes her learning strategies, but also illustrates the significant role of her social environment in guiding the self-organisation of her vocabulary learning system.

Tom

Initial conditions

Tom, a more mature student at the age of 27, already had extensive informal language learning experience before taking his Spanish class. He explains in his first blog entry, "Two years ago, I decided that I would learn Spanish no matter what, so I started searching the Internet for resources that can help me learn" (TB1). He finds YouTube to be an invaluable tool, both for advice on how to learn ("fast and without much unnecessary effort", TB1) and for language resources ("music, documentaries and stories based on real-life", TB1). Tom is less interested in Netflix, claiming to get bored easily by watching TV series. However, he admits having watched a few episodes of the romantic drama *Velvet*, "I'm a bit embarrassed to say so because Velvet is definitely a 'chick flick' " (TB1), and decides to continue watching the series for the project. The series aligns with his interests, he explains, "I can't resist a good romance story" (TB1). Also, it is based in Madrid, the destination of his upcoming university exchange.

The dynamic stage

Tom's language learning journey begins to shift as he embraces his enjoyment of the show. He states, "I like this series ... because of the style, the music, the actors who are very handsome by the way. In fact, I think I'm in love with the lead actress!" (B2). He also enjoys Castilian Spanish, and appreciates the exposure to the use of "vosotros", the informal second person plural pronoun predominantly used in Spain as an address form.

Initially, Tom is hesitant to deviate from his usual learning strategy of watching series without subtitles. However, after experimenting with LLN, he starts to appreciate the benefits of the glossed subtitles. With LLN, he is able to read more and has immediate access to unknown vocabulary. As Tom says, "The application gives me the ability to read much more in the same amount of time because the pace is not dependent on me. Also, instead of looking up unknown words on my computer, I can click on the word I want to know and immediately know it" (TB3). Thus, the LLN extension promotes continuous engagement with the series and vocabulary development.

Self-organisation

Tom's self-organisation process revolves around a regular viewing schedule, as he states, "My Netflix watching routine has been consistent after dinner, on Mondays and Wednesdays" (TB4). This regular pattern serves as a foundation for Tom to build on his past experiences by using his blog as a vocabulary journal, recording not just new words, but also the complete sentences they come from. He explains: "After a long time trying to learn vocabulary that wasn't worth the trouble with useless lists, applications like duolingo and only single words without context, I have found the way that works best for me" (TB5). The series he watches allows him to encounter words in various contexts, deepening his understanding of their usage. He notes, for example, the multiple meanings of the word "echar" and how it changes its meaning depending on the context:

> I was surprised that this word was used so many times in a very short time during the episode I watched, and how did I not notice it before? The word means many different things when translated into English; it can mean to throw, to throw out, to expel, to pour, to send, to add, to release, to produce, to estimate, to give, to lay off, to move ... and in the reflexive form *echarse* can mean to start, to throw oneself, to lie down or to apply something to oneself ... The phrase I heard at the beginning that included the word *echar* was 'to miss'. It was in the scene when the old designer came back to Velvet to greet everyone, he told them all how much he had missed them and in response they told him that they had missed him a lot too! A while later I heard the word again in

a very different context, "I'd rather not add fuel to the fire" ("*prefería no echarle más leña al fuego*") and again "I'm going to find someone who can give you a hand" ("*voy a buscar a alguien que te pueda echar un cable*").

(TB5)

Tom's reflective nature is a significant factor in the way he self-organises his system. He emphasises the importance of using "real language" in his blog writing activity, which requires him to review and revise his writing several times. He comments, "I had to spend about 4–5 hours writing every week" (TB7). This activity not only increases his exposure to Spanish, but also encourages him to reflect on his language use, fostering deeper learning.

New understandings

This exploratory study provided valuable insights into the personalised construction of vocabulary learning practices as the tertiary Spanish learners integrated Netflix viewing into their formal educational context. The findings revealed the emergent, adaptive nature of this process, aligned with key tenets of CDST. The learners' personalised approaches provided a window into the heterogeneous, context-dependent nature of developing vocabulary learning practices. Their varied experiences revealed the individual developmental variations inherent in dynamic systems.

Research question 1: Constructing personalised vocabulary learning practices

The case study illustrated how individual learners used the assigned formal activity of Netflix viewing to construct personalised vocabulary learning practices. As CDST recognises, learning is an emergent process shaped by learner-environment interactions (Larsen-Freeman, 1997). The learners' varied trajectories demonstrated the dynamism of vocabulary learning as a process dependent on contextual factors and learner motivations (Ellis, 2017; Godwin-Jones, 2018). Mario eagerly viewed his favourite show with dual subtitles to expose himself to authentic content. His compiling of colloquial vocabulary for sharing reflected a self-organised process of seizing affordances. Emma balanced scheduled viewing with social interactions, methodically expanding her vocabulary. Her organised integration of leisure and learning illustrated the bridging of formal and informal contexts. Tom paired intensive viewing routines with analysis of word usage through reflective writing. His structured analytical approach demonstrated deep personalised exploration. Despite differing motivations, all three learners used Netflix and the LLN extension in creative ways that bridged formal classroom instruction with informal digital resources. They actively participated in constructing personalised vocabulary learning practices shaped by their preferences. The learners' diverse self-directed approaches emphasise the heterogeneous, context-dependent nature of intraformal learning.

Research question 2: Individual factors influencing self-organisation

The learner experiences highlight how unique initial conditions including motivations, preferences, and prior experiences guided ongoing self-organisation, aligning with key CDST principles. Each learner's trajectory reflected dynamic adaptation as they interacted with the learning environment. Mario's exploratory approach reflected his strong intrinsic motivation and desire for immersive learning. Emma's organised routine balancing learning and leisure aligned with her cautious stance towards technology overuse. Her approach helped regulate engagement. Tom's intensive analysis of vocabulary usage matched his scholarly motivations. Their behaviours illustrate the integral role of adaptive self-organisation in shaping personalised approaches within intraformal learning contexts.

Research question 3: Interplay of contextual constraints and affordances

The learner experiences emphasise the multidirectional interplay between the individual and contextual factors perpetually shaping the evolving vocabulary learning trajectory. Points of tension were transformed into affordances over time as perceptions shifted, demonstrating the CDST concept of dynamism. Social viewing constraints for Emma were initially challenging but were mitigated through discussions with her boyfriend about the series' content and vocabulary. Initially hesitant about subtitles, Tom pivoted from wariness towards subtitles to embrace LLN tools. The experiences highlight the reciprocal evolution of learner goals and contextual affordance perceptions. The learner journeys reveal vocabulary development as an iterative negotiation of individual, social, and environmental elements within a complex system.

Implications

Exploring digital environments for personalised vocabulary learning

The study demonstrates the potential for purposefully integrating digital platforms like Netflix to promote personalised vocabulary development. Educators should guide learners in selectively utilising the array of informal digital resources to enrich vocabulary learning. This blending of formal and informal digital tools provides motivating opportunities for contextualised vocabulary expansion. Learners can be equipped to take control of their lexical development through flexible use of digital environments.

Fostering learner agency through digital reflection and sharing

Learners should be encouraged to take ownership of their digital vocabulary learning process through reflective and collaborative activities. Maintaining online vocabulary journals, exchanging insights on lexical patterns in digital texts, and sharing strategies on virtual learning platforms can enhance autonomy. Reflective practices allow learners to optimise their approaches to vocabulary development in digital spaces.

Accommodating learner differences in digital environments

The study highlights the need to align digital vocabulary learning experiences with diverse learner motivations, backgrounds, and preferences. Educators should recognise how factors like prior digital experiences shape affordance perceptions, guiding learners accordingly. Accommodating differences is key for enriching learner autonomy in digital environments.

Promoting dynamic lexical affordance exploration

Rather than prescribing set digital tools, educators should equip learners to understand and use lexical affordances in digital environments. This involves encouraging proactive yet flexible interaction with online resources, while recognising that affordance perceptions evolve. The goal is sustained lexical engagement through a changing digital landscape.

Further reading

Godwin-Jones, R. (2018). Contextualized vocabulary learning. *Language Learning & Technology*, 22(3), 1–19.
This article provides insights into vocabulary development through the lens of CDST. The paper highlights how mobile devices enable personalised, context-dependent vocabulary learning shaped by individual learner factors and their evolving interaction with digital resources. Godwin-Jones advocates teachers actively equipping learners to leverage mobile affordances. This involves providing adaptive strategies and scaffolding to help learners use digital tools for frequent, contextual vocabulary exposure aligned with usage-based approaches. The article offers useful perspectives on designing language curricula and the teacher's role in promoting autonomous lexical expansion.

Toffoli, D. (2020). Complex Dynamic Systems Theory (CDST). In *Informal learning and institution-wide language provision*. Palgrave Macmillan, Cham. https://doi.org/10.1007/978-3-030-37876-9_1

Toffoli applies CDST to examine the interplay between formal and informal language learning. The book profiles contemporary learners as autonomous agents directing their learning via both formal education and online leisure activities. It advocates integrating these spheres, with teachers drawing on knowledge of informal practices to support personalised language development. Toffoli argues that learner-driven integration of digital resources promotes self-directed learning and equips students with strategies for lifelong language development. The book offers insights into curriculum design and teaching approaches that develop autonomous lifelong learners.

References

Alm, A. (2019). Piloting Netflix for intraformal language learning. In F. Meunier, J. Van de Vyver, I. Bradley & S. Thouësny (Eds.), *CALL and complexity–short papers from EUROCALL, 2019* (pp. 13–18). Research-publishing.net. https://doi.org/10.14705/rpnet.2019.38.979

Arndt, H. L., & Woore, R. (2018). Vocabulary learning from watching YouTube videos and reading blog posts. *Language Learning & Technology*, 22(3), 124–142. https://doi.org/10125/44660/

Braun, V., & Clarke, V. (2006). Using thematic analysis in psychology. *Qualitative Research in Psychology*, 3(2), 77–101. https://doi.org/10.1191/1478088706qp063oa

Conklin, K., & Schmitt, N. (2012). The processing of formulaic language. *Annual Review of Applied Linguistics*, 32, 45–61. https://doi.org/10.1017/S0267190512000074

De Bot, K., Lowie, W., & Verspoor, M. (2007). A dynamic systems theory approach to second language acquisition. *Bilingualism: Language and Cognition*, 10(1), 7–21. https://doi.org/10.1017/S1366728906002732

Dizon, G., & Thanyawatpokin, B. (2021). Language learning with Netflix: Exploring the effects of dual subtitles on vocabulary learning and listening comprehension. *Computer Assisted Language Learning Electronic Journal*, 22(3), 52–65.

Duff, P. A. (2014). Case study research on language learning and use. *Annual Review of Applied Linguistics*, 34, 233–255. https://doi.org/10.1017/S0267190514000051

Ellis, N. C. (2017). Cognition, corpora, and computing: Triangulating research in usage-based language learning. *Language Learning*, 67(S1), 40–65. https://doi.org/10.1111/lang.12215

Feng, Y., & Webb, S. (2020). Learning vocabulary through reading, listening, and viewing: Which mode of input is most effective? *Studies in Second Language Acquisition*, 42(3), 599–623. https://doi.org/10.1017/S0272263119000494

Fievez, I., Montero Perez, M., Cornillie, F., & Desmet, P. (2023). Promoting incidental vocabulary learning through watching a French Netflix series with glossed captions. *Computer Assisted Language Learning*, 36(1–2), 26–51. https://doi.org/10.1080/09588221.2021.1899244

Folse, K. S. (2004). Myths about teaching and learning second language vocabulary: What recent research says. *TESL Reporter*, 37, 13–13.

Gass, S., Winke, P., Isbell, D. R., & Ahn, J. (2019). How captions help people learn languages: A working-memory, eye-tracking study. *Language Learning & Technology*, 23(2), 84–104. https://doi.org/10125/44684

Godwin-Jones, R. (2018). Contextualized vocabulary learning. *Language Learning & Technology*, 22(3), 1–19. https://doi.org/10125/44651

Henriksen, B. (1999). Three dimensions of vocabulary development. *Studies in Second Language Acquisition*, 21(2), 303–317. https://doi.org/10.1017/S0272263199002089

Hiver, P., & Al-Hoorie, A. H. (2019). *Research methods for complexity theory in applied linguistics* (Vol. 137). Multilingual Matters. https://doi.org/10.21832/HIVER5747

Hu, G., & Nassaji, H. (2016). Effective vocabulary learning tasks: Involvement load hypothesis versus technique feature analysis. *System*, 56, 28–39. https://doi.org/10.1016/j.system.2015.11.001

Karami, A., & Bowles, F. A. (2019). Which strategy promotes retention? Intentional vocabulary learning, incidental vocabulary learning, or a mixture of both? *Australian Journal of Teacher Education*, 44(9), 25–43. https://ro.ecu.edu.au/ajte/vol44/iss9/2

Larsen-Freeman, D. (1997). Chaos/complexity science and second language acquisition. *Applied Linguistics*, 18(2), 141–165. https://doi.org/10.1093/applin/18.2.141

Laufer, B., & Hulstijn, J. (2001). Incidental vocabulary acquisition in a second language: The construct of task-induced involvement. *Applied Linguistics*, 22(1), 1–26. https://doi.org/10.1093/applin/22.1.1

Liao, S., Kruger, J.-L., & Doherty, S. (2020). The impact of monolingual and bilingual subtitles on visual attention, cognitive load and comprehension. *The Journal of Specialised Translation*, 33, 70–98. www.jostrans.org/issue33/art_liao.pdf

Lunin, M., & Minaeva, L. (2015). Translated subtitles language learning method: A new practical approach to teaching English. *Procedia-Social and Behavioral Sciences*, 199, 268–275. https://doi.org/10.1016/j.sbspro.2015.07.516

Mohsen, M. A., & Balakumar, M. (2011). A review of multimedia glosses and their effects on L2 vocabulary acquisition in CALL literature. *ReCALL*, 23(2), 135–159. https://doi.org/10.1017/S095834401100005X

Montero Perez, M., Peters, E., Clarebout, G., & Desmet, P. (2014). Effects of captioning on video comprehension and incidental vocabulary learning. *Language Learning & Technology*, 18(1), 118–141. http://dx.doi.org/10125/44357

Nation, I. S. P., & Webb, S. (2011). *Researching and analyzing vocabulary*. Heinle.

Pellicer-Sánchez, A. (2016). Incidental L2 vocabulary acquisition from and while reading: An eye-tracking study. *Studies in Second Language Acquisition*, 38(1), 97–130. https://doi.org/10.1017/S0272263115000224

Peters, E. (2018). The effect of out-of-class exposure to English language media on learners' vocabulary knowledge. *ITL-International Journal of Applied Linguistics*, 169(1), 142–168. https://doi.org/10.1075/itl.00010.pet

Peters, E., & Muñoz, C. (2020). Introduction to the special issue: Language learning from multimodal input. *Studies in Second Language Acquisition*, 42(3), 489–497. https://doi.org/10.1017/S0272263120000212

Peters, E., & Webb, S. (2018). Incidental vocabulary acquisition through viewing L2 television and factors that affect learning. *Studies in Second Language Acquisition*, 40(3), 551–577. https://doi.org/10.1017/S0272263117000407

Rodgers, M. P. (2013). *English language learning through viewing television: An investigation of comprehension, incidental vocabulary acquisition, lexical coverage, attitudes, and captions.* [Doctoral dissertation, Victoria University of Wellington].

Rodgers, M. P., & Webb, S. (2017). The effects of captions on EFL learners' comprehension of English-language television programs. *Calico Journal*, 34(1), 20–38. https://doi.org/10.1558/cj.29522

Schmidt, R. W. (1990). The role of consciousness in second language learning. *Applied Linguistics*, 11, 129–158. https://doi.org/10.1093/applin/11.2.129

Schmitt, N. (2019). Understanding vocabulary acquisition, instruction, and assessment: A research agenda. *Language Teaching*, 52(2), 261–274. https://doi.org/10.1017/S0261444819000053

Sweller, J. (2005). Implications of cognitive load theory for multimedia learning. In R. E. Mayer (Ed.), *The Cambridge handbook of multimedia learning* (pp. 19–30). Cambridge University Press. https://doi.org/10.1017/CBO9780511816819.003

Teng, M. F. (2019). The effects of video caption types and advance organizers on incidental L2 collocation learning. *Computers & Education*, 142, 103–655. https://doi.org/10.1016/j.compedu.2019.103655

Teng, M. F. (2020). *Language learning through captioned videos: Incidental vocabulary acquisition.* Routledge. https://doi.org/10.4324/9780429264740

Toffoli, D. (2020). Complex Dynamic Systems Theory (CDST). In *Informal learning and institution-wide language provision.* Palgrave Macmillan, Cham. https://doi.org/10.1007/978-3-030-37876-9_1

Wang, Y. (2019). Effects of L1/L2 captioned TV programs on students' vocabulary learning and comprehension. *CALICO Journal*, 36(2), 204–224. https://doi.org/10.1558/cj.36268

Webb, S. (2020). Incidental vocabulary learning. In S. Webb (Ed.), *The Routledge handbook of vocabulary studies* (pp. 225–239). Routledge. https://doi.org/10.4324/9780429291586

Vanderplank, R. (2016). *Captioned media in foreign language learning and teaching: Subtitles for the deaf and hard-of-hearing as tools for language learning.* Palgrave Macmillan. https://doi.org/10.1057/978-1-137-50045-8

12 Using TikTok for vocabulary learning

Multimodal implications

Yeong-Ju Lee

Department of Linguistics, Macquarie University, Sydney, Australia

Pre-reading questions

1. What are the potentials of TikTok's multimodal aspects for vocabulary learning?
2. How is vocabulary learning organised on TikTok?

Background

Informal digital language learning and vocabulary acquisition

Informal digital language learning is understood as language learning that is not for formal institutional and instructional purposes and often involves resources designed for social and recreational purposes (Soyoof et al., 2021). In this context, research into vocabulary acquisition has explored incidental learning through out-of-class exposure to lexical knowledge, including via technological resources such as social media, without deliberate intention to learn (Peters, 2018; Teng, 2022a). Recent discussions further address how out-of-class experiences of technological resources can help learners to achieve a balance between incidental and deliberate learning opportunities (Godwin-Jones, 2018; Lai et al., 2022; Teng, 2022b). Moreover, a growing number of empirical studies have reported positive relationships between vocabulary knowledge and the use of social media not specifically designed for educational purposes. For instance, Sockett and Toffoli (2012) found French English as a foreign language (EFL) students improved their listening and vocabulary knowledge through engagement in messaging on social networking platforms including Facebook and Twitter. In the multilingual video-gaming practices of youth in Hong Kong, Benson and Chik (2013) observed frequent vocabulary acquisition when the participants actively sought opportunities for language use such as conversing with overseas players in chat rooms. Sundqvist (2019) reported

DOI: 10.4324/9781003367543-14

a correlation between experienced video gamers' collaborative use of digital technologies and productive vocabulary learning. These studies indicate how users repurpose social and recreational digital platforms for learning purposes. They also highlight the importance of users' perspectives to understanding informal digital vocabulary learning and how it involves autonomous or motivational uses of technology for learning.

Multimodality of social media and vocabulary acquisition

In the context of the visual turn from text-based to image-based social media (Burgess et al., 2018; Page et al., 2014), popularly emerging platforms such as TikTok often make use of the latest technologies supporting multimodal communication and networking (Lee, 2023). Recent research considers the modality of technological resources – the integration of multiple modes of communication such as textual, visual, and audial elements (Kress, 2010) – as a factor that motivates vocabulary learning (Teng & Zhang, 2023; Zou & Teng, 2023). This emerges from the consideration that diverse modalities may have differential vocabulary learning potentials (Lai et al., 2022). In their empirical research investigating whether modality influences the amount and aspects of vocabulary knowledge gained, Arndt and Woore (2018) compared the extent to which watching YouTube vlogs and reading blog posts supported vocabulary acquisition. They observed the potential of audio-visual plus textual information to promote greater vocabulary retention and recall. More recent exploratory studies have reported that TikTokers participate in language learning and teaching in the production of videos (Lee, 2023; Vazquez-Calvo et al., 2022). Lee (2023), in particular, observed that TikTok's in-application video editing features promoted the production of multimodal content, which supported the demonstration of pronunciation for multilingual vocabulary learning. This observation indicates how the latest image-based social media innovations can support vocabulary practices through the design and production of multimodal videos. It further indicates that current digital experiences of vocabulary learning occur with a multimodality that is supported not only by the platform but also by its users.

Despite numerous studies on language learning and technology, there is a lack of concrete examples and experiential data illustrating users' perspectives on how they benefit from technological innovations supporting the platform's richer multimodality for learning diverse language skills, including vocabulary. Moreover, language practices on newer platforms like TikTok occur in the process of producing multimodal content (Lee, 2023). However, little research has been conducted on TikTok, despite the potential of its innovations to afford opportunities for multimodal vocabulary learning, especially through engagement with multimodal digital content.

To fill these research gaps, this study examines the multimodal innovations of TikTok and how the platform is associated with vocabulary learning through the experiences and perspectives of five English language learners. It is guided by two research questions:

1. How do students identify the multimodal innovations of TikTok as affordances for vocabulary learning?
2. How do students organise their vocabulary learning using TikTok in accordance with these affordances?

A theoretical concept of affordances

To address the research questions, this study employs Gibson's (1979) concept of affordances – "what [the environment] offers" to particular organisms depending on need and perception (p. 127). For van Lier (2004, 2007), affordances refer to what is available in the environment for learners to potentially use for learning. This implies that learning, including language learning, depends on the learner's agency to engage with the resources available in the environment. These definitions are particularly related to Barton and Potts's (2013) approach to digital affordances, focusing on ways in which learners observe and negotiate language in use through digital communication.

Adopting this concept of affordances, studies of informal digital language learning have shown how social media environments support language use and practices. In an early study, Reinhardt and Chen (2013) examined a Chinese student's use of Facebook and RenRen (a Chinese social networking application) for English language learning. They showed how affordances of social and symbolic activities were perceived and acted upon by the student through the utilisation of features such as status update posting. More studies have focused on the language learning potential of social media environments with richer multimodality. Newgarden and Zheng (2016), for example, analysed the multimodal affordances of a multiplayer video game, *World of Warcraft*, for language learning. They observed that gamers' interactions were not planned, but emerged dynamically as the play went on. Recently, Lee (2023) analysed the language learning affordances of TikTok's technological innovations employed for the creation of multimodal digital content. She highlighted how affordances were manifested with individual learners who exercised agency and creativity to utilise non-linguistic, technological features to create linguistic opportunities. These studies suggest that learning involves interrelating with dynamics and multimodal innovations, distributed within the environment learners are exposed to.

In short, affordances can represent media sharing and social networking technologies consisting of possibilities for language learning that users would identify in particular features with their agency and creativity. Focusing on the use of TikTok, as one of the emerging multimodal media sharing and social networking platforms requiring more attention, this study uses this concept to examine how the use of the multimodal innovations of TikTok is realised and made available as affordances for vocabulary learning through digital interaction.

Methods

Research design

This study was designed as a multiple case study to explore in depth TikTok's multimodal innovations and implications for vocabulary learning from the participants' own perspectives (Barkhuizen et al., 2013; Benson, 2014). It adopted narrative inquiry as a method to collect and analyse narrative data. The data were collected for four weeks from three data sources to ensure triangulation: (a) journal entries, (b) stimulated recall interviews, and (c) TikTok posts. Journal entries and interviews were primary narrative data sources, whereas TikTok posts were supplementary data sources used to confirm intended meanings in journal entries. Using the concept of affordances, qualitative thematic analysis was conducted to identify insights that emerged from the coding process (Clarke & Braun, 2017).

Setting and participants

Participants were recruited from intensive language courses in a university in Sydney, Australia, offering English lessons as a prerequisite to an undergraduate/graduate degree. Recruitment was also carried out in the university English-speaking student club. Inclusion criteria were that participants: (1) voluntarily agreed to participate, and (2) were willing to engage with digital activities and resources for language learning. Table 12.1 summarises the five participants' background information and their previous experiences of using online resources for vocabulary learning. While participating in this research project, they frequently utilised TikTok to access multimodal digital content created by English speakers. No significant differences were observed in their learning needs and activities caused by discrepancies in their status, as they used TikTok

Table 12.1 Participants' background information

Name	Gender	Nationality	Educational status	Previous experience using online resources for vocabulary learning
Amir	M	Iranian	Pre-BA	Online dictionary and Google Translate
Prem	M	Thai	Pre-BA	Google, Wikipedia, online gaming, and Facebook
Joy	F	Chinese	Pre-MA	Online dictionary and Google Translate
Shasha	F	Indonesian	Pre-MA	Google and Duolingo
Jieun	F	Korean	MA	Online news and Naver (a Korean search tool)

MA = Master's degree; BA = Bachelor's degree.

to mainly create opportunities for conversational and practical language use, rather than for academic study.

Data collection

Participants were asked to write weekly journal entries about the digital resources and technologies they utilised, learning opportunities they engaged with, and linguistic knowledge they gained. Journal entries (n = 20) were used as written narrative data and an aid to recall during follow-up interviews. Following completion of each weekly journal entry, a one-hour interview was conducted to gain insights into each participant's perceptions of the value of the learning experiences they had recorded in their entries. Interviews (n = 20) were audio-recorded and transcribed verbatim. Individual narratives were extracted to use as narrative data in a sequential form of stories. TikTok posts included multimodal digital content the participants viewed or created for vocabulary learning and shared with the researcher as screenshots (or links). The three types of data identified are: posts created by the participants, posts created by others, and the participants' responses to the posts by others. Some screenshots are presented as examples of visual presentations in this chapter. Consent was obtained from each participant and each creator (whose content was perceived as useful by the participants) to be identified in screenshots and accompanying text.

Data analysis

Individual narratives that elicited multimodal innovations of TikTok and resulted in vocabulary learning were extracted from the data. These narratives were thematically analysed using the coding procedure in NVivo. Using the concept of "affordances"' to examine the platform's multimodal affordances for vocabulary learning, codes relevant to the research questions were classified under two categories: (1) multimodal technologies such as insertion of text, emojis, or images within a video and conversion of multiple photos into a video format; and (2) affordances such as subtitling or annotating a speech in a video and creating content consisting of image materials involving vocabulary knowledge. The analysis identified how users perceived the multimodal innovations of TikTok as affordances for acquiring vocabulary knowledge online (RQ1), and how users organised vocabulary learning using TikTok in accordance with these innovations (RQ2).

Results

The results section addresses the research questions regarding the multimodal innovations of TikTok particularly suited to vocabulary learning. The first subsection outlines the technological designs and features of TikTok that are not merely new, but also innovative in terms of supporting richer multimodality (RQ1). Analysis of these designs and features was based on what the students identified as useful for vocabulary learning in relation to multimodality, rather than the researcher's observation of the platform. The second subsection presents concrete examples illustrating how the students creatively organised opportunities and materials for vocabulary learning using TikTok in accordance with the multimodal innovations (RQ2). The findings identified that the multimodal innovations enabled them to create affordances for vocabulary learning and practice through interactions with online users. They perceived these affordances not as only users but also as content creators, which allowed them to become more active learners when creating their own content.

RQ1. Multimodal technological innovations of TikTok

Combination of multiple modes of communication

TikTok specialises in users sharing self-made videos via utilisation of user-friendly in-application video editing features to convey meaning primarily through images with support from written text. Users can, for example, insert text, emojis, and/or images within a video, alter sound, add music, and convert multiple photos into a video format. Analysis of the students' narratives identified three main affordances of these editing features for creating multimodal content. Firstly, TikTok provides sound-enhanced functionality to enable the expression of meaning in content through various sound effects. This makes the content more engaging for viewers by enhancing the video's audial impact as part of the overall experience on the platform. Secondly, the nature of TikTok's design emphasises visual storytelling, with users often using non-verbal cues in their videos, such as facial expressions and body gestures, to convey meaning and emotion. This encourages users to design content that emphasises meanings throughout contexts and evokes viewer reactions. Lastly, TikTok enables the content to be modified dynamically with multimodal elements throughout the video, supporting real-time-based interactions. The technology, for instance, that enables text to appear at the moment of speaking can create a sense of communication with online users.

Short-form videos with instantaneous integration of diverse modes

Analysis of the students' narratives identified the use of short-form TikTok videos, typically 15–60 seconds in length, in relation to multimodality. TikTok's short-form videos enable the efficient presentation of multiple modes of communication instantaneously within a single piece of content by leveraging user-friendly in-application video editing features. The ease of conveying meaning in a short duration supports users to be highly innovative in their use of multimodal elements to create engaging and entertaining content. They can easily tailor their content to be visually and multimodally appealing to viewers, with rapid integration of diverse modes, for example, by utilising sound, text, or emojis to convey emotion and humour. Moreover, the instantaneous access to short multimodal content enables viewers to engage with copious amounts of information as they navigate the platform, making their social networking experience both efficient and productive. As a result, the use of short-form videos to both view and create experiences encourages almost any user to become a content creator on the platform.

Algorithmic recommendation of multimodal content

TikTok's recommendation of multimodal content is based on algorithms leveraging the multimodal nature of the platform and providing personalised and engaging social networking experiences. According to the students' narratives, users can begin by searching for keywords and hashtags related to their interests using the "search" tool, which reveals the relevant multimodal content promoted by the search algorithm. The more the user searches these topics, the more likely they are to engage with the content by utilising the "liking" and "saving" features that enable them to store multimodal content within their user profile. These features enable the algorithm to identify the user's behavioural patterns, which then influences the recommendations for other videos of relevance

Using TikTok for vocabulary learning 237

to the user. The algorithm is also capable of recognising the connection between a user and different modes of representation in content, including how the creators express themselves. This, in turn, can also influence the recommendations for other videos provided to the user.

RQ2. Use of multimodal innovations as affordances for organising vocabulary learning

Combination of multiple modes of communication: Visual and multimodal learning

The students utilised TikTok's multimodal content, which was created and modified with user-friendly in-application video editing features, to improve their listening and speaking skills for vocabulary learning. Figure 12.1 presents examples of the multimodal content that they perceived as useful for vocabulary learning. This content was created for English teaching/learning that often requires an actual demonstration of speech such as pronunciation. Figure 12.1a is from a video post of

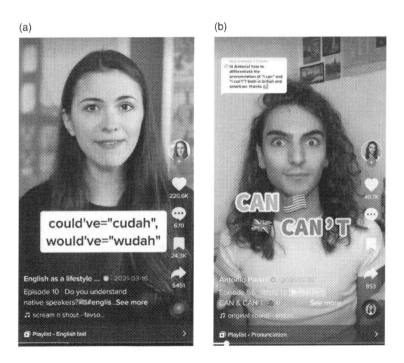

Figure 12.1a Multimodal content on pronouncing contractions

Figure 12.1b Multimodal content explaining confusing sounds

the creator demonstrating the sounds of contractions such as "could've [cudah]" or "would've [wudah]" in American English. Figure 12.1b is from another post in which the creator explains how to differentiate between confusing sounds, "can" and "can't", using a comparison of British and American English. Both videos include inserted text which indicates the sounds of words and emojis of national flags representing the type of English being taught.

Students drew on the multimodal elements of the videos to practise the pronunciations of words and phrases, which enabled them to "hear" the English speakers' speech and "see" the inserted text for sound. They stressed the benefits of the video's audial support for vocabulary practice. Prem commented: "videos include sounds I can hear and copy. I can practise pronunciations of words and phrases easily". Jieun commented on a specific sound effect which enhanced the video's overall impact on her vocabulary acquisition: "this content uses a 'ding' sound effect to highlight a certain word, which makes me focused on that word". They also utilised videos to practise the sounds of certain words in an Australian accent, which they were less familiar with. They listened to "a variety of English accents" from different creators to adjust their own speaking style. Jieun recounted how she practised saying confusing words in the Australian accent: "I've studied American English. Sometimes, I can't understand Australians' accent. It made me frustrated, but I listened to Australian TikTokers introducing confusing sounds like the [r] in 'here' or 'car'. I repeated after them aloud".

Furthermore, they benefited from the visual mode of a video by using the context of the image to guess the meaning of new expressions and idioms such as "hit the hay" and "I feel under the weather", and to pick up on subtle non-verbal cues. Joy observed: "videos are moving images. They are alive. I can see what people do through facial expressions and body gestures". Her use of descriptive words – "moving images" and "alive" – indicates her acknowledgement of the rich multimodality of TikTok videos, highlighting the visual experience of meaning-making. The students further benefited from exposure to different modes of visual communication to comprehend and retain new vocabulary knowledge. Shasha stated: "I understand how to use expressions better with visual supports while watching videos than by reading articles. Those stimulate my brain and lead to a long-term memory".

In addition, they perceived that the video content involving diverse modes enabled the demonstration of virtual vocabulary teaching while others view that content. They elucidated that this content supported "real time"-based teaching-learning interactions. They accounted for inserted text, emojis, or images in a video, conveying meaning in content and the creator's intention to engage with other users. They specifically pointed out the technology enabling "pop-up" text or emojis on the screen at the moment of speaking for emphasis, suggesting it provided them with a sense of actual communicative interaction. Jieun explained: "English-teaching contents use pop-up texts whenever introducing definitions, pronunciations, and examples of important words. I feel like actually interacting with the creator".

In short, the affordances of TikTok's rich multimodal video editing features enabled the students to engage with multimodal content, highlighting the audial and visual experiences of vocabulary knowledge acquisition supported with textual information. Interestingly, the multi-modal content supported them to practise listening and speaking skills, not only through viewing but also through real-time-based interactive experiences. This indicates how users created affordances for their content to indicate their intention to interact with viewers by integrating diverse modes of communication.

Short-form videos with instantaneous integration of diverse modes: Efficient and productive learning

The students perceived the affordances of TikTok's short-form videos for vocabulary learning to enable instantaneous integration and interpretation of diverse modes with the video editing features. They pointed to the English-teaching content delivering vocabulary knowledge with emotion and humour supported by multimodal elements, which captured their attention within a short time. Figure 12.2a shows the use of text phrases to teach synonyms such as "don't say", which students claimed were "eye-catching", as well as to teach about overused words in writing such as "very". Figure 12.2b shows the use of check mark (✔) and cross mark (✘) emojis for teaching the correct usage of the "commonly misused words" "fell down" and "fell over". The students also mentioned the creator's facial expression and intonation as part of the multimodal elements.

The creators' innovative ways of using multimodal elements to create short-form videos enabled not only "time-efficient" but also "inform-ative" and "intensive" learning. These multimodal elements "hooked [their] eyes", enabling them to learn new words and expressions "out of [their] comfort zone". Jieun specifically commented on Figure 12.2b:

> This creator's serious facial expression and eye-catching emojis grab my attention and make me focused instantly. Yesterday, I told my friend that I 'fell down'. However, I learnt that objects can 'fall down' and humans can 'fall over', which I've been using wrong. I realised that nobody fixes my mistakes but TikTok. I could have not caught my mistakes without it.

Figure 12.2a Short-form video content mainly edited with text

Figure 12.2b Multimodal content mainly edited with text and emojis

Jieun's story represents her acted-upon affordance of short-form multimodal content for improving lexical knowledge, which was efficient and effective. Prem also commented: "TikTok's short videos enable time-efficient learning, especially when I am busy with assignments. They are easy to understand because they are multimodal. [They] require low energy but provide high-quality learning". Shasha further noted how useful short content was for the recall and retention of acquired knowledge: "TikTok videos have only a few new words I need to learn in one video because they need a punch line to attract viewers, which helps me to remember even after watching".

As the students became more exposed to short multimodal content, they began to create their own content utilising video editing features to share the vocabulary knowledge emergent in their daily lives. For instance, Figure 12.3 illustrates how Jieun applied editing features to create content to share the expressions she learnt when taking a train; that is, "tap on"

Using TikTok for vocabulary learning 241

Figure 12.3 Screenshots of Jieun's short-form multimodal content

and "tap off". She described the meanings: "people need to tap on and off like tap the opal card (a contactless smart card) to pay based on travel distance when using public transport in Sydney". She converted multiple photos taken while on the train and the station into a video format. She presented definitions and example sentences of the expressions in English and Korean (her first language) in text, with images of the Australian and Korean national flags. She inserted various emojis including the thinking emoji (🤔) to raise the question, "How do you say (교통) 카드를 찍다 in English?". She used the round-shape (O) and cross mark (❌) when describing differences between a train and subway. She also added video descriptions in text using relevant hashtags such as #englishvocabulary and #languagelearning, which she reported was helpful for articulating content in keywords in English. Jieun commented that this multimodal content creation activity provided an opportunity to practise and retain acquired vocabulary knowledge efficiently and effectively.

Taken together, TikTok's short videos, created and modified with multimodal elements, enabled the students to craft opportunities for learning that was efficient both in time and quality. The content creation activity highlights their initiative to create learning opportunities through interactions with viewers. Importantly, their created content was often oriented towards "situated vocabulary learning" in everyday life experiences. These findings represent current online learning experiences adaptive to technological innovations that support efficient and productive social networking.

Algorithmic recommendation of multimodal content: Personalised learning spaces

The students acted upon the affordances of TikTok's algorithms supporting personalised and engaging experiences as they realised the algorithmic recommendations presenting multimodal content were relevant to English learning, especially vocabulary learning. They began by searching English learning-related keywords and hashtags such as Australian English, #englishlearning, and #englishvocabulary, which returned extensive relevant multimodal content. The more they searched and engaged with such content, the more they received recommendations for content providing vocabulary knowledge. They also searched for content not designed for, but involving, English language use, using keywords or hashtags based on their personal interests. Joy recounted a specific example of how she engaged in vocabulary learning on TikTok by responding to the algorithms that quickly "customised with [her] interest" based on her searches:

> I love watching English movies and dramas. One day, I searched them as key words to see if TikTok has relevant videos. From the next day, TikTok started showing me videos using scenes or segments of English movies and dramas.

Prem pointed more directly to the affordances of TikTok's algorithms which he found to enhance his overall experience of English learning on the platform, saying: "TikTok recommends contents based on algorithms tracking what I search, watch, or like. This means I can play with it. I made it show contents about Australian English and cultures. This helped my vocabulary, listening, and speaking".

Furthermore, the students saved the content they found useful – involving new words, expressions, or idioms – within their user profile through the "liking" and "saving" features (Figure 12.4).

The students' TikTok user profiles – within which all the selected content was saved – allowed for instantaneous engagement with a variety of multimodal content and interactions on the platform. As such, it supported them to revisit and review the content whenever they needed to. This enabled them to create a connection between their online and

Using TikTok for vocabulary learning 243

Figure 12.4 Shasha's user profile within which all the selected content is saved

offline learning. Jieun recounted a specific example of how she applied the vocabulary knowledge she acquired from the multimodal content in a conversation in her daily life:

> I had COVID-19 last week and wanted to message my friends that I was sick. I remembered that I saw the video about alternative phrases for feeling sick, but I couldn't recall what they were. I simply accessed my profile on TikTok through my phone and found the phrases, 'feeling off' and 'feeling not 100 percent', in seconds.

Amir described his TikTok profile as "[his] own learning space" which he constantly crafted based on his specific interest in learning practical words and expressions he could use in daily conversations. Joy's TikTok profile also served as "a convenient space" which she regularly visited "to review and keep learning until [she] actually remember[s]".

As a result, the students utilised the TikTok platform as a "customised" space for learning in accordance with the algorithms that identified their behavioural patterns and the connections between diverse modes of communication from the content they had watched. Their searches for English learning- and vocabulary-related keywords and hashtags to seek out specific multimodal content that taught or involved English language use highlights how they exercised agency to engage with English speakers. Interestingly, the use of a user profile enabled them to visually organise all the selected multimodal content which, in turn, supported a visualisation of online networks. This indicates that their user profile served as a highly interconnected personalised space comprised of multimodally rich content across diverse audiences.

New understandings

This chapter has shown that the multimodality of TikTok is particularly suited to vocabulary learning in accordance with its innovations, highlighting audial and visual experiences with support from textual information. Multimodally rich videos were useful for audial demonstrations of words and phrases such as pronunciation and speaking, and the visual demonstration of meanings of expressions and idioms in context. These findings not only identify modality as a factor that motivates vocabulary learning (Arndt & Woore, 2018; Lai et al., 2022; Teng & Zhang, 2023; Zou & Teng, 2023), but also enhance understanding of differential vocabulary learning potentials that diverse modes support. This chapter thus advances our understanding of the concept of affordances for vocabulary learning, supporting van Lier's (2004, 2007) emphasis on the role of learners and agency. It further enhances Barton and Potts' (2013) approach to digital affordances by particularly demonstrating the current state of social networking facilitated by multimodal innovations.

Importantly, the findings related to the acted-upon affordances of these multimodal elements represent how creatively the students organised their vocabulary learning using TikTok, which shed light on two key insights of this study. Firstly, they created their own content that was oriented towards "situated vocabulary learning"; that is, situated in everyday life experiences. While utilising the multimodal content specifically created for English vocabulary teaching/learning online, they created the opportunity to practise and retain vocabulary knowledge emergent and acquired in daily life. Acted-upon affordances of short-form videos and user-friendly in-application video editing tools enabled the students to engage in both efficient and productive digital learning in highly innovative ways, connecting everyday life and the digital learning. These findings contribute to current understandings of autonomous or motivational technology use for vocabulary learning (Benson & Chik, 2013; Sockett & Toffoli, 2012; Sundqvist, 2019), and also reveal that technology use is about both agency and creativity. Adding to previous research on creative uses of digital technology for informal language learning (Lee, 2023), this study provides insights into the modern reality of digital activity that is situated and integrated within individual users' everyday life experiences.

Secondly, the students created spaces on TikTok to organise their learning. Upon realising that the algorithmic recommendations are based on their search and viewing behaviours, they oriented their choices of multimodal content towards those that are more relevant and engaging for vocabulary learning. As a result, they were able to "customise" the TikTok platform as a space to learn vocabulary. The use of a user profile especially enabled them to organise their own learning spaces on the platform, comprised of all the saved multimodally rich content across online networks. Each student's TikTok profile served as a digital space for continuous learning and practice both *within* and *outside* the platform. This was accomplished in particular by applying acquired vocabulary knowledge from multimodal content into conversations in daily life. In other words, their vocabulary learning occurred not merely within the platform itself, but also within their everyday life experiences through acted-upon affordances of the digital spaces they crafted.

Therefore, this chapter has provided insights into not only how TikTok users make use of its multimodal innovations for vocabulary learning, but also how they creatively bring online vocabulary learning into everyday life. These insights add to the line of research that adopted the concept of affordances and showed the utilisation of particular social media features for language learning (Newgarden & Zheng, 2016; Reinhardt & Chen, 2013; Lee, 2023). This line of research is further expanded through the understanding of the uses of the latest innovations of multimodal social media which enable learning to occur in both digital and physical spaces.

Implications

This chapter has explored TikTok's multimodal affordances for vocabulary learning, and students' creative articulation of their use to organise their learning. It offered new insights into situated vocabulary learning and the creation of highly personalised digital spaces on the platform which interconnect digital and everyday life learning. Given these insights, this chapter provides practical implications for teaching. It would help language educators to understand TikTok's creative potential as a medium for multimodal vocabulary learning and incorporate it into lesson planning and teaching strategies to make learning more visually and multimodally engaging for students. In particular, educators can guide students to craft their own digital space using a user profile comprised of multimodal content involving vocabulary knowledge relevant to a certain lesson topic. This content can be used for class discussion. Educators can also encourage students to create their own multimodal content using vocabulary knowledge emergent and acquired in everyday life experiences. This can help educators to see how this multimodal content creation activity develops students' ability to recall and retain vocabulary knowledge and to further test out the amount and extent of their vocabulary knowledge gains. These suggestions allow educators not only to better equip students with new and innovative ways of vocabulary learning, but also to achieve a balance between informal out-of-class and formal in-class learning through technology use.

Further reading

Dressman, M., & Sadler, R. (2020). *The handbook of informal language learning*. Wiley-Blackwell.

This book covers theoretical and empirical research for out-of-class technology use for language learning in areas of vocabulary acquisition, multimodality, and virtual contexts. It also explores the implications for integration between formal and informal learning.

Jensen, S. H. (2019). Language learning in the wild: A young user perspective. *Language Learning & Technology*, 23(1), 72–86.

This article examines users' explorations across a range of multimodal digital platforms, revealing incidental vocabulary learning as a result of motivated use of learning strategies in navigating the digital wilds.

Webb, S. (2020). *The Routledge handbook of vocabulary studies*. Routledge.

This book covers approaches to and studies on learning vocabulary using technologies before 2020. While it establishes a foundation in vocabulary learning research by addressing key issues and challenges throughout history, our book further explores technological advances that support multimodal communication through the visual turn of social media like TikTok.

References

Arndt, H. L., & Woore, R. (2018). Vocabulary learning from watching YouTube videos and reading blog posts. *Language Learning & Technology*, 22(3), 124–142. https://doi.org/10125/44660

Barkhuizen, G., Benson, P., & Chik, A. (2013). *Narrative inquiry in language teaching and learning research*. Routledge.

Barton, D., & Potts, D. (2013). Language learning online as a social practice. *TESOL Quarterly*, 47(4), 815–820. https://doi.org/10.1002/tesq.130

Benson, P. (2014). Narrative inquiry in applied linguistics research. *Annual Review of Applied Linguistics*, 34, 154–170. https://doi.org/10.1017/S0267190514000099

Benson, P., & Chik, A. (2013). Towards a more naturalistic CALL: Video-gaming and language learning. In B. Zou (Ed.), *Explorations of language teaching and learning with computational assistance* (pp. 75–88). IGI Global.

Burgess, J., Marwick, A., & Poell, T. (2018). *The SAGE handbook of social media.* SAGE Publications.

Clarke, V., & Braun, V. (2017). Thematic analysis. *The Journal of Positive Psychology*, 12(3), 297–298. https://doi.org/10.1080/17439760.2016.1262613

Gibson, J. J. (1979). *The ecological approach to visual perception.* Houghton Mifflin.

Godwin-Jones, R. (2018). Contextualized vocabulary learning. *Language Learning & Technology*, 22(3), 1–19. https://doi.org/10125/44651

Kress, G. (2010). *Multimodality: A social semiotic approach to contemporary communication.* Routledge.

Lai, C., Liu, Y., Jingjing, J., Benson, P., & Lyu, B. (2022). Association between the characteristics of out-of-class technology-mediated language experience and L2 vocabulary knowledge. *Language Learning & Technology*, 26(1), 1–24. https://hdl.handle.net/10125/73485

Lee, Y.-J. (2023). Language learning affordances of Instagram and TikTok. *Innovation in Language Learning and Teaching*, 17(2), 408–423. https://doi.org/10.1080/17501229.2022.2051517

Newgarden, K., & Zheng, D. (2016). Recurrent languaging activities in World of Warcraft: Skilled linguistic action meets the Common European Framework of Reference. *ReCALL*, 28(3), 274–304. https://doi.org/10.1017/S0958344016000112

Page, R., Barton, D., Unger, J. W., & Zappavigna, M. (2014). *Researching language and social media.* Routledge.

Peters, E. (2018). The effect of out-of-class exposure to English language media on learners' vocabulary knowledge. *International Journal of Applied Linguistics*, 169(1), 142–168. https://doi.org/10.1075/bct.109.itl.00010.pet

Reinhardt, J., & Chen, H.-I. (2013). An ecological analysis of social networking site – Mediated identity development. In M.-N. Lamy & K. Zourou (Eds.), *Social networking for language education* (pp. 11–30). Palgrave Macmillan.

Sockett, G., & Toffoli, D. (2012). Beyond learner autonomy: A dynamic systems view of the informal learning of English in virtual online communities. *ReCALL*, 24(2), 138–151. https://doi.org/10.1017/S0958344012000031

Soyoof, A., Reynolds, B. L., Vazquez-Calvo, B., & McLay, K. (2021). Informal digital learning of English (IDLE): A scoping review of what has been done and a look towards what is to come. *Computer Assisted Language Learning*, 1–27. https://doi.org/10.1080/09588221.2021.1936562

Sundqvist, P. (2019). Commercial-off-the-shelf games in the digital wild and L2 learner vocabulary. *Language Learning & Technology*, 23(1), 87–113. https://doi.org/10125/44674

Teng, F. (2022a). Incidental L2 vocabulary learning from viewing captioned videos: Effects of learner-related factors. *System*, 105, 102–736. https://doi.org/10.1016/j.system.2022.102736

Teng, F. (2022b). The effectiveness of multimedia input on vocabulary learning and retention. *Innovation in Language Learning and Teaching, 17*(3), 738–754, https://doi.org/10.1080/17501229.2022.2131791

Teng, F., & Zhang, D. (2023). Vocabulary learning in a foreign language: Multimedia input, sentence-writing task, and their combination, 1–26. *Applied Linguistics Review*. https://doi.org/10.1515/applirev-2022-0160

van Lier, L. (2004). *The ecology and semiotics of language learning: A sociocultural perspective*. Kluwer Academic Publishers.

van Lier, L. (2007). Action-based teaching, autonomy and identity. *Innovation in Language Learning and Teaching, 1*(1), 46–65. https://doi.org/10.2167/illt42.0

Vazquez-Calvo, B., Zhang, L.-T., & Shafirova, L. (2022). Language learning hashtags on TikTok in Chinese, Italian, and Russian. In L. Klimanova (Ed.), *Identity, multilingualism and CALL: Responding to new global realities* (pp. 104–134). Equinox Publishing Ltd.

Zou, D., & Teng, F. (2023). Effects of tasks and multimedia annotations on vocabulary learning. *System, 115*, 1–15. https://doi.org/10.1016/j.system.2023.103050

13 Conclusion

The next generation of studies in multimodal, multilingual, and multi-agent vocabulary learning

Agnes Kukulska-Hulme

Introduction

Mastering new vocabulary often involves tasks that are both motivational and cognitive in nature (Laufer & Hulstijn, 2001), while a lack of appropriate tools to practise vocabulary learning can be a real barrier to success in language learning (Meara & Miralpeix, 2016). It is therefore encouraging to know that researchers as well as practitioners are continuing to innovate and are investigating ingenious ways to optimise and facilitate vocabulary learning, as well as conducting rigorous research studies to evaluate effectiveness and understand experiences. The research establishes links between theory and practice, and generates increasingly intricate and insightful models of the cognitive, psychological, social, and dialogic processes involved. The present volume, with its focus on recent innovations in digital research, pedagogy, and learning practices in multiple contexts, enables a celebration of recent achievements and a reappraisal of what still needs to be investigated and improved.

In many countries and regions – though admittedly not all – there are continuously expanding possibilities afforded by technology-enhanced methods and tools, online communities, and openly available resources that are supporting learners in the processes of encountering, noticing, and paying attention to vocabulary; memorising, internalising, and remembering; comprehending nuances and contexts; and incorporating all that knowledge and experience into productive use. Mobile phones and other technologies, such as digital role-playing games (Zou et al., 2024), have improved access and support and have extended digital learning opportunities beyond geographical and school boundaries (Kukulska-Hulme et al., 2023b). At the same time, their use has created new expectations and practices, particularly in respect of how self-directed technology-assisted learning outside class can relate to classroom learning and which language learners are most likely to benefit from such activity (Laufer & Vaisman, 2023). Deftly combining classroom-based activity

DOI: 10.4324/9781003367543-15

with learning beyond the classroom is one of the foremost contemporary challenges in language education, hence it is of key importance in vocabulary learning and in research studies that increasingly need to straddle these two domains.

Learning from past and current studies

The present volume provides critical reviews of existing bodies of research, including on word glossing, word-level checking, and captioned video viewing. Several reviews note a relative lack of studies on how learner behaviours and learning outcomes may change or evolve over a longer period of time. This echoes past calls for more longitudinal studies, which have been heard in the fields of language learning, digital learning, and related areas over many years (e.g., Arciuli & Torkildsen, 2012; Harju et al., 2019). There has also been sound advice on how to conduct such studies in language learning (Ortega & Iberri-Shea, 2005) and in other fields where longitudinal studies are considered important (e.g., Zhao et al., 2024). The calls seem to have resulted in more longitudinal research, including a few recent studies on vocabulary learning with technology (e.g., Lei et al., 2022; Lyrigkou, 2021) or without technology (Teng & Zhang, 2024); however there are still relatively few such studies. Longitudinal research is challenging to conduct, and it requires analytical expertise that may be less available among researchers or teacher-researchers who have a language discipline background. Besides, the studies may not produce conclusive results due to participant attrition as well as difficulties incorporating or controlling for extraneous factors such as fluctuating social or personal contexts and greater exposure to language sources outside class. Many languages are evolving at a rapid pace, such that some word usage and meanings could even change during the period of the study. There is no doubt that longitudinal studies are needed, but they may require a team effort, with multi-disciplinary expertise as well as the capacity to take account of the broader contexts in which people now learn with technologies.

Theory-informed perspectives that can underpin vocabulary studies are highly diverse, as can be seen in the theories and concepts mentioned and employed in the studies reported in this book. The theories and concepts originate from numerous disciplines, including:

- education *(constructivism, socio-cultural learning, incidental learning, game-based learning, data-driven learning)*;
- psychology, cognitive psychology, or educational psychology *(working memory, affordances, emotions, noticing, cognitive load, involvement load, dual coding)*;

- ecology or cognitive science (*Complex Dynamic Systems Theory*);
- sociology or philosophy (*agency*);
- communication studies (*body language*);
- linguistics (*usage-based perspectives, meaning negotiation, semantic preference, semantic prosody*).

This again highlights a desire to draw upon knowledge from across disciplines, yet any individual or even a research team may be constrained in this regard. Resulting risks include only partial engagement with a theory, or choosing an approach that happens to be familiar from previous studies. Theories and concepts relating to informal language learning beyond the classroom will become increasingly relevant, because informal settings emphasise experiential and social learning, motivation, contexts, self-direction and self-regulation, multimodality, communities, interest-based and recreational learning (including games and entertainment programmes), translanguaging, and superdiversity (see Dressman & Sadler, 2020).

As vocabulary studies delve deeper into the cognitive, affective, and social processes of learning, it will be helpful to pay close attention to what research is being done in the fields of first language acquisition and in vocabulary learning in occupational, professional, and specialised domains (e.g., Martín-Monje et al., 2016). There is also much to be learnt from studies conducted with marginalised populations such as migrants and refugees (e.g., Bello et al., 2023). Furthermore, studies involving people with disabilities and impairments can provide inspiration for new perspectives, technologies, or methods (e.g., Urrea et al., 2024). Indeed, in this volume our attention is drawn to how video captions, originally intended for people who are deaf or hard of hearing, came to be adopted for more diverse and widespread uses.

The present volume illustrates very clearly how the affordances of particular technologies and learning environments support vocabulary studies and vocabulary learning. As can be seen in the chapters on gloss studies, corpus-based research, and captioned viewing, the advent of specific technologies enabled a step-change in what could be done. It is equally evident that widely used digital resources and tools such as messaging apps, translation tools, social media, and video streaming platforms are being appropriated for language learning and vocabulary development with promising results. It seems like the right time for concepts such as cultures-of-use (Thorne, 2016), learning cultures (Kukulska-Hulme, 2010), and intercultural competence (Liu et al., 2023; Zhang et al., 2024) to play a more central role in vocabulary studies.

Diversification and integration are two opposing trends, yet both are needed in contemporary education and research. Reflection on case studies in mobile assisted language learning (Kukulska-Hulme, 2021) led to the conclusion that there was a strong theme around "Multiplicity of technologies, methods, and modalities": digital services are accessed from multiple devices, there are multimodal communication and creation media being used for learning, and people frequently switch channels or media in the course of an activity or as their needs evolve. A trendy word for this type of phenomenon – "multi-everything" – could be used to describe what teachers and learners are experiencing in language learning, and it is reflected in some overarching themes we can identify in the present volume. Three of these are briefly discussed in the next section. They align quite well with the three emerging areas for technology-enhanced vocabulary learning (Metaverse, ethics, and AI) signalled in the introduction to the book.

Multimodal, multilingual, and multi-agent vocabulary learning

Multimodal pedagogy, which has been described as "enhancing learning by diversifying communication and representation" (Kukulska-Hulme et al., 2023a, p. 18), harnesses the potential of resources such as images, words, gestures, and sounds, enabling different means of expression and ways of knowing for vocabulary learning (Teng, 2021). Nevertheless, a challenge to enacting this pedagogy is that teachers "need to have knowledge of multimodal literacy practices in order to design and assess learning experiences" (op.cit. p. 20). Multimodal literacy practices are constantly evolving, as new technologies emerge and are incorporated into social, educational, and working lives. In the present volume, multimodal teaching and learning and associated literacies are in plentiful evidence, while immersive literacies (Pegrum et al., 2022) have been highlighted in relation to the emerging worlds of augmented reality and the Metaverse (Wu et al., 2024).

A second theme worth exploring further in vocabulary studies concerns opportunities for learners to explore new vocabulary through the lens of multiple other languages that they know (Bartolotti & Marian, 2017). Plurilingual learners have been poorly served in the past, with systems and methods typically confining them to definitions and comparisons in the target language or one chosen language. The ability to explore vocabulary across multiple languages, and the ability to express oneself in multiple languages (and be understood), can be considered under the banner of ethical concerns, because it enables learners to realise their potential and validates their unique linguistic resources. It is also incumbent on researchers to address the issue of the strong tendency for researchers the world over – in all disciplines – to confine themselves in literature reviews to papers published in English. With the help of advanced technologies and AI (and perhaps with a hefty dose of cultural change), it should be possible to alter these practices so as to understand and embrace all the literature that is published in other languages and enable more researchers to express themselves and communicate their ideas, methods, and findings ("Scientific publishing has a language problem", n.a.).

The third, and currently most topical, theme concerns the multi-agent nature of teaching, learning, and assessing with the aid of artificial intelligence. AI is now seen as a partner that can perform many roles. Several studies have investigated how AI may help in the process of vocabulary learning and use, for example through the provision or generation of stories with target vocabulary, combined with interaction with the learner. For instance, Alsadoon (2021) explored chatting with an AI bot ("an interactive storytelling chatterbot") as a means to vocabulary learning through stories in an adult EFL Saudi context. The chatbot engaged in simple conversation and offered a selection of stories from a database, while the learners had access to several tools, namely a dictionary, images, an L1 translation tool, and a concordance, with differential effects on their vocabulary learning and retention. In a study by Jeon (2023), several types of assistance were provided by a chatbot to Korean EFL primary school learners, and the interaction records were analysed. Dynamic chatbot assistance proved to be beneficial in terms of vocabulary gains, while the interaction records showed learner development that could be used for diagnostic purposes.

A separate, but related strand of research on AI in vocabulary studies focuses on ubiquitous learning with AI-enhanced, multisensory technologies facilitating embodied learning and exploring dual-coding theory. Hsu et al.'s (2023) approach to vocabulary learning involved AI-supported image recognition and aimed to improve the "learning climate" for young (aged 10–11) EFL learners in Taiwan, to support self-regulated learning, as well as to help narrow the gap between vocabulary knowledge and physical objects. The app used in this study detects objects through captured images and displays relevant information on the user's device; it offers translation, pronunciation, a text-to-speech function, and a dictionary database, as well as "tactile enhancement" (in the sense of touching objects). Learners followed a short story from their textbook and engaged in associated physical tasks in the classroom. There were reported benefits in terms of vocabulary learning, self-regulation, and anxiety-reduced learning. A similar study by Liu and Chen (2023), also with young learners in Taiwan, employed object detection using mobile phones, combining pictures, text, and pronunciation, and it focused on 10- to 12-year-old learners with different abilities. The AI-based approach supported vocabulary attainment (learning names of fruit and vegetables) and emphasised active learning; it benefited higher-ability students more than lower-ability students. In another study that also explored embodied learning, Huang and Wang (2023) used a motion-sensing system for teaching simple French words through gestures to college students (trainee teachers) in Taiwan. It was found that meaningful body movements can reinforce students' vocabulary retention. The approach seems to have significant limitations (learning simple words connected to gestures) but demonstrates the potential of embodied learning of vocabulary.

From all the above reflections and highlighted themes, it is possible to conclude that future research studies and designs for vocabulary learning will need to maintain awareness of a wide range of ideas and methods as these emerge from across multiple disciplines, languages, cultures, and technologies. A "multi-everything" approach is not a bad starting point when designing a learning activity or a study because it opens up many new possibilities.

References

Alsadoon, R. (2021). Chatting with AI bot: Vocabulary learning assistant for Saudi EFL learners. *English Language Teaching*, 14(6), 135–157.

Arciuli, J., & Torkildsen, J. V. K. (2012). Advancing our understanding of the link between statistical learning and language acquisition: The need for longitudinal data. *Frontiers in Psychology*, 3, 324.

Bartolotti, J., & Marian, V. (2017). Bilinguals' existing languages benefit vocabulary learning in a third language. *Language Learning*, 67(1), 110–140. https://doi.org/10.1111/lang.12200

Bello, A., Ferraresi, P., Stefanini, S., & Perucchini, P. (2023). L1 and L2 vocabulary and word combinations of preschool children from migrant families in Italy. *International Journal of Bilingualism*, 27(4), 486–503. https://doi.org/10.1177/13670069221099324

Dressman, M., & Sadler, R. W. (Eds.). (2020). *The handbook of informal language learning*. John Wiley & Sons.

Harju, V., Koskinen, A., & Pehkonen, L. (2019). An exploration of longitudinal studies of digital learning. *Educational Research*, 61(4), 388–407.

Hsu, T. C., Chang, C., & Jen, T. H. (2023). Artificial Intelligence image recognition using self-regulation learning strategies: Effects on vocabulary acquisition, learning anxiety, and learning behaviours of English language learners. *Interactive Learning Environments*, 1–19. https://doi.org/10.1080/10494820.2023.2165508

Huang, T. H., & Wang, L. Z. (2023). Artificial intelligence learning approach through total physical response embodiment teaching on French vocabulary learning retention. *Computer Assisted Language Learning*, 36(8), 1608–1632. https://doi.org/10.1080/09588221.2021.2008980

Jeon, J. (2023). Chatbot-assisted dynamic assessment (CA-DA) for L2 vocabulary learning and diagnosis. *Computer Assisted Language Learning*, 36(7), 1338–1364. https://doi.org/10.1080/09588221.2021.1987272

Kukulska-Hulme, A. (2010). Learning cultures on the move: Where are we heading? *Journal of Educational Technology & Society, 13*(4), 4–14.

Kukulska-Hulme, A. (2021). Conclusions: A lifelong perspective on mobile language learning. In V. Morgana & A. Kukulska-Hulme (Eds.), *Mobile assisted language learning across educational contexts* (pp. 122–133). Routledge.

Kukulska-Hulme, A., Bossu, C., Charitonos, K., Coughlan, T., Deacon, A., Deane, N., Ferguson, R., Herodotou, C., Huang, C-W., Mayisela, T., Rets, I., Sargent, J., Scanlon, E., Small, J., Walji, S., Weller, M., & Whitelock, D. (2023a). *Innovating pedagogy 2023: Open university innovation report 11.* The Open University.

Kukulska-Hulme, A., Giri, R. A., Dawadi, S., Devkota, K. R., & Gaved, M. (2023b). Languages and technologies in education at school and outside of school: Perspectives from young people in low-resource countries in Africa and Asia. *Frontiers in Communication, 8,* 1081155. https://doi.org/10.3389/fcomm.2023.1081155

Laufer, B., & Hulstijn, J. (2001). Incidental vocabulary acquisition in a second language: The construct of task-induced involvement. *Applied Linguistics, 22*(1), 1–26. https://doi.org/10.1093/applin/22.1.1

Laufer, B., & Vaisman, E. E. (2023). Out-of-classroom L2 vocabulary acquisition: The effects of digital activities and school vocabulary. *The Modern Language Journal, 107*(4), 854–872. https://doi.org/10.1111/modl.12880

Lei, X., Fathi, J., Noorbakhsh, S., & Rahimi, M. (2022). The impact of mobile-assisted language learning on English as a foreign language learners' vocabulary learning attitudes and self-regulatory capacity. *Frontiers in Psychology, 13,* 872922.

Liu, G., Ma, C., Bao, J., & Liu, Z. (2023). Toward a model of informal digital learning of English and intercultural competence: A large-scale structural equation modeling approach. *Computer Assisted Language Learning,* 1–25. https://doi.org/10.1080/09588221.2023.2191652

Liu, P. L., & Chen, C. J. (2023). Using an AI-based object detection translation application for English vocabulary learning. *Educational Technology & Society, 26*(3), 5–20. https://doi.org/10.30191/ETS.202307_26(3).0002

Lyrigkou, C. (2021). *The role of informal second language learning in the spoken use of discourse markers by Greek adolescent learners of English.* PhD thesis. The Open University.

Martín-Monje, E., Elorza, I., & Riaza, B. G. (Eds.) (2016). Technology-enhanced language learning for specialized domains. *Practical applications and mobility.* Routledge.

Meara, P., & Miralpeix, I. (2016). *Tools for researching vocabulary.* Multilingual Matters.

Ortega, L., & Iberri-Shea, G. (2005). Longitudinal research in second language acquisition: Recent trends and future directions. *Annual Review of Applied Linguistics, 25,* 26–45. https://doi.org/10.1017/S0267190505000024

Pegrum, M., Hockly, N., & Dudeney, G. (2022). *Digital literacies.* Routledge.

Teng, M. F. (2021). *Language learning through captioned videos: Incidental vocabulary acquisition.* Routledge.

Teng, M. F., & Zhang, L. J. (2024). Ethnic minority multilingual young learners' longitudinal development of metacognitive knowledge and breadth of vocabulary knowledge. *Metacognition and Learning*, 19(1), 123–146. https://doi.org/10.1007/s11409-023-09360-z

Thorne, S. L. (2016). Cultures-of-use and morphologies of communicative action. *Language Learning & Technology*, 20(2), 185–191.

Urrea, A. L., Fernández-Torres, V., Rodríguez-Ortiz, I. R., & Saldaña, D. (2024). The use of technology-assisted intervention in vocabulary learning for children with autism spectrum disorder: A systematic review. *Frontiers in Psychology*, 15, 1370965.

Wu, J. G., Zhang, D. & Lee, S. M. (2024). Into the brave new metaverse: Envisaging future language teaching and learning. *IEEE Transactions on Learning Technologies*, 17, 44–53. https://doi.org/10.1109/TLT.2023.3259470

Zhang, D., Wu, J. G., & Fu, Z. (2024). Improving pre-service English teachers' native cultural knowledge and English language knowledge of native culture in a PBL classroom. *Innovation in Language Learning and Teaching*, 1–15. https://doi.org/10.1080/17501229.2024.2318568

Zhao, H. H., Shipp, A. J., Carter, K., Gonzalez-Mulé, E., & Xu, E. (2024). Time and change: A meta-analysis of temporal decisions in longitudinal studies. *Journal of Organizational Behavior*, 45(4), 620–640. https://doi.org/10.1002/job.2771

Zou, D., Lee, J. S., & Zhang, R. (2024). Digital RPG-Based Vocabulary Learning. In Lee, J. S., Zou, D. & Gu, M. M. (Eds.), *Technology and English language teaching in a changing world. New language learning and teaching environments*. Palgrave Macmillan.

Index

academic vocabulary learning 194, 195, 200, 201, 202, 206, 207, 208
academic writing 135, 146, 148, 149, 150
affordances 7, 53, 134, 135, 146, 147, 148, 150, 151, 213, 214, 218, 219, 220, 224, 225, 226, 232, 233, 235, 237, 239, 242, 244, 245, 250, 251
AI chatbot 6, 115, 136
algorithmic recommendation 236, 242, 245
aptitude 96, 212
asynchronous CMC 154
autonomous lexical expansion 226
autonomy 8, 26, 113, 188, 189, 226

bibliometric analysis 8, 41, 42, 52
Blackboard 157

capitalized letters 181, 182
captioned audiovisual input 35, 95
captioned videos 20, 24, 34, 36, 94, 95, 96, 97, 98, 99, 100, 103, 105, 106, 108, 109, 110, 111, 112, 113
captioned viewing 5, 6, 15, 16, 17, 19, 21, 23, 26, 27, 35, 93, 94, 95, 96, 97, 98, 102, 106, 110, 111, 112, 113, 251, 113, 251
ChatGPT 6, 8, 9, 128, 136, 137, 139, 140, 141, 144, 145, 146, 147, 148, 149, 150, 190
clarification 100, 165, 167
cognitive-affective model of language learning 16
cognitive faculties 112
cognitive load theory 18, 62, 95

cognitive processing 3, 19, 35, 102, 167, 212
cognitive theory of multimedia learning 19, 63
collocate 62, 99
collocations 39, 96, 139, 170, 189, 211
colloquial vocabulary 224
communication strategies 127, 165, 167, 169
complex dynamic systems theory 6, 211, 213, 214, 251
compounds 183, 184
comprehension 2, 17, 18, 19, 21, 26, 29, 30, 34, 35, 54, 61, 62, 93, 94, 95, 98, 103, 105, 106, 107, 108, 109, 110, 133, 211, 213, 215
computational linguistics 51
computer-aided instruction 51
computer-mediated communication 2, 154
concordance analysis 99, 100, 108
content words 100, 159, 160, 167, 188
contracted forms 182
corpus-based discourse analysis 98, 99
corpus linguistics 5, 99
coverage rate 175, 185, 186, 187, 190
critical thinking 8, 109, 143, 150, 207
cross-cultural communication 154
cultural awareness 106, 108, 111, 112
cyber language 167

data-driven learning 174, 188, 250
DeepL 6, 132, 136, 137, 139, 140, 141, 144, 145, 146, 147, 148, 149
deep learning 9, 49, 51, 54
digital competence 206, 207

digital reflection 226
dual coding theory 18, 95
dual processing 103
dual sensory input 110

emotional trajectory 112
English for academic purposes 6, 194
eye-tracking 71, 72, 74, 75, 79, 80, 81, 82

facial expression 117, 126, 127, 236, 238, 239
flashcard 133, 147, 190, 194, 205, 208
flemma and lemma counting methods 174, 190
formal educational contexts 213
frequency of access 80

game-based learning 8, 40, 46, 48, 55, 194, 197, 250
gloss 5, 60, 61, 62, 63, 64, 65, 66, 67, 68, 69, 70, 71, 72, 73, 74, 75, 76, 77, 78, 79, 80, 81, 82, 136, 212, 223, 251
Google Translate 6, 132, 136, 137, 139, 140, 141, 144, 146, 147, 148, 149, 234

human–chatbot interaction 119
human–human interaction 119
hyphenated words 183, 184

idioms 147, 222, 238, 242, 244
individual differences 20, 33, 34, 53, 113, 211, 212, 216
individual learning strategies 151
instant feedback 151
intentional vocabulary learning 5, 15, 26, 27, 116, 212
interlanguage lexical development 168
intonation 124, 126, 127, 147, 239
intraformal learning practices 211
intrinsic motivation 166, 225, 241
introspective processes 112
involvement load 63, 64, 116, 188, 211, 250

Kahoot! 40, 194, 199, 200, 202, 205, 207, 208
KakaoTalk 157, 159

L1 glosses 71, 74, 76
L2 glosses 61, 76
language-related episodes 168
learner agency 226
learner management system 157
learning style 67, 70, 89, 150, 169
lemmatization 180, 181
lexical competence 154, 156
lexical complexity analyzer 158
lexical density 120, 121, 127, 156, 158, 159, 160, 167, 169
lexical sophistication 157, 158, 159, 160, 161, 167, 168
lexical variation 158, 160, 162
linguistic pattern 99
long-term memory 33, 34, 184, 238

machine learning 34, 49, 54
machine translation 6, 132, 133, 136, 151
meaning negotiation 159, 168, 169, 251
metalinguistic awareness 168
mobile-assisted vocabulary learning 168, 194, 196, 197, 202, 206, 207, 208
modelling of words 164
Moodle 198, 199, 204
multimedia learning theories 17, 21
multimodal content 231, 237, 239, 240, 241, 242, 243, 244, 245, 246
multimodal glosses 60, 73, 77
multimodal innovation 232, 233, 234, 235, 237, 244, 245
multimodal learning 237
multiple case study 233
multi-word units 183

Netflix 6, 97, 211, 212, 213, 214, 215, 216, 218, 220, 221, 222, 223, 224, 225
New Word Level Checker 6, 174
nonverbal cues 124, 126, 236, 238

peer modelling 168
personalised learning spaces 168, 242
polysemous 147
positive reinforcement 220

prior digital experience 226
productive knowledge 32, 116, 125

qualitative case study approach 194, 216
Quizlet 150, 194, 196, 199, 200, 202, 203, 204, 205, 207

recall 10, 217, 231, 233, 234, 243, 246
receptive knowledge 32, 116, 117, 125
redundancy effect 80
reflexive form 223
Replica 119
retrieval 34, 51, 94, 95, 127, 129, 146, 149

self-compiled corpus 99
self-directed learning 206, 227
self-organisation 213, 214, 215, 216, 219, 220, 221, 222, 223, 225
self-reflective learner 207
semantic preference 99, 103, 108, 109, 251
semantic prosody 99, 251
single-mode glosses 60, 77
slang 99, 147

situated vocabulary learning 242, 244, 245
subtitles 15, 16, 21, 36, 93, 212, 213, 219, 221, 222, 223, 224, 225, 229
synchronous CMC 6, 154, 158, 170
synonyms 146, 147, 164, 239

text analysis 120, 127, 158
think-aloud methods 80, 81
TikTok 230, 231, 232, 233, 234, 235, 236, 237, 238, 239, 240, 241, 242, 243, 244, 245, 246
tone interpretation 146
training model 137

vocabulary profiling 137, 174, 175, 177, 187, 190, 191

willingness to communicate 118, 126
word association 164
word counting units 179, 183, 185, 191
word frequency list 99
word lists 174, 175, 176, 177, 178, 180, 183, 185, 186, 187, 188, 190, 191, 192, 195
working memory 18, 19, 70, 71, 88, 96, 212, 250

Printed in the United States
by Baker & Taylor Publisher Services